Appalachian Travels

Appalachian Travels

The Diary of
Olive Dame Campbell

Edited by
Elizabeth McCutchen Williams

K UNIVERSITY PRESS OF KENTUCKY

Diary and Photographs from the John C. and Olive Dame Campbell Papers in the Southern Historical Collection at the University of North Carolina.

Scholarly publisher for the Commonwealth,
serving Bellarmine University, Berea College, Centre College of Kentucky, Eastern Kentucky University, The Filson Historical Society, Georgetown College, Kentucky Historical Society, Kentucky State University, Morehead State University, Murray State University, Northern Kentucky University, Transylvania University, University of Kentucky, University of Louisville, and Western Kentucky University.
All rights reserved.

Editorial and Sales Offices: The University Press of Kentucky
663 South Limestone Street, Lexington, Kentucky 40508-4008
www.kentuckypress.com

16 15 14 13 12   5 4 3 2 1

Library of Congress Cataloging-in-Publication Data

Campbell, Olive D. (Olive Dame), 1882-1954.
 Appalachian travels : the diary of Olive Dame Campbell / edited by Elizabeth McCutchen Williams.
    p. cm.
 Includes bibliographical references and index.
 ISBN 978-0-8131-3644-8 (hardcover : alk. paper) —
 ISBN 978-0-8131-3668-4 (pdf) — ISBN 978-0-8131-3992-0 (epub)
 1. Campbell, Olive D. (Olive Dame), 1882-1954—Travel—Appalachian Region, Southern. 2. Campbell, Olive D. (Olive Dame), 1882-1954—Diaries. 3. Appalachian Region, Southern—Description and travel. 4. Appalachians (People)—History—20th century. 5. Mountain life—Appalachian Region, Southern—History—20th century. 6. Appalachian Region, Southern—Social life and customs—20th century. 7. Appalachian Region, Southern—Social conditions—20th century. 8. Appalachian Region, Southern—Economic conditions—20th century. I. Williams, Elizabeth McCutchen. II. Title.
 F217.A65C36 2012
 917.504—dc23   2012029582

This book is printed on acid-free paper meeting the requirements of the American National Standard for Permanence in Paper for Printed Library Materials.

♾

Manufactured in the United States of America.

Member of the Association of
American University Presses

To my daughters,
Elizabeth, Lucy, and Mary Boykin,
who think I can do anything.

CONTENTS

Illustrations follow page 128

ACKNOWLEDGMENTS

I offer my sincere thanks to my colleagues at Appalachian State University who so kindly supported and encouraged me in this pursuit. The W. L. Eury Appalachian Collection has provided most of the resources cited in this book. Many of them would have remained undiscovered without the gracious and expert help of Dean Williams and Dianna Johnson of the Belk Library Interlibrary Loan Department, who dug deep to obtain rare and obscure documents and monographs for my research. Thomas Main helped to decipher the various formats of the text in order to replicate the diary as closely as possible. Those who have written histories of their families, towns, churches, and schools have my hearty thanks; without them I could not have provided the detailed commentary about the places Olive Dame and John C. Campbell visited and the people they met on their trip through the region. Lastly, I gratefully acknowledge the expert advice and guidance of my advisers and colleagues Sandra Ballad, Thomas McGowan, and John Alexander Williams.

EDITORIAL METHOD

Olive Dame Campbell's original diary of the pioneering trip that she and her husband made through the Southern Highlands in the fall of 1908 and the early months of 1909 is in the John Charles and Olive D. Campbell Papers in the Southern Historical Collection at the University of North Carolina. It is a small volume, handwritten, and is in fragile condition. The Southern Historical Collection makes this valuable primary source about Appalachian history available only as a microfilmed copy of a transcription of the diary by an unknown person. I used a digitized copy of the original diary to attempt to authenticate the text and present it as it was first written as closely as possible without sacrificing clarity.

The parentheses and dashes the diarist used, common in diaries, are generally retained. Punctuation has been corrected only when the failure to do so would be distracting to the reader. Olive Campbell's sometimes inconsistent spellings of place and personal names have been retained (those spellings also vary in maps and other documents of the period), but most other irregular spellings have been silently corrected, to help the reader concentrate on the diary's content. Words that are in full capitals in the diary appear here in small capitals. Following the writing style of her day, Olive Campbell often failed to provide given names in her diary; when I am able to provide them, they are included in a note.

The initials JCC (John C. Campbell) are used in the text by the diarist as an abbreviation and appear in the notes as well.

This transcription of the diary is separated into chapters based on the months of the trip. Each chapter's diary entries are preceded by biographical material from chapter 4 of Olive Dame Campbell's biography of her husband, *The Life and Work of John Charles Campbell.* Along with a discursive narration, chapter 4 of the biography included numerous excerpts from this diary about the exploratory mountain trip.

Although Olive Campbell was unable to finish *Life and Work* before she died in 1954, the Dame family decided to complete a "working version," which was copied in 1968 and placed in "certain libraries" for the use of persons who wished to study the Highland Region. Edith R. Canterbury, John Campbell's former secretary in the office of the Southern Highlands Division of the Russell Sage Foundation in Asheville, was a literary executor for Olive Campbell's estate, along with Louise Pitman and Lois Bacon.[1] Footnote 15 in the biography refers to the typed transcript of the diary, contained in the Campbell Papers on microfilm: "There is an early dittoed version of the diary which at times differs somewhat in wording or content, though not in meaning, from the original handwritten one. Usually, but not always, the original version has been used for the extracts appearing in Chapter IV. Many of these extracts have been slightly edited—for punctuation, breaking up of long paragraphs and completion of sentences—to make reading easier."

Neither the diary nor the biography has been widely published before this publication of the diary. *Life and Work* is more than six hundred typescript pages long and includes much of Campbell's correspondence with the Russell Sage Foundation and with denominational and educational co-workers in the region. Even though most scholars writing about the southern Appalachians have mentioned the pioneering work that Olive Dame and John C. Campbell accomplished, full information about the Campbells' lives and their work together has never been made available in published form.

Some of the findings chronicled in the diary appeared in *The Southern Highlander and His Homeland*,[2] the first major survey of the Appalachian region, which Olive Campbell compiled and completed in her husband's name after his death in 1919. Her diary of their investigative trip is a valuable primary account of conditions in the Appalachian region during the Progressive Era, when major changes—social, educational, religious, and economic—were taking place.

INTRODUCTION

Olive Dame Campbell is generally remembered as the founder of the John C. Campbell Folk School or as a ballad collector—a "songcatcher"—but she also played a key role as a social reformer at the turn of the century in Appalachia. On a trip with her husband, John C. Campbell, through the Southern Highlands region to survey social and economic situations in mountain communities, she unearthed some of the old folk songs preserved by women perpetuating the traditions of their ancestors. This discovery inspired her to collect and document both the music and the lyrics of old ballads that had their roots in England and Scotland. Thus Olive Dame Campbell was a songcatcher in the vernacular of the mountaineers.

She is less well known for her part in the social and educational history of Appalachia. However, for the better part of her life she was one of the leading women social reformers of the period and part of the Progressive movement in America. Although much of the work done by women in establishing craft workshops and cottage industries in the mountains took place in the 1920s—the John C. Campbell Folk School was opened in 1925—the Campbells and the Southern Mountain Workers Conference, which they were instrumental in founding, had a significant impact on the movement. Both of them saw a fundamental connection between the preservation of Appalachian culture and the attainment of the educational and social goals of the schools and churches; mountain culture, they believed, should be a source of pride to the people and should be embedded in the educational and social life of communities: the Campbells promoted "the recognition and preservation of all that is native and fine."[1]

It is remarkable that the young woman who fearlessly embarked on this pioneer-like adventure of discovery was from a middle-class family in the Northeast. Olive Arnold Dame was born in 1882 in Medford, Massachusetts, "a daughter of New England: child of a talented teacher of botany and a gifted mother who early taught her to love music."[2] After her graduation from Tufts College in 1903, she taught literature for several years. On a vacation to Scotland with her family, she met John Charles Campbell, who was traveling to his ancestral homeland to recover from overwork and the death of his first wife. Campbell was born September 14, 1867, in La Porte, Indiana, and spent his youth in Wisconsin. After graduating from Williams College in 1892 and from Andover Theological Seminary in 1895, he taught for three years in a small school in Joppa, in northern Alabama. He subsequently served as the principal of Pleasant Hill Academy in Tennessee and then as president of Piedmont College in Demorest, Georgia (1901–1907).[3] The couple was married in 1907 and embarked on a lifetime of collaboration in social and cultural projects, beginning with the trip they took in the fall of 1908 and the spring of 1909 in the southern Appalachian Mountains—through eastern Kentucky, eastern Tennessee, western North Carolina, and parts of West Virginia and northern Georgia.

The Campbells wanted to survey educational and religious agencies working in the southern mountain region.

After collecting substantive data, they hoped to encourage cooperation between these groups, which were often in competition with one another. John Campbell asked Olive to keep a diary, or daily journal, of their trip, recording information about the places where they went and the people they met, as well as descriptions and details about mountain culture and the state of living conditions. The turn of the century had brought exponential changes to the region: religious conflicts, educational changes, and rapid industrialization. In *Miners, Millhands, and Mountaineers,* Ronald D Eller wrote, "What had been in 1860 only the quiet backcountry of the Old South became by the turn of the century a new frontier for expanding industrial capitalism."[4] Documentation of the struggles that mountain people were experiencing with these transitions was a vital step toward any solution.

Olive Campbell's day-by-day description of their trip is entertaining and fascinating reading, affording an intimate glimpse of mountaineer life and the problems being confronted at the turn of the century in Appalachia. Abundant information about the time period is conveyed in its pages—particulars about family life, diet, housing, buildings, hotels, roads, and railroad travel. She meticulously recorded harrowing details about bitter winter weather and travel challenges, all the while exclaiming enthusiastically about the scenery as they journeyed over the countryside by wagon, on horseback, and sometimes on foot, on roads or trails that were, as often as not, creek or river beds. Acutely aware of her surroundings, she furnished descriptive, candid comments about the individuals and issues they encountered along the way. Her rendition is invaluable documentation of mountain society in that period.

In the latter half of the nineteenth century, Americans were fascinated with interesting and unusual places; tours of the southern mountains were popular with both southerners and northerners before the Civil War. Periodicals such as *Harper's, Atlantic,* and *Lippincott's* were publishing travel and human interest stories that often focused on the quaint, old-world characteristics of mountain people. A prominent example is the much-quoted 1872 article in *Lippincott's* by Will Harney with the captivating title "A Strange Land and a Peculiar People."[5] Novels like John Fox's *Little Shepherd of Kingdom Come* and *In the Tennessee Mountains,* by Mary Noailles Murfree (pen name Charles Egbert Craddock), capitalized on this fascination with the exotic. Although many of these novels were sympathetic to the Appalachian people, such authors reinforced the stereotypical image of the mountaineer as a remnant of a former century. Writers of nonfiction also took a sympathetic, often sentimental approach, for instance, Emma Bell Miles in *The Spirit of the Mountains* and Horace Kephart in *The Southern Highlanders.*[6]

At the turn of the twentieth century, northern Protestants in general imagined the mountaineers as backward, degenerate, and lawless. But because many of them had supposedly been loyal to the Union during the Civil War, they were considered worthy of salvation. In a publication by the Home Missions Council in 1933, Elizabeth R. Hooker and Fannie Wyche Dunn stated that the interest of northerners in mountain people was due partly to their obvious neediness but also to the belief that they had been sympathetic to the North in the war.[7] More recent discussions of missionaries and their motivations can be found in *Appalachia: A History* by John Alexander Williams: "The Appalachian region presented an inviting field for missionary activity. . . . They were also worthy, according to the myth of wartime Appalachian Unionism, which made mountain missions fundable in the eyes of northern congregations and philanthropists."[8]

A chapter by John C. Inscoe in *Reconstructing Appalachia* outlines the scholarly discussion of the "myth of Appalachian Unionism." Inscoe states that early scholars showed relatively little interest in the Civil War in Appalachia: "Only from about the mid-1880's did regionalists come to acknowledge highlanders' role in the war, and then only as Unionists, whose loyalty became a valuable means of winning favor for southern mountaineers."[9]

In an effort to raise support for his own missionary activities, William Goodell Frost, president of Berea College in Kentucky, widely preached another theory. He maintained that physical isolation and the lack of good roads had preserved the pioneer days. He wrote a popular piece in the *Atlantic Monthly* in March 1899, entitled "Our Contemporary Ancestors in the Southern Mountains." Mountaineers were worth saving because the Scotch Irish in Appalachia were the direct descendants of the original settlers and still had pure white Anglo-Saxon blood, as Frost's term "contemporary ancestors" implies. Other scholars found their rationale in the same argument. In 1898 George E. Vincent published an article, "A Retarded Frontier," in the *American Journal of Sociology,* saying the region had "survived in practical isolation until this very day," although he admitted that he had based his generalizations on visits to only three Kentucky counties. Willard Hayes's physiographic description of the region in 1895, "The Southern Appalachians," and Ellen Churchill Semple's article in the *Bulletin of the American Geographical Society,* "The Anglo-Saxons of the Kentucky Mountains: A Study in Anthropogeography" fifteen years later reinforced the concept of Appalachia as an entity of its own, distinct and different from the rest of the country.[10] John Campbell disagreed with this assumption and argued that the highland South, like the rest of the country, had various parts and peoples—the mountains and the valleys, the rural and the urban, the farmers and the factory or mine workers. Not until outsiders came to understand the lack of uniformity in mountain life could they help the mountain people achieve a better life. Williams wrote, "In contrast to most other writers, Campbell emphasized the diversity of Appalachia, both in its class structure and its geographic features."[11] H. Davis Yeuell, in *Moving Mountains,* noted that Campbell pointed out the lack of good roads and railways, prevalent throughout the country prior to the 1850s. The mountain South was not that different from or more isolated than many other parts of America; but by the 1870s, industrial expansion had created the need for better transportation everywhere but in Appalachia. Yeuell further maintained that it was "theological understandings and cultural expectations with an assist from local color writers and mission interpreters that created 'Appalachia.'"[12] Marcia Clark Meyers found in writing her master's thesis, "Presbyterian Home Missions in Appalachia: A Female Enterprise," that the church used contradictory images: the "Appalachian people were a problem, a threat, and, at the same time a source of hope"; sometimes "barbarians and people of strong moral fiber" and at other times "lazy degenerates."[13]

Henry D. Shapiro's *Appalachia on Our Mind: The Southern Mountains and Mountaineers in the American Consciousness, 1870–1920* is probably still the quintessential study of the mythical image of Appalachia as a "Strange Land and Peculiar People." He observes that both local-color writers and missionaries had a practical stake in promoting the idea of Appalachia as a strange land; otherwise, they had no justification for their efforts. He further comments, "It was this irony inherent in the practice of benevolent work in Appalachia (that it destroyed what it pretended to value) against which

John Campbell directed his most strenuous and systematic efforts."[14] But local-colorists and missionaries had the power of the printed word, and they dominated public discussions of mountain life. And those who came to minister to the needs of the mountaineers often had little understanding of what their real needs were.

Campbell knew that programs to improve the situation in the region would have to be customized to meet the needs of a population that was remarkably diverse. Campbell wrote: "The Highland country is in truth a land of paradoxes and contradictions, because here in a restricted area are taking place all the changes that are going on in the world elsewhere."[15] In 1910 Samuel H. Thompson spoke of "three distinct classes" and in the flowery, colorful prose of the period described them: "valley dwellers, the true, worthy, mountaineers," and the "'poor whites' . . . the drift, the flotsam . . . shiftless, ambitionless degenerates, such as are found wherever men are found."[16] There was little disagreement with the view set forth by Samuel T. Wilson, that the problems of the southern Appalachians were the lack of communication due to "gully-gashed roads leading from one settlement to another," the lack of money due to "the prohibitive distance from all markets," and the lack of schools due to "the small school funds of the states involved." He quotes the Southern Education Board's 1902 statistics, stating that 16.34 percent of the white voters in the Southern Appalachians were illiterate.[17]

Campbell's work was sponsored by the Russell Sage Foundation, which had just been founded in 1907 by the wealthy widow of financier Russell Sage to promote benevolent and charitable projects. Russell Sage was not enthusiastic about his wife's interest in charitable work, but after he died, she inherited his fortune and invested much of it in the foundation she named for him.[18] John Glenn was one of the first trustees of the Russell Sage Foundation and its first director. He had earlier practiced law in Baltimore and was active in public service in his state, also serving as president of the National Conference of Charities and Correction in 1901. At the time of his appointment as director, he was on the boards of several charity organizations in Baltimore and a lecturer at Johns Hopkins University.[19] As the social survey movement was well established in the early part of the twentieth century, he believed that Campbell's idea for an investigation of the Southern Highlands was right in step with the foundation's Pittsburgh Survey and similar projects elsewhere. Social surveys usually involved firsthand collection of data within a specific area for the purpose of social reform. Most of the individuals conducting the early surveys were not academics, but reformers with practical projects in mind for political or charitable purposes.[20]

With a three-thousand-dollar grant from the foundation, Olive and John Campbell set out in September 1908 to travel across the Southern Highlands. They wanted to get to know the inhabitants and to collect factual data to help determine what might be done about the educational and social situation there. Sixteen separate denominations with church-related mission schools operated in the mountain region.[21] There were also public schools in some sections, with little or no communication or cooperation between them and the church schools. The Campbells visited independent, church, and public schools and engaged church and school workers in the field in conversation, collecting data about rural life, health conditions, educational issues, and denominational friction.

Olive Campbell very carefully recorded particulars about traditions and customs—such as permissive child-rearing, especially of boy children; the expectation that women would ride sidesaddle and would wait on the men; and the nature of what could be called hotel accommodations: when one stayed overnight with a local family, it was not uncommon to share a bed with strangers, even those "expectorating freely."[22] As an educated, refined New Englander, she occasionally expressed aversion to some of the social customs and religious viewpoints she encountered among the mountaineers. As she became more familiar with her surroundings and the people she met, she became more acclimated to their traditions, such as "frolics." She always felt that her role and that of the missionary workers was to instill "a better understanding of what is worthwhile," but when she later established the Folk School in Brasstown, North Carolina, it was evident that she planned for the native culture to be the basis of the school's educational efforts.[23]

The Russell Sage Foundation hoped that the discoveries the Campbells made would facilitate coordination among the southern mountain region's religious and educational workers, who often belonged to very different institutions. After the investigatory trip, John Campbell was employed by the foundation to compile the results of his study. For four years, he and his wife traveled extensively for the foundation, attending educational and religious conferences and conferring with the participants. When the results of the survey were presented, the foundation established the Southern Highland Division in Asheville, North Carolina, in 1913 and appointed John Campbell as director. In this role, he was instrumental in the formation of the Conference of Southern Mountain Workers (later called the Council) to help bridge differences and improve communication among the mountain workers.[24] Perhaps alternative ways could be found to meet the needs of mountain people. If church and independent schools could adapt their programs to a mountain environment and advocate the introduction of public schools in many more locations, they might be able to "work toward the ideal of a better rural life through church and other community activities, rather than purely academic activities."[25] The council held yearly conferences to encourage the exchange of ideas for the most effective methods for working in the mountainous areas. Campbell served as executive secretary until his death on May 2, 1919; his wife then assumed the position as secretary, and she cofounded the official publication of the council, *Mountain Life and Work* in 1925.

Olive Campbell was an accomplished author as well as a significant player in the social and cultural history of Appalachia in the first half of the twentieth century.[26] Suffering from angina, and never having been strong, John Campbell died in 1919. Olive Campbell gathered her husband's collection of notes and took them to a family cottage in Nantucket, where she finally completed *The Southern Highlanders and Their Homeland* in his name in 1921. Although Campbell was reluctant to publish his findings for a wide audience, he often shared his data with other workers in the region. As Olive Campbell writes in the preface to *The Southern Highlander,* he was "ready to give confidential information confidentially to those who may be social physicians and who will hold to the social and professional code."[27] Dr. Samuel T. Wilson, a prominent Presbyterian minister and educator, dedicated the 1914 revision of his book *The Southern Mountaineers* to Campbell, citing his generosity and his "epoch-making study" of the region.[28]

The Southern Highlanders and Their Homeland was a compilation of the findings of the survey and a documentation of John Campbell's perceptive and sensitive observations about the southern mountains and mountain life. It was the first comprehensive history of the region and the definitive study of its time. First published by the Russell Sage Foundation, it was reprinted in 1969 by the University Press of Kentucky with an introduction by Henry D. Shapiro and a foreword by Rupert B. Vance, a noted sociologist at the University of North Carolina.[29]

After *The Southern Highlander* was published, Olive Campbell traveled to Denmark to investigate the methods employed by Danish folk schools to educate adults. P. P. Claxton was also an advocate of Scandinavian schools and had often discussed the concept with the Campbells.[30] The principles of the Scandinavian folk schools, which attempted to encourage creativity and the spiritual life, could possibly be adapted to a mountain environment. The worst mistakes that most schools made, John Campbell wrote, had "arisen from the assumption that what was good for the city school, or the school in the Lowland rural sections . . . was, without change, good for the Highlands." He added: "There is a native culture in the mountains that has been too much ignored, which should be given expression in any educational system intended for the mountains."[31] Olive Campbell used the data from the mountain survey to apply her husband's philosophy of education to a real-life situation when she established the John C. Campbell Folk School in Brasstown, North Carolina, in 1925, finally fulfilling one of their dreams—a school to teach adults how to preserve their native heritage and to function and even prosper at the same time. Alvic credits their careful study of appropriate educational systems with the school's long-term success when she writes, "The John C. Campbell Folk School . . . stands alone among mountain schools for its organizational structure, which is based on the Danish folk school model."[32]

Beginning with the trip in 1908, Olive Campbell had an

abiding interest in the native culture of the mountain region. She contacted the foremost English ballad collector, Cecil Sharp, about the Scottish and English ballads she had discovered in the hills and valleys of the Appalachian Mountains. Sharp, traveling in America and lecturing on the Child ballads, was pleased to learn that many of them were still being sung.[33] With him, she published *English Folk Songs from the Southern Appalachians* in 1917, a collection of both lyrics and music.[34] After retiring as executive secretary of the Conference of Southern Mountain Workers, she focused her attention on the distinctive and varied work of the mountaineer craftsmen. Both of the Campbells were charmed by the native artistry, so much a part of mountain life, hidden in the coves and hollows where few outsiders wanted or dared to go. The Campbells believed that the talents of mountain people should be encouraged and that their creative projects could be a source of supplemental income. David Whisnant devotes a chapter of *All That Is Native and Fine: The Politics of Culture in an American Region* to recounting Olive Campbell's prominence in the cultural history of Appalachia. But Whisnant opines that although her efforts were worthy, she did little to improve social or living conditions for the mountaineers.

Other scholars disagree, believing that Olive Campbell made a substantial contribution to the betterment of mountain lives. At the Russell Sage Foundation, she met Allan Eaton. With Eaton and others at craft schools, she was instrumental in the formation in 1930 of the Southern Mountain Handicraft Guild, which changed its name to the Southern Highland Handicraft Guild in 1933 and is now known as the Southern Highland Craft Guild. In his authoritative work *Handicrafts of the Southern Highlands,* Eaton drew attention to her part in the promotion of crafts, as did Philis Alvic in the more recent *Weavers of the Southern Highlands.* Alvic champions Olive's work with the Conference of Southern Mountain Workers and states that many of the "most progressive ideas concerning crafts development can be traced back to her."[35] There is a comprehensive summary of her life, work, and cultural and educational contribution in "Olive Dame Campbell and Appalachian Tradition," by William Bernard McCarthy, in *Ballads into Books: The Legacies of F. J. Child.* In describing her discovery of the Child ballads in Appalachia, he writes that she "was to become an influential educator and developer of craft production in the southern mountains, the host of Cecil Sharp and his Southern Appalachian folk-song expeditions . . . and a significant ballad collector in her own right. Indeed, she was one of the first to discover that the popular ballad was far from dead."[36]

As time went on, Olive Dame Campbell took her place among the notable women of the period, alongside other social reformers such as Katherine Pettit and May Stone of Hindman and Pine Mountain Settlement Schools, Frances Goodrich of Allanstand Industries, and Lucy Morgan of the Penland School. *North Carolina Women Making History,* by Margaret Supplee Smith, chronicles the work of these women in the chapter "Culture, Altruism, and Exceptionalism." A short biography of Olive Campbell is also included, in which she is described as the woman who introduced "cultural studies—likely to be one of the major themes of the twenty-first century."[37] She was esteemed for her wise and practical approach to sometimes controversial social and educational issues.

Olive Campbell's diary, recording the day-by-day, systematic study of educational, religious, and social conditions among the southern highlanders, is a significant artifact in the history of Appalachian culture. It offers the vivid, entertaining, and personal account of the tireless efforts of dedicated individuals, devoted to their cause and to each other, who were involved in a project that produced the primary investigation of mountain society at the turn of the twentieth century in the southern Appalachians.

1

OCTOBER *1908*

VIRGINIA, TENNESSEE, NORTH CAROLINA, GEORGIA

The beginning could hardly have been made under more favorable conditions. Mr. Glenn, head of a new organization with untraveled ways to chart, was ready for experiment. Conscious of the full weight of his responsibility, he yet placed great reliance on the personality of the worker.

Being in New York rather seldom, we were somewhat in the nature of guests of Mr. and Mrs. Glenn while there, and often stayed at their house when they had room. Thus we came to know them in a social as well as a business relation. They had many influential friends, largely in the lowland South, and knew almost everyone prominent in social work. To these they introduced us when they thought it might be of help. A little typed sheet, signed and explaining who we were, helped to vouch for us whenever we needed such an introduction.

"RUSSELL SAGE FOUNDATION
"September 22, 1908
"This will introduce Mr. John C. Campbell who is to make an expedition through the southern mountains with a view to studying conditions there for the Russell Sage Foundation.

"*Any attention shown him will be greatly appreciated by the Foundation and by*

[Signed] "John M. Glenn, Director"[1]

. . . *Such letters, evidencing interest and a desire to help, and at the same time careful not to interfere with the free action of the investigator, were to be characteristic of our whole relation with Mr. Glenn. John kept him and Mrs. Glenn informed of our main steps and experiences, and asked advice from time to time. In this way the study went forward to the best advantage and, I believe, to mutual satisfaction.*

. . . *I have here the detailed diary which John asked me to keep, that first year of the study, as an aid to his memory. I had made a short record in my Line-A-Day the previous spring at Demorest, but now, with most of the South new to me and everything of interest, I recorded experiences faithfully, in detail as requested—from weather and character of the terrain to persons and personalities, what was said and how it all seemed to me personally. I am impressed, as I read it over, by our almost constant activity day after day for months at a time; traveling by train, by wagon, surrey, "hack," buckboard or buggy, horse or mule—even on foot—absorbing new sights, new information, making planned and chance contacts, gathering material of all sorts.*

The larger private and denominational schools were our first goals. They were not primarily, most of them, denominational in the aggressive sense but had been established by different boards and philanthropic groups to meet the great poverty of public education throughout the rural areas. Beginning with "day schools" and elementary boarding schools, they had gradually broadened their scope until the larger ones offered an "academy" or full high school course, often the only such course to be secured in the county. "Colleges" had naturally followed, not always standard in equipment and curriculum, but certainly institutions of higher learning, and important out of proportion to their size and equipment. They were, too, very hospitable and, whatever their academic standing, could give us information which it would have taken us long to have gathered elsewhere. More

16

important still were the friends we made—friends who were to become the foundation of later work.

From larger and more accessible schools we reached out to the smaller and more remote, public and private, and stopped by little one- and two-roomed public schools and high schools, where there were any. We talked with teachers, county superintendents, doctors, ministers of all sorts, where John was almost invariably called on to speak. We asked about resources, farm practices and income, and if there was an established industry besides farming, we tried to get data on it and knowledge of conditions associated with it. We took many pictures, and bought or were given many more. We inquired into local history, ancestry, travel-routes.[2]

THURSDAY, October 1st, 1908: Back again in Dixie by a new road—Richmond, Petersburg, and Potomac, which carried us along the James River for miles through country red with battles. One cannot get away from the war, with the Wilderness at one point and Fredericksburg and Stonewall Jackson's dying place. The type changed too. Some of the poor whites got in and off at small stations. We saw one horrid old man and boys—17 or 18—loaded down with whiskey in jugs and bags. A brakeman had to stop one from drinking, and then he tried to bluff the conductor by pretending sleep while the former collected tickets—an unsuccessful effort.

The rural aspect of the South strikes one immediately—no large cities and stretches and stretches of woodlands and corn fields. It makes one wonder how the education problem is ever to be solved, complicated as it is with the negro question.

We drove down to the station at Washington with an old negro (the taximeter was late) and with a little encouragement, he regaled us all the way with conversation on these lines. The Presidents made no difference to him. He was second stable boy under Cleveland, and he could not see that

Cleveland was any different from Roosevelt. A negro did not have much chance anyway. Once they used to let the negro cabmen solicit fares—now a white taximeter company from which the negro was barred out, was formed, and everything was planned so that the taximeter got all the business. If a negro solicited trade, rode up and down the streets, etc.—he was (presto) clapped into prison, fined or called down. He said it was up to the colored man to do the best he could and keep quiet. He reckoned a colored man might work and earn a living and be respected in his place—but the trouble was that some of them got an education and tried to push up higher. They couldn't get there and it made it harder for all the rest. Poor things, it is hard all round.

I was all ready in spirit for Richmond, which was full of the past to me. However, outside the Capital Square and isolated houses, we did not see many attractive parts. Much of it is new and flat—brick blocks and modern dwelling houses. Confederate White House, however was very charming, and though we rushed the interior, it brought up the whole tragedy. We posed as from Georgia and were shown the Georgia relics by a sad young woman dressed entirely in black (The Lost Cause?). Also an old Confederate soldier showed us about, grieving that we did not have more time. It made me feel a little like a hypocrite. One is so sorry for them, and the tragedy seems deeper the more you see. Yet I think the young ones, at least, ought not to keep up the feeling. I cannot blame the ones who really saw and suffered, but the young ones should live it down if they can. We didn't have time to see the cemeteries or battlefields, and I cannot see why the city should make such an impression—but it did—perhaps through the appeal to the imagination.

October 2nd, Friday: Richmond to Charlottesville: Such pretty country all through here, and Virginia seems much richer and better cultivated than I remember Georgia to be. There were many nice looking Southerners on the train— the type unmistakable. The young ones are generally lean, with narrow faces—slightly unshaven—large grey eyes. They wear soft collars, large ties and black felt hats, and so many of them chew! I wish they wouldn't. Spittoons everywhere in evidence. Every seat in the car has one and every room in the hotel. The coaches have a prevailing smell of tobacco juice.

Charlottesville is quite a neat little town for the South, though they say that the poor live in town and the rich in the country. We saw many beautiful country residences—some old ones tucked back among the trees. The town has a general aspect of old Colonial (red brick and tall white columns) for many of the new houses are built in the old style. The entire University of Virginia around the rectangle is so built and is very dignified and effective. One can walk around three sides entirely under colonnades.

The people are immensely cordial. We met an old D.U. friend of John's—who has married and turned into a typical southerner; says he "couldn't live north now."[3] His wife was originally from Chicago, but brought up abroad. She was most elaborately coiffured and gowned, and they have a lovely stone house out of town on a hillside. I imagine, by the residences and get-ups I see, that there must be quite an aristocratic society here.

Professor Payne was, however, one of the most attractive men we have met.[4] He is a southerner and extremely good looking—dark and well built though not tall. He talked along easily (though with a certain shyness) to me, while John was busy with the baggage, and I never noticed until John got back, that he was bareheaded all that time, his hat held behind him. John told him to put it on, and I apologized as well as I could. He talked to me mainly of the country and county, its race horses, etc., but John says he found him full of knowledge and interest in the mountain situation. He speaks of it as not being our best stock, about 20 percent good, which should be kept in the mountains to develop them. He told of an old mountaineer who got hold of some agricultural information and improved his apples. Now he gets several thousand ($3000) a year from his Albemarle Pippins which were sent abroad—too expensive to eat on this side of the water. Queen Victoria ate them for years. He said he could sell the man's estate for a big sum ($20,000), but he did not think it well to urge him. Such people should have the development of the mountains. Peaches and apples were perfectly possible—even best in the mountain hollows.

In educational lines, he had found the churches hard to deal with. He was not for propagating Episcopal, Baptist or any other denomination—much as their social effort might appeal to him. But the State could help them if they wanted to create local boards which were self-perpetuating. The trouble was that most churches did not wish to give up the doctrinal grip. Found the workers broad-minded and liberal—ready to take the advanced steps. A question of support troubled them. The Sage Board might use its influence to buy Boards to right view. Mayo he wants as County Superintendent.[5]

We had a beautiful drive Friday afternoon to Ivy where Archdeacon Neve lives.[6] The fertility and beauty of this Virginia country is a constant joy, and gives one a better idea of the old days than any other part of the South I have yet seen. We met constantly people on horseback and driving blooded horses. They say the county is famous for its thoroughbreds. One livery stable keeps nothing but them. The Archdeacon's house was unpretentious and [he] a tall awkward man, 6 feet 2–3 inches, I should say. His eyes turn in opposite directions, which seems to cause him as much embarrassment as you. He does not look at you directly. We had to hurry our talk as he was due to leave at 5.45, but we sat over a very grateful open fire, and he and John feet in. He likewise believes in keeping the people in the mountains—in orchards, stock raising (the dairy idea seemed a new one to him). The Episcopal work is arranged in districts and his includes this part of Virginia. He said the railroad ran near enough the Blue Ridge in places to take care of the fruit, but most of the travelling must be done on horseback. Their P.E. [Protestant Episcopal] work began in small ways. They generally first got some refined educated woman to go, from missionary impulse, into some mountain community and by her method of living show the people how. He said they needed a standard of living, something which was not attained by the district school. In fact the district schools were many of them farces. In their work they had frequently had to take up schools that had been closed. When educational matters were left entirely to local settlement, a school degenerated—became useless and was dropped. One school in a near hollow had been running for years, but few of the inhabitants could read or write—showing its usefulness or uselessness.

We found our ride back, 5.30–6—decidedly cool with a suggestion of frost in the air. Such weather makes one think twice of horseback + sleeping bag. I should want a heavy sleeping bag. We came back in double quick time. I do like good horses, though I cannot say I like the careless way the people leave dangerous R.R. crossings unprotected. These were as bad as the ones about Mendenhall, Pa.

OCTOBER 4th, Sunday: Natural Bridge, Virginia: The quiet of this country seems good after the roar of trains. Such a typical station, too, at Lynchburg—with upstairs waiting room literally packed with men, women and crying babies.

This combined with trains running on either side of the station (junction of C & O and Southern) made the noise quite deafening. John and I escaped to the lunch room which was quite deserted and quiet in comparison, and spent our hour wait in eating and directing cards. They don't seem to have any idea how to manage things down here—I do not know exactly why. Maybe it is the fault of the travelling public. The hotel, however, is as nice as one could wish—quite magnificent—and when we drove up—a fine twilight mile through woods and up hill, it was all a blaze of lights (they have their own plant).

This morning was so cold that John and I started with our coats into the glen. We needed them too, though it grew warm before we got back. The path along the brook, under the bridge and to the falls is charming—especially so at this fall season, when the steep slopes of the hills were streaked with color. The bridge itself is most impressive, especially from the further side. It seems doubly wonderful when one looks at the little insignificant stream below—which was its author. We had a great time craning our necks to discover G. W. [George Washington's] initials. He chose a hard though not very high place to put them over the water. Some one climbed up last year and stuck a little chain above. It marks the place quite conveniently. I believe he fell into the water before finally succeeding. Much as I love my old reader story of the boy who climbed to the top, I am afraid it is not true. It would not seem to be borne out and looks quite impossible—at least above G. W.'s initials.

We had the maddest ride I ever took—to the station. We were a little late, owing to someone being left, and our driver, a mountain boy with Sunday clothes and mountain hair-cut, let out the two great brown horses. If we did hustle down that steep hill! The horses did not walk a step and most of the way they galloped. How we rattled over those little bridges and around those steep curves! My heart sat behind my teeth, but it certainly was great! All the men of the town were at the station—indeed we noticed that all along the line. In places it seemed as if the whole town had flocked to the train—amusing, entertaining and pathetic.

OCTOBER 6th, Tuesday, Knoxville: A wait of two nights here in order to get at Dr. Claxton and Dr. Duncan, both of whom were out of town, after all our Sunday hustle.[7] The city (the business part of it) has a suggestion of Springfield, though on an inferior scale. The soft-coal smoke is spoiling it too. I have not taken such a fancy to this country. I do not think it nearly so pretty as Virginia, and our car ride to Fountain City today did not show us pretty suburbs. John says that Maryville is not so pretty as Virginia nor nearly as fine as the Asheville region. I shall be interested to see the Blue Ridge and Murphy section tomorrow.

We had a tiring ride here from Bristol though it was interesting too in showing the people. Nothing could have been more different from New England—the towns were small and straggling—unattractive mostly, and the men unkempt. At one place we took the whole town aboard, old soldiers, mountaineer loafers, everybody—and in a body they left at Jonesboro—where it appeared there was court to be held that day. We had a number of girls aboard, each one dressed in her best; even those, apparently well acquainted, took separate seats, where they could look out of the window and wave to acquaintances at every station. Some Washington College boys who were on the train, got off at every station to yell to some acquaintance.[8] They were like children—and chewing gum! Every one chews—the men tobacco, I suppose—but the women and children gum. I suppose I ought to be thankful it was not tobacco or snuff. I became quite worn watching a little baby, in front of me chew and chew and chew—rolling the gum inside and outside, winding her finger in it, etc. It is not an alluring performance. Such conditions must make a woman of Miss de Graffenreid's culture sigh for her poor South. Miss de Graffenreid is one of the first I have met of the old stock and I found her charming.[9] She appeared to be in touch with all the old southern aristocracy—said she could give influence if not money. Her great desire was to see not the individual development of small colleges and academies, but a big federated control, which should not foster local prejudice, etc. For that reason she would give nothing to separate schools, like Rabun Gap.[10] She said another thing which interested me—that she found the southerner (the old South, I suppose) and the New Englander were really closest of all sections, when their misunderstanding was wiped away. She refused to go to the Hallowell's to meet some colored celebrity—laughed and said she thought too much of herself! I fancy the Hallowells must have been annoyed.

OCTOBER 7th: Dr. Duncan, Synodical Missionary of the synod of Tennessee, which includes the mountain Presbytery of western North Carolina.[11] His view is that the mountain schools must give way to State schools when conditions permit; some schools to be given up entirely—others activities changed to home industries, etc. He believes that the investment made by the church boards should not be lost but by transfer and change made to minister to the soul and body needs of the people. He is not very hopeful regarding the agricultural future of the mountain region and feels that the best will be drawn away. He also feels that there is a religious asset in the mountains which should be drawn upon to supply the thinning ministerial ranks in other sections. He feels that the Women's Board under whose charge the mountain work mainly is in the U.S.A. Presbyterian Church, is retreating from the field too quickly in their desire to do work in Cuba and elsewhere—advised writing to Dr. Wilson, of Maryville for data as to money-values, etc.[12]

P. P. Claxton, Superintendent of Secondary Education (in Tennessee): He emphasizes the good stock of the mountain people; thinks their education should be of a nature to keep them in the mountains to develop the natural resources of East Tennessee and North Carolina, with which he is familiar; has great faith in the industrial future of the mountains—coal, iron, marble, timber. Furniture factories could be established. He feels the time for the church school is almost past—on its present basis. Perhaps still some work along the present lines in the remote sections. Church schools and the secondary departments of the colleges hinder the growth of county high schools and a healthy local atmosphere of self support. They are tending to pauperize the poor and are patronized very largely by well-to-do farmers with a false pride which leads them to send their children to a "pay private school" rather than to the public school provided by the state which they look upon as a sort of poor charity school where anyone can send his children for nothing. Three ideas to emphasize—Adapt the school's curriculum to life of people; Let all effort from outside tend to build up a spirit of self-support; not to be antagonistic even unconsciously; To establish schools for grown-ups; cites grown-up schools of Denmark and Sweden.[13] Sage fund a mediator—a go-between to bring about these things.

President Alderman, of the University of Virginia: Has had a struggle with the church schools—narrowness of religious leaders.[14] Says they are much more liberal than they used to be. Rather favors the idea of getting people out of the mountains—no one but a hero really wants to go back there and help them. Heroism is exceptional in human nature. Admits that they are a magnificent asset that should be incorporated into our life as a people.

OCTOBER 8th: I found the other side of Knoxville much more attractive and the views going toward Maryville grew prettier when we finally struck the Blueridge line. Saw plenty of small frightened pigs and in one place a man with a gun sitting on the R.R. platform and holding a live possum by the tail. At Blueridge we held a conference with the hotel keeper and Colonel Bass and decided to go through to Murphy. The scenery continued pretty and the grade up—although it did not equal the beauty of the ride in the morning round the mountain and along the Hiawassee River. We did, however, have three very drunk young fellows roaring and whooping on the back platform (only one coach to the train and one freight car—the coach divided into smoking and non-smoking compartments). They drank white-moonshine copiously, and were watched by three train officials who finally shipped them safely at a small station. There were some Young-Harris students (unattractive) aboard who advised us not to try to go through that night, and as it turned out, we couldn't leave Murphy anyway, as all the horses were busy, it being horse-swapping day.[15] Ten or more of us—with baggage, crammed into a crazy old hack which creaked in a dangerous way up a steep hill to the Dickey Hotel—alluringly known as the Drummer's Home. It proved to be very comfortable, as well as picturesque, and the food was excellent—heaps of fried chicken, hot biscuit, meat etc, etc. John trotted off first thing to the horse swapping convention—ostensibly to make arrangements for morrow with the livery keeper. I stayed at home as women do not go (to the swappings here.) I had fun, however, watching the groups pass the house. There were all sorts and conditions of mounts as well as cattle. John came back much amused, and had also had a talk with County Commissioner

Norval.[16] He said [there were] fruit, cattle raising possibilities in the mountains. Can't let the church schools go yet—doing good work. Mountain people do not want an education unless they can get it for nothing. (He was under criticism for spending too much on schools and felt sore.) In North Carolina they get appropriation from general State fund. County can tax itself for high school. District can also tax itself.

We had a pleasant chat, after tea and short walk, with our landlady who said there were plenty of natural resources in the region—mineral, timber, fruit and a number of good farms. There was also good hunting and some fish.

OCTOBER 8th, Continued: Up before light—we boasted an electric light in our room—a small one but real—and off again on the road. We had a most dilapidated surrey and the horses were not "right peart" in appearance. They went however very well and covered the rough twenty miles to Young-Harris before 12 noon. These were the worst roads I have struck yet—great ledges of rock jerking up in the middle or side of the road indifferently; up and down hill with a rising grade and many times a steep drop off on the side. We had to keep turning out and out, for we met fifty odd men, horses, mules, teams, oxen, etc. on the road, most of them bound, I suppose, to the horse swapping convention which lasts three days. There was the sorriest collection of animals on parade—to be swapped, but also we met many smart mounts, mules and otherwise. In one place—passing a team of steers, our surrey had to be half-lifted—quite exciting. I would also add that we passed plenty of pigs and hens galore.

The country all along was of the prettiest and glorious with color. I never saw such gorgeous reds as there in the black gums, sourwood and dogwood. There were maples too and woodbine and oak in rich color. Especially along the first half of our way the road was massed with laurel (ivy) and rhododendron (not the "big laurel"). It must be beautiful in June, and even now the rich green was in handsome contrast with the autumn color. Now one would be riding along in a valley, fording a creek or branch, now high on a mountain side, looking parallel into the branches of a tree whose trunk was hidden. We saw some nice farms—quite prosperous in appearance, bottom land and other scraggly corn fields high up, that did not look as if they would yield more than five bushels an acre. Our driver, Charlie Lance (I called him Spear), a rather good looking mountain lad with a heart trouble which I lay to indigestion, said some acres would yield 50 bushels and they got about $1.00 per bushel.

The cabins looked very attractive tucked in along the roadside, though I can't help thinking that in spite of their picturesqueness and the beauty of their position backed by blue mountains—they must be desperately lonely in winter when these roads are well-nigh impassible. Hard on the women and children. It is very pretty now. We passed a sorghum mill where the cane was heaped high and the horse was going around the tread mill. There were lots of children about and there was an air of festivity and cheer. John called a little boy to bring us a piece of cane—and he came running across the field and through the branch with two great long pieces. We broke and chewed some—a sweet rather acid pleasant flavor.

At another place where the road was high, we looked down into a hollow by a creek to a mill, where children were playing. On the opposite side, alone under the bushes, one little girl sat solemnly fishing. I wonder how much schooling she gets a year.

There were plenty of persimmons along the road, and I tried my first ones—a candy-like odd flavor—also some wild grapes which were not very good. We varied these with chestnuts, of which Charlie had his pockets full.

Young-Harris has a lovely situation in a small valley surrounded by mountains, but itself makes a rather dismal neglected impression. There is one big recitation hall, built of
brick with white columns. The columns are pieced out with
tin which is splitting open, and the building near at hand
does not live up to its distant impression. There is an old dormitory for the boys and a new one this summer, of wood covered with tin to simulate red brick for the girls. Then there
is a little red brick chapel and some odd shanties. There
was no green about nor apparently any effort to keep things
picked up and in shape. No one came out as we drove up, so
John got out and went in. He appeared presently with a thin
worn looking woman in red calico (dressing jacket type) who
turned out to be the President's wife Mrs. Sharpe. She took
us to her room to clean up, then excused herself to prepare
dinner. She came back in twenty minutes or so and had a talk
with us while we waited for her husband.[17]

She felt that they had done their share in the work there
(10 years) and should change. They had worked like slaves
and she had lost her health (had one child). She could get
no kitchen help and it was slow work teaching the mountain girls. In fact, she had to direct and do most of the cooking (the matron looked quite fat and cheerful). They have
a number of girls (8–10) who wait on table and wash dishes
to partially pay their way through. They keep their own cows
for milk and butter and raise their own vegetables. They start
their farm in the spring and Prof. Sharpe over-sees it (he was
trying to get in hay before the rain). They have a large summer school and many of the students stay all the year round.
She gets no rest or change (two weeks last year at Washington
D.C.) and seemed discouraged. I don't wonder. Later, she
said, they wanted Domestic Science for the girls and wished
to make an industrial school of it.

Pres. Sharpe was very late in coming in (had not gotten our letter) and seemed rather brusque in manner—evidently like Mrs. Sharpe thought us out for a job. On explanation he warmed up and talked for an hour after dinner (a sad one—dinner). He is a big rather powerful man with an unkempt appearance (all were unshaven) and unpolished manners. He evidently felt some lack. Said he could not beg—had to run the school on the income—about $2–3,000. Last year he persuaded his Board to put out part of endowment in a farm with timber and bottom land. He has made this pay about 6%. Mrs. Sharpe had told us that they had practically no mountain pupils—only 10–15 boarding—out of the 400 to 500 total. Most were from the lowlands—beyond Atlanta. He said they had had the greatest difficulty in getting mountain students. Many of the remote mountaineers did not want an education—others looked with suspicion on Methodism. The county had always been Baptist, and an old Baptist preacher of considerable influence in the county, resented Methodists coming in. The school bells made him mad, and he had publicly told the mountaineers that the sound of those bells was "the clatter of the devil's tongue." It had taken a long time to overcome this prejudice, but it had been overcome—practically all, he thought now. The mountain students were beginning to come in—in all about 50. However he gave no definite numbers, and Mrs. S. had said that although they had a special fund for 10 mountain girls, they had only been able to get 6 and had to go further south for the others. He said the mountaineers were suspicious of anything new or educational. Also they do not like to get into debt—and as I understood the scheme—they were asked to borrow in order to pay in advance. The mountaineers felt they might be asked to pay these notes any time, lose their farms, etc. He said one winter they burned 400 cords of wood—wood getting scarce.

He induced authorities to buy a tract for $3000 with some cleared land—the rest heavily timbered. In the winter he uses his own team and hires men to cut and haul the wood. In the spring he lets each of these men have a horse to farm the old and recently cleared land on shares, half and half. In this way he makes the investment pay 6%. (John recalls, at this point, that a county superintendent in Georgia brought about the consolidation of two schools by buying a team, drawing the pupils of the community where the school was given to the other school which had furnished a farm. The driver worked the team on the farm during school hours and made a crop paying for the keep of team and some over. When school was out, the children were taken back home.)

Drove in P.M. to Hiawassee through high country. Spent the night at the Hooper House—and had to wait a long time while John went out to see Prof. Greene, of the Academy, and the people got our feather-bed ready.[18] He found the Professor a cripple and a most interesting man—full of courage and optimism as to the situation. Said the school leavened the whole country side. His pupils were teaching to right and left. Twenty-five of the 27 teachers in the county were his graduates. Can do anything with a mountaineer when you get his confidence. Wanted $1000 to put up cabins where his pupils could batch it. Agreed to send us a statement of where his pupils came from and where went, but has not done so. Admitted that those most highly educated did not come back, but, therefore emphasized the need of good secondary schools. These pupils went back.

OCTOBER 9th: Had a good night but woke to find it still raining after a showery night. Charlie was cheerful and we resolved to go ahead. I heard a screech as I was finishing dressing, and John prophesied a chicken for breakfast. We had it sure enough—an improvement on the pork of the night before. These mountain people spread their tables most bountifully, chicken, rice, biscuit and corn bread (Charlie ate enormously of the former which were strong of soda—poor weak heart!) dried peach sauce, sweet potatoes, some breakfast food and various odd things which are spread out at angles all along the tables. You pick and choose.

This day's drive was the best yet—in spite of the showers ending in a heavy downpour as we arrived at Nacoochee about 2:15 P.M.[19] All along the clouds shifted over the top of the mountains alternating with flashes of sunshine. For half the way the road mounted steadily till we reached the highest point in Indian Grave Gap. Fortunately the roads had not softened and we made fine time. From there on Charlie let the horses go and we galloped cheerfully down the mountain side passing Mr. Glenn and his grandson who had camped there that night after chestnuts—by three nut wagons (nearly tipped over in a mad rush by the 3rd which did not move aside) and down amid a pour to the Chattahoochee. Made a mistake at the cross roads and went 4 miles out but finally got in safely. We passed such a funny old sow with a crowd of little squeaking pigs which ran under our wagon.

Had a jolly dinner at the Glenn House. Col. Bingham who has an interest in the Sal Asbestos mine was there and there was much jollity over the open fire.[20] We didn't care to start out in the rain—but Charlie had gone back to cross the ford before the river came up and we wanted to make town [Demorest].[21] So we got a man to take us back behind Frank and George, two big ugly looking mules, who trotted neatly along amid the mud. Home about seven to find Miss Santly and Wells waiting.

Charlie a thrifty lad, had earned $1.50 a day logging—very hard work. Had $150 in the bank and had just bought a farm of good bottomland for $350. Owned saddle horse. Now earning $20 a month and board—at livery stable driving, but preferred it to logging as it was not so hard. Drove the horses hard—saw everything—no remarks or details lost. Told me instantly names of all trees which were used for tan bark etc. Described a farm of ginseng owned by his uncle—1/4 acre now—valued at $3000. Would sell none until he had an acre. Seeds worth a lot apiece. A beautiful plant with red berries— required a lot of care and shade—900 berries on one plant.

OCTOBER 28th: Atlanta: State Superintendent Jerry M. Pound: Georgia has no law for creation of high schools. In sympathy with church schools. Can help out if they do not teach denominationalism. Problem of mountains = problem of more people. Same as rural lowland problem with a little more isolation—mountain children get as much pro-rate from State fund as lowland practically. (Perhaps lowlands get a little more as some of the negroes go to them?) Lowlands have to divide with negro fairly evenly. Noticeable that as you get to mountain counties, more schools and more teachers, but oftentimes a 3rd grade teacher in lowlands gets as much as 1st grade teacher in highlands. Notice the smallness of some mountain schools. Hard to get mountaineer to consolidate schools. Each wants school at own door yard because of individualism, lack of community spirit due to environment—also due to danger for children of crossing streams etc. (Good roads and bridges will obviate. JCC)—Multiplicity of schools due to another fact. Mountain boy hears of outside world and wants to get into it. Needs money to get a start. Can't earn much. Gets up a school—gets a little money til he can go elsewhere. Consequently multiplicity of schools taught by boys and girls instead of grown men and cannot influence community (notice proportion of male teachers in mountains). Teachers are temporary—these schools among which the state fund is divided, last a shorter time than would if there were fewer schools among which to divide funds.

Comparatively few people in remote parts of the mountains. Cluster in mountain valleys, and there could be established good schools for long terms with good teachers with good salaries—in these valleys within walking distance of large numbers of children. (JCC—Winter storms, laying by time too short for lengthy schools). Another influence sending children away to lowlands—fathers expecting too much work (JCC—boy not his own man until he is 21). Boys want to get away. Parents need to be educated—social and community life made better. Long slow process. Thinks teachers trained to teach for country life will solve situation—text books, etc. are based on commerce and banking—examples, etc. should be based on life the people live. JCC suggestion—based on ideas suggested by Supt. Pound—In the mountains get teachers to give examples, lessons, etc—based on material sources of section.[22]

Rev. John E. White, Second Baptist Church Atlanta—formerly of Mars Hill College N. C. See his opinions in pamphlets: Home Mission Board South, Baptist Convention, Mountain School Work. Pamphlet No. 4—1905–1906—A solution of mountain problems of our Southern mountain region. A dollar in the mountains.

Believes the Sage Foundation can do its best work through sociological and neighborhood work with enlightened school communities as centers. Recommended articles by Judge Pritchard in Asheville Citizen—June 12th, 1907—Address on Intellectual Development.[23] Recommended my seeing Judge Pritchard, Rev. A. E. Brown, Supt. Of Baptist Mountain Missions Asheville—suggest our reading "At our Doors" by Supt. S. M. Morris of Southern Presbyterian Church Atlanta—suggested going to see President of Presbyterian Normal College Asheville. Suggested reading article by Alvin Horton—*Raleigh News & Observer* September 16, 1906, "Mountain Revivals."

R. E. Wright, Assistant Commissioner of Agriculture, Atlanta, gave material on resource of Virginia and suggested reading "Historical and Industrial Virginia"—1890–1902, Department Agriculture, by O. B. Stephens, Commissioner and B. G. Wright, Asst. Resources set down by counties. Bureau of Entomology will send horticultural report of 1908 by December to Demorest. S. W. McCallie, State Geologist, sending 17 reports October 29th to me at Demorest, giving mineral resources. Write to Prof. M. B Waite, Pathologist, Bureau of Plant Industry, Washington D. C., for mountain resources and ask him to refer us to people who can tell us of fruits, vegetables, etc. that will grow in mountains.

Quoted from "At Our Own Door," by S. L. Morris, D.D., Secy. Of the General Assemblys, Home Missions, Presbyterian Church in U.S. South: "The Northern Presbyterian Church in doing noble work in this (mountain) section, as appears from Doyles' "Presbyterian Home Missions": Presbyterian Home Mission Work among the mountain people of the south was begun in 1879. The first mission school was Whitehall Seminary established near Concord, N. C. and Miss Frances E. Ufford was teacher. The work has extended from that beginning over the mountain region of the four States—N. C., Tennessee, Kentucky and West Virginia. There are today, as a result of the Home Board's work, 31 churches, 1378 church members, 76 Sunday Schools, 6172 Sunday school scholars, 37 mission schools, 108 mission school teachers, 3000 pupils, 21 ministers, and 16 Bible teachers. The principle agencies in advancing missions have been churches, mission schools, Sabbath Schools and Bible readers."

(JCC note added in his handwriting: Very good article on origin and classification of the mountains. Rev. R. F. Campbell, *Home Missions Herald*, Presbyterian Church in U.S., April

1908. Note possible reasons for their going to the mountains. John Temple joins in same issue as above—Ozark work also.)

Mrs. J. K. Ottley, Atlanta, October 29th, much interested in the situation, but had most to say on Rabun Gap, explaining Mr. Ritchie's struggle. U.D.C. and Federation idea was to start industrial training in small schools, the Federation providing building and industrial teacher, and the town supplying the regular teacher. When the town was able to support both, Federation wished to drop its share. New school at Tallulah, but Federation here was obliged to support the whole thing owing to the local situation. Was suspicious of Mrs. Gielow and the Southern Educational Board—said they instituted themselves as a Board and rendered account to no one. Had collected money in the name of the Rabun school and never given it.[24]

OCTOBER 30th TO NOVEMBER 3rd, Rome, Georgia:

Miss Berry's School:

Arrived at 8:00 P.M. and were met by Henry Gaines, one of the boys, and quite a character—loquacious if nothing else, who drove us four miles out in the country to the school.[25] Were met by Miss Berry and several teachers and conducted to a charming model log cabin which serves as a center for the school, a home for some of the teachers, and a place to put visitors. There was a red lantern on the porch, which dimly showed logs, vines and rustic furniture, and when we pulled the old-fashioned latchstring we found a large room, with a cozy fire in the grate, a big carved four-poster, old fashioned bureau and wardrobe—latticed windows. We left our grips and sat down before a huge open fire in the main room, while they got dinner ready for us. The teachers generally meal with the boys but there is a nice little kitchen in the cabin where they can cook for visitors or themselves if they feel so inclined. One of the boys wipes dishes, cleans up, sweeps, dusts, etc., every day. Miss Berry sat down with us and Miss Neal who is one of her secretaries. A delicious supper of fried chicken, toast, tea and jelly—gelatin with real cream and nice tea. A fire also in that room. Then we adjourned to the front room, met several teachers and talked.

Miss Berry is a Southern woman in the region of forty—dark and rather heavily built with sweet voice and vivacious animated manner. She belongs to an aristocratic old family, was brought up with nursery maids and governesses, lived abroad and had a busy society life. Her sisters are now in the run of fashion. One has married an Italian nobleman and lives out of Rome. None understand her interest in the work. Her mother we met twice—a little erect old lady, with sparkling dark eyes, a dignified manner and deep voice. She ran the whole plantation during the war—a mere girl—her husband being 20 years older. The work started from a cabin on the old place (Miss Berry has given her share of the estate to the school), where she saw children playing in the woods, gradually found their need and ignorance, started a chain of Sunday Schools and finally this school—from the first on a working agricultural basis. There is no endowment or regular income except [a small annual amount] given by the town. She has to raise it all herself by speaking, writing, etc. She will have nothing but the very best teachers she can find—and they are a splendid corps—all absorbed in the work and devoted personally to her. She is a woman of great personal power—a leader.

No boys are taken from the town or from districts where there are more than 5 months' schooling—none except the needy and these from rural places—lowland and highland. All are obliged to work two hours a day at the rate of 6 cents. They have an academy (?) training and instruction in farming—building—dairy work (they make their own butter which is delicious and this last summer sold $100 worth a month of cream and butter to the town). They have a steam laundry where the boys do their own washing and pressing, their own power house, a shop and open work shed, a barn and poultry yard, where they also raise pigeons. There are several small houses—5–6—which are used as dormitories—one of them a charming old Southern mansion which they hope to eventually become Miss Berry's home, they hope. At present she has no regular abiding place—but lives in her trunk between school and home (her mother is alone). There are about 150 boys, all fine looking. They have musical training and make an excellent impression in church with their quiet manners and good singing. They also sing well our old Northern college songs. We heard them after supper Saturday night around the old tinny piano.

They tell most amusing stories of the place. Miss Neal gave me an account of how they got their bathroom in the log cabin. A fussy old lady who complained of every draft and pointed out every crack, took up Miss Berry's offer of a bath. Miss Berry sent to her old home for an old zinc tub. Mr. McLean brought it in the cold pale dawn—and the young teachers got up and scrubbed it on the porch of Brewster Hall (there being no water at the cabin). Then they warmed the water and lugged it over. This old lady had given a scholarship of $50 but no more. A demure little charity worker staying at the same time left $300 as she wanted to "help toward a bathroom which seemed their greatest need."

The school is beset with foreign missionaries—one spoke Sunday after John finished—urging all to enlist and quite looking down on those who stayed on the farm—just opposed to Miss Berry's idea and training.

They have had amusing mission barrels—among donations a whole black Bishop's coat.[26] It went to a big fellow who came in a grass green shirt and coat almost up to his elbows. He looked well though odd in it, especially when he danced a clog dance, as he could inimitably. Another donation was a good tuxedo coat, and another fine white coat. They had had two installments of out-of-style Rogers Peet's—the first all of one bright tan color![27] One came full of bonnets and another of children's clothes in spite of repeated statements that the school was for boys. Old theological books of course and old text books of no use—express paid by the school.

John told his story of the pretty child and plain father, the child naively remarking "God is doing better work now." The boys—to our amusement—applied it to John and me. They all clustered about John on Sunday and listened absorbed to Alabama tales. They had a Y.M.C.A. testimony meeting— all sitting on cushions on the floor in front of the big cabin dining room fireplace. Miss Berry has the boys there for a special talk every Sunday night. Then singing after supper at the table—the evening service is a pleasant feature. The boys also work in the kitchen—cook and wash under direction of a Mrs. Grawther(?), and wait on table. There are 17 teachers, including Mr. Berry, practical farmer, Mrs. Berry nurse, etc.; Miss Brewster (who has been here since the beginning and is specially close to Miss Berry) in English; Miss Neal in office; Miss Brooks in music; Mr. Adams head of school academy; Mr. McLane general superintendent of grounds, buildings, etc.

Miss Berry believes in waking a boy up by taking him from his old environment into a new atmosphere. Better school in Rome than among mountains. Wants same for girls on cottage plan.

2

NOVEMBER 1908

TENNESSEE AND KENTUCKY

John was insatiable. He pushed travel as fast as he could and let no op-
portunity slide for gathering new information. From my diary one may pick
almost at random a characteristic series of days. For example, from Novem-
ber 7 to November 11 we were travelling by buggy—John driving—over the
Cumberland Plateau in Tennessee to Pleasant Hill, Grassy Cove, Jewett,
Grandview, Ozone, and so to the train which would take us to Knoxville for
the opening meeting of President Roosevelt's Rural Commission. We started
from Chattanooga, on November 3, 1908.[1]

NOVEMBER 2: Off very early—6.30 AM—for Chattanooga. Henry Gaines with his English siders, drove us to train and regaled us with tales of his old affairs and top buggy. He is a
quaint soul.

Engine broke down on way up and we were an hour or
more late. Went to the Patten which was really quite grand.
J. went to Mormon headquarters for information on their
work. Very cordially received by Elder Sec.—shown through
buildings and given a number of books—asked to call again—
and promised to send account of mission work in mountains.

Said people were coming to understand them better—less prejudice. All they wanted was to do good. Their missionaries report to them every week. Support selves or are supported by own people for five years—paying even for pamphlets they distribute.

We had an amusing old negro guide on Lookout Mt—who talked of the rock formation as "hetogenous conglomeration." He had lived in Chattanooga, was a slave originally belonging to General Wheeler. We had a really quite terrifying ride up the incline and a heavenly view on top, especially on the sunset rock side—though the day was very misty and blue. Went home early and I had a regular orgy of washing—hair, etc.

NOVEMBER 3: Off again early in the morn—Arose at 3.45 for 5.05 train. It was absolutely dark when we left and we could not see much before six. It seemed odd enough to rattle along in that dark silent city behind the fat old negro—our lantern beaming as if it were early in the eve. We had to wait five hours at Rockwood for our Tennessee Central train—most of which time we spend at Hotel Mourfield—a neat looking structure without but dark and cold within. My first picture, as the door opened [in] "the best hotel in town" was a dusty room with a stove in the center surrounded by seven chairs (all rockers but two, and these were well tilted.) There seemed to be several women, a baby and a number of drummers on hand and no one looked as if he had any interest in life. The drummers were rather bored as they could do no business—it being election day—and neither could they get any returns.

We strolled out along the main street—a typical one with its scattered papers, unkempt stores, with negroes hanging at the corners. Judging from the wagon marked "Taft," that gentleman was drawing most votes. "Bryan" seemed fairly occupied, but poor "Debs," in spite of his red streamers, quite empty. John went out to look for the pastor of the Christian

Church, and presently returned with him to the hotel, having picked him out by his wife's description—"A little short chunky man with black eyes—looks like a preacher." His name was Ferguson and he was a kindly pleasant old gentleman. He spoke of the fineness of mountain boys. Gave special credit to Milligan and its head—the makers of good men. Kimberly Heights, 12 miles from Knoxville—President Johnston–(John met President Johnston casually on the train several years ago and was promised by him two good hogs as a start, if he would buy a farm for Demorest.)

After he left, a Jewish drummer from Austria fell into animated discussion on Bible subjects. Was much concerned as to whether Jews could become Christians. Said you couldn't tell a Jew from a Turk—usual American characterization not fair or true—a Semitic not a Jewish feature. Said he did not meet much prejudice. At the station we talked with a man who was starting out shooting. Said there were plenty of wild turkey, a few deer and even bear at Cany Creek. His little daughter reached up and took hold of my red and silver locket (from Mary K)—asked if it wouldn't hold a picture. The men hanging around the station seemed rather rough to me—even the young boys chewing tobacco.

The rode to Pomona Stand was very pretty—through country new to the R.R. The stations very small and woods and hills close above. Mostly oak in this region—some already in winter garb, and some still in brilliant color. We saw in the lowland some good pines. Beyond Crab Orchard, was a nice big orchard, and I began to notice grass (hay on the stalk)—a fine range for cattle. Indeed they say there is nothing like it for sheep and cattle. The only trouble with sheep is the "filth" (briars) and the dogs, which kill so many. Mr. Wheeler told us that cows did better on this grass than on finest timothy clover.

43

At Crossville John got off to give trunk check to the mail-carrier and met there three of his old pupils, Nora Southard, Baxter Southard and Frank Santley. Met Mr. Southard on the train—Mr. Stanley met us at Pomona Road with a buggy and a horse (to ride himself). Then we drove 6 miles of a fierce road—trail, rather, of rocks and stumps—which brought us into Pleasant Hill about 2–3 PM.[2] Mrs. Wheeler met us and put us into a comfortable room, while all the boys hung out of the dormitory windows to watch our movements. Found Mrs. W. a tired, worn, little woman with two big babies (starting on whooping cough) and an easy-going husband.

All the teachers were very cordial and we had a chance to see some of their work. Miss Morley in Music seemed to me an excellent grade-instructor, as well as a sweet personality. Miss Blair in sewing (salary not paid by A.M.A.) had a course beginning with paper folding, weaving in worsteds on little looms and gradually working up thru embroidery (button hole stitch—she said when she came, all the girls pinned their clothes) to making of simple shirt-waist suits.[3] She has two sales every year—the proceeds going to the school and through them and a few home donations last year she raised $200 toward a new building in which to have her classes. She wished to get Mrs. Brown, one of the town women, to set up her rag carpet loom in the sewing room and work on it Saturdays so that the children might learn. We visited Mrs. Brown (who also makes home-spun) and Mrs. Mercer who makes crocheted mats ($2–$2.50 for medium size). Mrs. Lundy also makes fine rag carpet at 50¢ a yard. Coverlets here run up to $10. I did not see one for sale—but bought three lovely mountain baskets at Miss Frye's—$1.00—.75 and .65 respectively—was charmed with them. There is such a chance for self-support in these old industries.

Other teachers were Miss Hanson, primary, Miss Daniels, 3rd, Mrs. Boyce, 4th and 5th, Mr. Boyce—Treasurer—Miss Leavens, preceptress, Miss Dodge, Miss Jones in Literature. I visited Miss Jones' Julius Caesar class and heard questions given and answered by the class. The work was excellent—some of the questions being most interesting. One was whether a man should ever sacrifice a friend for country. Most of the answers were in the negative. One boy asked—why Caesar refused the crown and questions led as to whether anyone under the circumstances would not wish the crown. A firm democrat said Bryan would not, while an ardent republican denied this. The discussion unfortunately had to be stopped. Miss Jones called on my valuable opinion several times as to ghost—Brutus sincerity, etc. I also made two speeches in Miss Leaven's class. As it happened her history class was just talking about Sicilian expedition of the Athenians and I spouted on Syracuse. In the afternoon John and I gave the Geography class a little spiel on Sicilian and Italian life.

They have a strict discipline at Pleasant Hill—read postcards. Examine letters (if necessary) etc. It seemed to me also that the type of boy was different from Georgia. Country seems different also—more oaks to the exclusion of pines—more grass and more rock. Rock creeps through everywhere—in fact bursts through as one finds in the roads.

NOVEMBER 6: I never saw such roads as those from Pleasant Hill to Grassy Cove, especially the last few miles near Grassy Cove.[4] The horses fairly slid on their haunches and would sometimes have to jump to clear a gully. It seems they had been hauling lumber from Grassy Cove to Crab Orchard. Also they were cutting lime-stone and hauling that. In places we fairly bounced down rocky stairs instead of stony hills. I enjoyed the ride immensely, however.

Just beyond Crossville, we stopped to water our horses and were most cordially invited to "come in and warm," while a tow-headed baby cried "Good-bye" until we were out of sight. Further along we asked the way of a Mrs. Music who was pretty and had quite properly a sweet voice—"eight miles to Grassy Cove and an awful road." Just beyond her house, we ran into a little forest fire partially under control—a number of men were fighting it. It seems that it has been fearfully dry in this region for weeks and weeks. All the water is very low and woods dry and roads very dusty. John drove the horses right thru, though we found it pretty smoky for a bit.

We had our lunch near a creek and christened Mabel Weeks' kit by making tea—very convenient. I took a picture of John trying to boil the water—then another of a pine tree foot-log further on and still another of a fearfully rough stretch of hill. We passed rougher still further on. There was still bright foliage in many places.

I forgot to say that in passing Pomona, which is quite a nice looking place—large houses and painted—we called on Rev. Patridge. His wife was away but a Mrs. Taylor was helping him and she urged us to stop on our way back, said she would do everything, and that it would be "great fun."

Grassy Cove itself is one of the prettiest little valleys I have ever seen—prettier than Nacoochee for it is smaller. Very green and level and shut in close by high blue hills or mountains. The first houses we came to were all log-cabins with handmade shingle roofs—most picturesque. The land, most of it, seems to be used for meadows and hay. Some corn, which seems to be shocked in this country, and a number of good orchards.

We drove by Mr. Kimmer's store and found a note from Mr. Beecham who had been called to Crossville and advised us to make Jewett.[5] Decided to look up teachers, found the man had gone home, as it was Friday night, and the woman, a Miss Redding, was staying 1 1/2 miles up the road at a Mr. Hamby's.[6] So we rode up there and had a short conversation with her—a pretty girl with her shirtwaist pinned by common pins in front. She said they had about 58 pupils—but school was not up to the old standard.

Mrs. Hamby said she could not take us in for the night, and as it was nearing four we decided it was too late to try for Jewett—so drove by Mr. Kimmer's.[7] There found open fire and a table of magazines—mostly Cosmopolitan and Womans Home Journal. I amused myself reading while John looked about the horses. He had an amusing time with the daughter. Mr. Kimmer called out for Frank to take care of us, and as we went to the porch, a boy came out, "Frank" as we supposed. John called him Frank, told him to grease the axles and feed horses (they had had no dinner) then corn later. In the morning he ask Frank to harness up, and it then appeared that Frank was the nice grownup daughter—and John the boy—both much amused.

It was growing dark when we arrived and quite dark by five—smoky too. By 5.30 it seemed seven o'clock. A wonderful moonlight night with mountains clearly to be seen. We had a very nice and bountiful supper and retired to a clean room with two beds at 7.15. All was very nice though my bed was a feather one and both had but one sheet. However, we slept hard—to awake before light at five for a 5.30 breakfast. Another bountiful meal—fried chicken, scrambled eggs, coffee, biscuits, blackberry jam, fried potatoes. All the family were very nice and Miss Kimmer promised to show me her kodaks of the valley.

We were off at 6.30—the horses very lively and gay, particularly the crabbed sorrel, who was full of interest in everything. A few rods down the street we were stopped by a fine looking old man on horseback, who wanted a word. He proved to be Mr. Hamby—much concerned that his wife had not taken us in the night previous—particularly when we were on the business (school) that he supposed we were. Said he didn't like that way of doing. Yes—they did have company—the school teacher was there, his daughter and son-in-law (five of them and I don't believe that there were that number of rooms in the little house)—but he thought that they could have found a peg to hang us on. "You see, my wife's a Baptist! (as if that explained all!). I told her the next time, whether it was a Baptist preacher or not, to take him in." He told us the school was not doing very well; that they hadn't appreciated the other Presbyterian school until it was too late. Now they would like it back.

A few rods beyond a nice white house, we turned to the left, down into an insignificant little lane, bordered closely by Virginia rail fence and trees. It was wonderfully pretty, backed by the blue mountains, behind which the sun had not risen. There were plenty of stumps and rough places, but we did not strike roads until we began to climb Walden's Ridge.[8] I am sorry I have left no words to describe that ride.

The road (over which they told us there was travel perhaps once in two months) was hardly a trail—beset with rock and so covered with fallen leaves that it was hardly distinguishable. We wound round and round and up—even the big bay beginning to sweat, while I hung over the wheel, both in interest and to keep the buggy balanced from the edge. The woods were wonderfully pretty—oaks and some chestnuts and other woods here—with great ropes of grape vine climbing high up in the branches. We kept getting glimpses through—but the smoky air and morning mist kept us from getting distinct views. Reached the top of the first ridge in about 35 minutes and took a picture of me coming in the buggy under the arch of a bended tree. From there on, the road just "busted" itself. We slipped over flat rock, crumbled down over bubbled rock, knocked over stumps and finally crashed down two terrible places leading into dry creek beds. At the last, the least bad of the two, I took a picture of John descending in the buggy.

About 9 o'clock at last we sighted the store on the main Spring City road and were rejoiced to hear that our worst was over, our left hand road—the right one—and that Jewett was hardly 3/4 of a mile beyond.

We swung to the left and before long, sighted a little white building on the edge of the road. The house, a nice looking one, was set a little back—a corn field around and a little deserted log cabin. I held the horses, while John went up the plank walk to the house. He returned saying the teachers were there—then drove the horses back a 1/2 mile to get in through a gate.

In the meanwhile, Miss Vickery had come out to meet me and I walked in with her. She was from some place in South Carolina and had been in Jewett the former year. The other teacher was a young Illinois girl (from Paris)—had been at Huntsville one year—but was new to this. These two girls live alone up there in their house, doing their own work. They got their mail once a week, had no telephone connections and could get no horses to drive themselves. In her 1 1/2 years, Miss Vickery said they had horses once, and a week before, the minister and his wife, Mr. and Mrs. Beecham, had ridden up on horseback and had let them use the horses for a while. Mr. Beecham preached there once a month—otherwise they saw no one from the outside world. Were glad to see us.

Said they had great difficulty in getting supplies; had some shipped from Chattanooga. Could always get eggs and Irish potatoes, the best butter there was, and sometimes chicken at the store. They had a hard time to get any milk. Also at this time they could get only 1/2 bucket of water from the well—such a drought in the region.

They had 53 scholars enrolled, from a vicinity of five miles—some of them coming about that distance to school. The community people were all proud of the school and well-disposed and children were eager to come—but the winter presented great difficulties—mountain torrents, mud, etc. The children would come if possible and were often soaking wet when they arrived. Would be so more or less all day. Also as soon as it began to be decent in spring—they must help on the farm. Little girls 6–7 must dig potatoes, plant, etc. Some were out now because of the fall crops, ploughing, etc. were not entirely ready.[9] She said the children were bright and right sweet—not dirty though poor and incredibly ignorant. The girls had a great fondness for color and dress hair with three different colored ribbons where possible—the dress in keeping.

Miss Vickery spoke at length on the health question—first the ignorance and carelessness as to exposure, the great amount of tuberculosis resulting—her apprehension for those who would come in the wet to school and sit there all day. One boy had died the preceding year and another had just gone west—too late she feared. A doctor could be secured only at Spring City—and sometimes at Crab Orchard. Even then he would only come when pay was guaranteed, and he charged $25.00—a prohibitive price of course—though as she said, he had to start at dawn and arrive at home late, after a drive of thirty miles, and his rig cost him $5.00. She told of a man who had had his jaw broken by the kick of a mule. He couldn't have a doctor so simply bandaged it without having it set. After a day it became so painful that he took the bandage off. After some days, an attempt was made to get a doctor at Crab Orchard—14 miles—but he was not there and they let it go. In about a month the sore had come through to the outside. The family had sold their little—sewing machine, old trunk and all—and the wife came to Miss Vickery with tears in her eyes, begging her to get the doctor. As it chanced, the weekly mail had just started—and she got a phone message through to Spring City. The next day the doctor came. He could do nothing but lance the sore and shook his head. The poison was already in the man's system. He came that once—$25.00 and Miss Vickery paid the charge (the friends of hers made it up to her later). After a terrible sickness the man got well and his gratitude was unbounded.

She told another case of a little child with the "white swelling"—one of a family of 14—fearfully poor. Again the doctor came—once only—and left directions. Told them to keep on a bran poultice. A week or more later when Miss V. came—the mother showed the same poultice on—declaring the doctor meant the same one. The child simply dragged its life out—after a long sickness—during which it was allowed to have anything to eat that it could swallow. Now the family were trying to get money to pay the doctor. Miss V. wished so much for a medical missionary. I couldn't but think that a trained nurse too would be helpful.

We left about 1.45 P.M.—and came through pretty scenery and across more rough road to Grand View, about 4–5.[10] Prof. Woodworth and wife were expecting us and we had a nice room in their house. Had meals at the dormitory—as the baby was sick and kept Mrs. Woodworth busy.

Got rather an indefinite idea of the work here. Met a number of teachers—one a Miss Chick, from North Tennessee—a mountain girl. They have sewing and domestic science, though I could not tell to what extent or what lines, as I did not meet the teacher. Also they have bought a farm which they are beginning to work as a first step toward industrial department for boys. They have about 200 here—80 boarders. Over half of these are from the mountains proper.

NOVEMBER 8th, Sunday: Lovely day—though smoky so we could get no view. After breakfast at the dormitory, we came back to the house and packed up. Mrs. Woodworth was busy and except a few minutes walk behind the house to look off at a blur of smoke, we whiled away time until 10. At Sunday School John made a short strong address on future for the mountains—mountain children. Many of the audience were in tears. Miss Chick especially could hardly speak afterwards. A great many came out afterwards and thanked John—just as we were starting off. Both felt fearfully sleepy and stupid and the roads had come to be such an old story that we rattled and ground over them without comment. Part of the way is exceptionally pretty—along a creek where the hollies grew both low by the road and into tall trees only overtopped by fine great hemlocks. There was plenty of laurel as well and rhododendron.

Mrs. Woodworth had put up a lunch which we ate as we went along. We stopped a few minutes to take a picture of a footlog (railed and braced) the stream beneath a mere puddle now. At the forks of the road we stopped again to ask our direction and a pleasant looking man stepped out and asked us in. Said his name was Knox. We said we had to reach Crab Orchard and asked if he would sell us a dime's worth of apples. In a minute he came back with arms full—refusing the money, however. Was sorry we would not come in.

Reached the Kimmers between 1–1.30 and found them dressed for Sunday and expecting us. Miss K. had on a white dress and looked pretty and fresh. We fell at once to discussing our cameras and she showed me her first pictures which she developed and printed herself—gave me two. As they had prepared some dinner for us I felt we had to eat, though neither of us was hungry. Miss K. told us about her last summer's visit in Texas, while Mrs. Kimmer said she never took money of ministers if she knew it. John said he wasn't a minister—but she only charged us 50 cents for horses feed and our own—as he wasn't a travelling man and was out for the schools.

Got off again before 2.30 and again rattled up the fearful road leading out of the cove. On the way out, we found that Mr. Beecham had preached there that day and was to preach at Meridian at 3.00—on the way to Crab Orchard.[11] So there we overtook him and stopped in the little one-roomed school house where he was speaking. He guessed who we were and stopped to invite us in. The place was full—women in sunbonnets, men, boys and children (mostly nice looking) and he was exhorting them to take thought of the girls and boys, stop jealousies and have a regular church. He was a nice looking man, slim and dark with beard and mustache—38 to 40 I should say. He looked to me like a Scotch Presbyterian, also like J. S. Kingsley.[12] After he closed, he asked John to speak—which John did—along the same line—asking them to join in making Christians, not put stones in the way.

Mr. Beecham's district is all through these mountains—Ozone, Crab Orchard (where he lives), Meridian, Grassy Cove, Jewett, and another mountain. He has no horse and sometimes walks 25 miles a day or more. Said he had a horse once but feed was too expensive to pay him to keep it. He was full of perplexity as to the situation—and felt himself so helpless—his duties scattered over so wide an area. The people were fearfully poor, with crops mortgaged ahead, were afraid to be seen [in] church by their creditors. The lack of medical treatment was a constant source of distress to him. He told how one night he had tramped eighteen miles over the mountain to the call of a dying woman, and when he came he could do nothing. He felt strongly that the first help must be material, and that would lead to spiritual uplift. He had a set of stereopticon slides which he was planning to give—was trying to organize a poultry association, was eager to seize on anything that might lead to the mental, spiritual or material needs of the people. Every Friday he and his wife had house full—not in prayer meeting—but a neighborhood meeting where everyone took part in entertaining the others. The tears stood in his eyes as he talked of his helplessness. He had almost planned to leave but felt such a course cowardly.

He took us to the Melrose House to supper and for night as Mrs. Beecham did not know we were coming—told us he would come in the morning. We got through supper somehow, talking to Mrs. Brooks (née Parker) who ran the house. She had been christened by A. E. Barton and was a pretty dark woman with a rather sad face. Was glad to talk to us. After supper went to bed and on looking at watch, discovered it to be 6 P.M. Dead tired and slept directly.

NOVEMBER 9th: Up again for 6.30 breakfast and Mr. Beecham appeared about 7.45. We then went to call on Mr. Klein, the County Superintendent. Had to pass through cowyard, where Mrs. Klein was milking the six cows—a disheveled looking woman, originally from Iowa—but as she had nine children in addition to the cows and house, her appearance could be explained. Mr. Klein it appears has a farm on Crab Orchard mountain, runs a saw-mill, teaches county school, is County Superintendent and is building a new house—the "busiest man in the county." His house bore witness—at least the room into which we were ushered—the dining-room, where a seedy open fire was burning, table half cleared, bare floor so dirty, and such a smell! I thought at first I couldn't stand it. Some half dozen children—likewise dirty—ran back and forth. Mr. K. was in his shirt sleeves—preparing for school—and seemed quite vague as to ideas. Thought the Crossville school would not interfere with Pleasant Hill—and agreed that it would be a good thing if the church schools should supplement the county schools—by industrial work.

We then went down to old Presbyterian school house, where Miss B. has a little private class for the sake of her daughter. All was neat, pleasant and quiet. Stayed there a bit and then had a long talk with Mr. B. along lines already described. We then went to the county school, which was a sight. Mr. K. had senior grades—so odd in big room. His costume bore evidence of hurry and his black dangling tie was up under one ear. He snapped boys and girls up in good shape—"Stand up there! Don't you hear what I say?" etc. etc. There was discipline at least in the room if not order of the housewife kind. Below where the young assistant was struggling, conditions were worse. A crowded big room with heavy wooden settles instead of desks. Rows of dirty little children—twisting and turning. One corner was doing everything but study, and one boy was asleep. She seemed to have one book to a class and had to copy work on the board. Children climbed up on seats to reach the board. One row sat on the back of settle on the platform while they did examples. Poor girl—she couldn't help it—and such a litter on the floor! I noticed most of the children here had buttons and buttonholes on their clothes. Some pinned them—and what looking shoes, where there were any! The whole thing was quite in contrast to Mrs. B's where at least order reigned and refinement.

We went to Beecham's to dinner, where we met a Mrs. Niles, from Ozone, and a Mrs. _____ formerly a teacher. Got off about 3 o'clock and drove gingerly along the track watching for trains. Got through safely and landed in Ozone about 4. Fires burning all through the forests and my eyes were sore with smoke. Road ran through several creeks and some pretty rhododendron and hemlock woods. Felt tired, with the talk and doings.

(Mr. B. told us several stories—among them, an experience of Miss Fish who was at Jewett last year. She was called to a sick woman, supposedly dying, and found her with 18 other people and 4 dogs in a one roomed cabin. Six men were on one bed, son and wife and five children on another. Man alone was up and waiting on sick wife.)

At Ozone—Mr. Young took us in—a fine looking old man, originally from Adelphi, Indiana. Came 18 years ago for his health. His wife too was a nice old lady. Miss Rankin turned out to be a gentle dark little woman, with big eyes and a hard cough that sounded dangerous to me. She did not have much to say except that people were not so poor as a rule in this region. When mines were going, men got $2–3 a day and upwards. Were very wasteful—particularly in food, and needed instruction along that line. Of course mines had not been running for some time.

Mines not worked scientifically here—scratched on surface—coal being in pockets. The other teacher Miss Beasley entertained a young man over the piano while the rest of us talked very sleepily in eve. Had a nice room and good night.

NOVEMBER 10th: Up for 7 and breakfast of fried pork, fried potatoes, and soda biscuit. I chewed carefully and felt no ill results. Then over to see the school—a neat pretty little building—not many scholars. They want a boarding-school there—but I doubt expediency with two large ones so near. John gave a little talk to children—then back and got horses harnessed up after some time. Mrs. Young put up a lunch for us, and we got off about 10.

Had a rather uneventful and pleasant drive to Crossville. Warm and smoky—with an unfulfilled promise of rain. Fires burning in the woods. Avoided train at Crab Orchard and got to Mrs. Music's at 2.00 P.M. Then while John fed the horses, I sat inside in a smelly room, about which Mrs. M. was very apologetic, hadn't had "time to clean up." There were only two bare beds and two chairs in the room, a pile of comforts, and a most ancient rickety piano, which I insulted by playing "Hiawatha." Five children (three belonging to Mrs. Gyentanner) were playing in and out, and a large turkey and a number of hens kept invading the room. Mrs. Music, in the meantime, insisted on making us corn-bread and coffee (postum), took milk out of the churn, and cooked some horrible looking meat. She kept apologizing, so we put it down, in spite of delay in our start. We took a picture of the crowd of children, to whom John had brought some candy. The oldest, a dirty but pretty little wretch, took a shine to John and as we were leaving, thrust up a coy face saying, "I'd like to kiss somebody." The mother was looking on and of course the "somebody" (John) had to come up, which he did with apparent outward enthusiasm. I couldn't help laughing.

At Pomona we met Mr. Patridge and had a few minutes talk with him, before continuing home. It grew entirely dark before we got half way, and we had to trust pretty much to the horses. Passed two big hay wagons on the road. Home about six—late for dinner, but got some after the others.

NOVEMBER 12th: Had a long drive over to Pomona, in very cold weather. An hour's wait in the combination station and store. I sat with my feet on the stove rail, getting warm until the various loungers spit so near my feet and so persistently on the hot ashes that the fried tobacco smell was too much for me. I then found John, who was talking to a tall humorous mountaineer outside on the track. Flagging the train seemed to consist of putting our trunk near the track and waving arms to the engineer.

NOVEMBER 13th: Hearing of President's Committee, Rural Research, at Knoxville, Tennessee: Points and deductions: Farming must be made to pay on economic and human side—good roads (by convict labor, by U.S. Government subsidy supplementing state or community amounts raised). Easier to combine county schools where roads are good—(inspirational leadership most important—J.C.C.). Compulsory education must carry with it provisions for better and more teachers and schools. If simply compel the children to attend under present conditions may overwork teachers already overworked. Other statements lead one to suppose this is not so. Corn robs land of fertility year by year—decreases steadily in fertility unless there is rotation of crops. But even this poor land increases in price when roads and R.R.s come near. Rotation in crops should be one of the provisions in contracts for tenancy. Too much tenancy. Frequent moving—a class moving frequently from place to place. These are the more inefficient—do not rise readily into ownership. Regular tenant class arises perhaps. Pioneer suspicion of each other—hence difficult to bring about co-operation. Need to supply inspiration to rise out of disadvantaged class. (J.C.C. suggests neighborhood leader in each school). Provision should be made for rural men of character to borrow more easily and save more easily. Postage savings banks. Illiteracy and consequent inability to avail oneself of credit, etc. and to secure confidence.

Dr. Charles Wardell Stiles, Geologist, U.S. Public Health & Marine Hospital Service, has spent better part of seven years in studying factory conditions and operatives.[13] Report to be submitted to Bureau of Labor in January. Says mountain and rural people are drawn to cotton mills—not only by better wages but by better home and sanitary conditions provided by company. Country question largely a medical question—note privies. Soil and water contamination typhoid (Tennessee 4th state in typhoid, high up in tuberculosis). Lack of ambition in mountain people and mill operatives is result of disease, hookworm, etc.—anemia. One out of 5 going to Alabama from Tennessee (that he had examined) below normal in blood (12%?). By treatment could be brought up. U. S. government purposely sending out bulletins to schools to teach ordinary sanitary arrangements. Send out women to teach cookery, food-chewing. Mothers and daughters must be saved. Biological, hygienic, physiological knowledge should be spread. Fifteen kinds of tape worms—one transmitted by soil pollution, fourteen by food. Idea of individual liberty hinders compulsory education. "My child is my child."

Find out what southern states have compulsory education laws. (Two? Kentucky and North Carolina? Not well operated—optional?)

Citizenship we are after, not merely raising more crops, and good citizenship is making the best man one can be in the place one is. Education is adaptation to life where one is. Agricultural and industrial training should be not taught as something separate on a money basis, but in through all studies. Beauty of the common things—the aesthetic and spiritual values of common things should be shown. Help toward doing those things must come from outside. One of great things is to teach country man who wants better things that a local tax to get them is not robbery.

Various suggestions for training teachers. Head of Peabody Fund—said question a big one—head work and faces of nature applied in city work, as against hand and mule labor in farm work. County needed to apply inanimate forces of nature before it could compete with city in attractiveness.

Combination as against individualism. Need of teachers with feeling toward country and with proper spirit could turn children's attention back home even if city taught.

(J.C.C. thinks possibly a publication giving what is being done, once a year, might be helpful).

(Copied by John's request, from letter to M.W.K., November 13th, Knoxville): "I wish I could make you see the picture which lingers in my mind—a little plain house and a white two-roomed school house in a lonely hollow at the mountain top. Near it a field of corn and an empty log cabin—no other signs of habitation—just miles of woodland. You drive along leaf-scattered mountain roads, over boulder, pebble, dust and mud. Here and there you come to a little cabin in its clearing of corn—the mother with a baby in her arms (or one coming) digging potatoes, with a troop of carefully graded (in size) dirty faced, barefooted youngsters. It is all picturesque and fascinating enough in the fall, when the woods are rich with autumn color, mountains blue—plenty of fat chestnuts dropping in one's path, big shagbarks and persimmons! What difference if one is in danger of dropping off a ledge down a steep trail into a stony creek—or is joggled and shaken and jolted till his dinner is down at the toes of his stockings? It is all in the game, and the air is crisp and golden! But let it come on winter (and I tell you it is *cold* here!) and rain and rain-ice forms on the ledges and thick mud clogs your wagon wheels in the interims; when pools of dark water stand in the furrows of the decaying corn and a winter wind comes through the big log chunks of the houses; when the creeks are swollen way above the danger point and water literally rolls down the mountain trails in torrents. I tell you it is a reversible picture! How to get to the log school? How to keep dry? How to pay $25.00 for one doctor's visit if you get sick and have the white swelling, or the lung fever or get kicked by a mule? You are alone—your next neighbor shut off as you are and perhaps another mile or two down the road."

(Copied from a letter of John's to Miss Sheak, Rockwood, November 13th:) "I have just conquered breakfast. The picture is more pretentious than the breakfast was. Lined down the center of the table were—

Left end—milk,
Left half—pepper   Left tackle—vinegar
                              Left guard—catsup
Quarterback—mustard   Centre—sugar
Right guard—Worcestershire.
Right half—salt   Right tackle—pepper,
Fullback—butter   Right end—sorghum

"Opposed to this team and playing alone in its own strength was a lone piece of cheese. In true foot-ball style, the butter had not had its hair cut since the season opened. It promised to be an interesting game, but mustard got hotter when the cheese let out its 'mite' and I had to leave as the coffee was coming in to settle the grounds of dispute."

NOVEMBER 15th, Sunday: Got up about seven—a cold though brilliant morning. A "nigger man" built us a fire which heated our stove red hot and enabled us to dress in some comfort. After breakfast followed up an old unused narrow-gage to the left of Pinnacle Mountain—and took—according to direction—a road off it to the left. It was an old road but no worse than many others of the past week. We stumbled along up and down one path after another—but finally decided we would go up direct. It was a pretty stiff proposition—tooth and nail. Both John and I felt a little sick at the turning toward the last and my head felt dizzy enough. However we took breath, ate some chestnuts, braced against a tree—and finally scaled the last steep rock. Found a magnificent view—mountain beyond mountain—blue in the crisp morning and partially covered with snow. The other side of our steep ridge was still well covered. To the back of us lay Middleboro and in front the Gap, Swanee, etc. I took a mountain view from the highest rock I could find—through pines to the right of the Gap proper. Then we crunched along, looking for the government stone which marks the corner of Kentucky, Virginia and Tennessee. We found by the bye that our hotel was all in Virginia—only one piazza post being in Tennessee. On the left side of the ridge we discovered a good road, which we followed on a bit, until it led to a big cleared space at the mountain top, then turned back and followed it toward town. Just above it to the left some distance on—John discovered the stone. He thereupon took a picture of me sitting on it. Then, while I took a view of snow, trees and mountains in the Middleboro direction, he sat down and wrote a line to Gavin. Had a lovely easy walk down.

Had only been back a few minutes when the team of mules arrived from Lincoln Memorial School—to drive us over. A pretty drive through lovely country. Passed on the way the Grace Nettleton Memorial Industrial School.[14] The Lincoln Memorial is beautiful—situated on rolling valley ground surrounded by mountains. It has about 25 buildings of varied sorts on the 600 acres—the grounds having been those of a hotel (very grand), and the girls and boys dormitories former hotel buildings. They are really very grand—stone, steam heat, etc., etc.

Mrs. Stooksbury received us (the President being in N.Y.) and drove round to the various buildings—then to girls dormitory for dinner. Met a number of the teachers—matron Miss Morton—primary teacher, Mrs. Nichols (son?) a former missionary in coal mining region—and a Mrs. Hale—a visitor. Had quite a talk on mountain conditions, all testifying to poor health conditions, amount of tuberculosis, scrofula, eczema etc. Had several cases of first in school—tried to isolate them. Said if girls had an idea of sickness, gave up at once all as lost. They make a great feature of the music here—conservatory, etc.—wish to attract students from all South; evidently are bent on a big thing—though have developed little so far industrially. Have a farm and are hoping for a domestic science department. About 250 students registered now. More later on. Evidently expect a big thing though I couldn't seem to feel that they had a vital interest or hold on the mountain situation. Get many mountain students they said—but gave no proportion. Didn't seem to think they would go back. Said there was not much sentimentalism between girls and boys. Had few girls—found it hard to get and keep them.

At three we went to Auditorium and froze while Presbyterian preacher preached and John spoke. Then drove Miss Stooksbury to Grace Nettleton Home—in charge of an old lady and former friend, parishioner, etc., of Dr. Moxom. It is combination orphanage and school. About 30 children in school—all Miss W. can take care of—and all mountain girls. Three workers in house which was built for hotel in other hotel boom. Arrangement etc. interesting and appealing. Miss W. makes $700 a year off sales of mission barrel goods. Has no endowment as yet.

Left Miss Stooksbury there and drove back to Gap for the night. Dead tired and John celebrated by having a bad attack of indigestion.

NOVEMBER 16th, Monday: Arrived at Barbourville about ten and went up to Union College.[15] They have several very nice buildings—brick and modern. President Easley was in his office and we had a conference with him—a rather severe and didactic old man who confessed to a short knowledge of the mountains, but suspiciously advised John against ones settling the situation quickly. It needed a *long* study. Get many mountain students—perhaps 50% though it is not exclusively a mountain school. Plans all laid for a *big* university on purely academic lines—no industrial work or side lines. Has at present 104 pupils (few boarders) but get twice or more that number after Xmas. Spoke of prevalence of tuberculosis and in a rather condescending way of his acquaintance with mountain cabins—sickness, etc. Said there was *nothing* in the mountains to develop—except little mining and failing timber. Nothing else. Bad feeling between Baptists and selves (Northern Methodists), or rather no cooperation.

We then walked over to the Baptist minister's house—a rather unkempt place without—and decidedly dirty within. A disheveled young woman in gingham and sunbonnet invited us cordially in and asked us to "have off your hats and coats." The "parlor" had a very dirty carpet—large bed—two chairs and low grate fire. An obstreperous fat dirty black eyed baby whooped about—followed by a forward older brother. In time the Rev. Arvin awkwardly appeared, tall—black-eyed (whites dark and bilious looking), sallow faced, black mustached. He got another chair and picked his prominent gold teeth with a toothpick while hunting for something to say. School about 80 now—more after Xmas. At length he and John fell into a religious discussion—he most exasperatingly narrow. All the world to become Baptist: would take no other candidates from another church unless reimmersed. Was not "narrow," only doing just what Christ said. Was *not* inconsistent. Felt it right to establish Baptist schools in every community—even if previously occupied by excellent school of another denomination. Would co-operate? Yes—but never join of course until all would become Baptist. Would like to be obliging and not hinder education, but must follow Bible. Spoke of ignorance of country Baptist preachers—and by inference, his own education!

We were both glad to shake the dust of this squalid mining and R.R. town from our feet—a study of denominationalism rather than mountaineers. Five churches to 300(?) people. (Spoke quite fanatically and savagely of M.E.S. and M.E.N.)[16]

NOVEMBER 17th, Tuesday: Got up early and followed our landlady's daughter to P. E. School. Another mining town, or preeminently Railroad. Prof. Banks—the nice young Englishman in charge—told us that the aristocracy of the town (which came to their school) were children of engineers, conductors and firemen. They have two nice buildings and carrying up to eleventh (?) grade—some basketry and cooking. Have had no opportunity so far to reach real mountain class. Need of horse to get out—and also scholarships, etc. to help boys and girls through. Great poverty in country, but had not had chance for careful investigation. Felt however that the small R.R. mining town also needed education and uplift. People wasteful—homes a mere roof to sleep under. One of teachers was trying to teach girls home cooking, home economy, and how to make home attractive. She also taught the boys some sloyd work, using tobacco boxes—old slats and whatever she could lay her hands on. Difficult to get lumber, particularly thin wood for sloyd purposes, but thought it well to teach boys to make use of what they could get. Only about 80 pupils there now; 10 churches in town; a public school of low grade and a Catholic school (practically parochial). Rev. Crusoe said he had to combat idea of Catholicism—especially raised by his vest. His vested choir was for first meeting an object of great curiosity. He is himself quite a singer and was organizing choirs and orchestras—Sunday School on modern lines etc. Talked freely with other pastors and found his school a general leaven. All were braced up. Did not object to cards and dancing—to objection of older people. Was working with the younger generation mostly. Baptist element aggressive (narrow) rather than progressive.

We also called on Congregationalist minister, Mr.—, (Presbyterian minister not at home)—a discouraged, half-sick, silent man, with a monotonous tired utterance. Uphill work for Congregationalism and I fancy he was worn out in spirit.[17]

WILLIAMSBURG [Kentucky]: Took train at 3.15, landing in Williamsburg about 4.[18] President Wood and Rev. Hibbs met us cordially and took us to a nice modern little hotel. Running water in the room—nice bath-room and good table service (with too much fry as usual). I had a pretty woven mountain "kiver" on my bed. Two white iron beds and all comfortable. Rested and went to bed early, though John talked a while with Mr. Hibbs after supper.

NOVEMBER 18th: In the morning, Mr. Hibbs and Dr. Ellison (treasurer) called for us with team and drove us to chapel. They use the fine Congregationalist building as their main building. John made a fine address. We met all the various professors—then again with Dr. Hibbs and Ellison drove around town to other buildings. They have a good plant— fine boys dormitory and good girls. They own considerable land and are eager to buy a farm. Are contemplating an industrial department—wood-work and cooking—but are trying for an endowment. Are questioning what to do in regard to public schools—whether to keep on with help of public money—or build up independent scheme which will not be as good as theirs at present, lease one building to the town for a graded school. The work as far as I could judge seemed good—also the spirit. Considerable enthusiasm among faculty. The art teacher says she finds great appreciation of natural beauty, flowers, etc. among students as soon as their attention is called. Great desire to put it on practical basis.

Had an interesting talk with old trustee, Dr. _____. Was delighted with John's compliments to climate. Said there was not much tuberculosis in this section—a good deal of typhoid and great ignorance of the sanitary and culinary side. Need of teaching cooking especially. Had little food and did not know how to cook—that this is a great source of the sickness.

Dr. Hibbs also felt great need of farm work—great ignorance of farming.

Williamsburg has a beautiful situation in a little valley surrounded by mountains. The river has high wide palisades which I suppose some day will be crowned by fine residences. Town however has some good houses now and looks progressive. We drove across creek to heights beyond where we had a fine view of the town—then back to the big saw mill and home about 11.30. In P.M. they drove us way up to Mount Morgan. Rather too smoky or misty for a clear view but there is a magnificent stretch there. In evening went to Prayer meeting—where John again spoke. Tired and home to bed.

Prof. Wood in for a talk, mostly on college plans. Wishes to develop industrial side—discussed dairy possibilities, etc—farm.

Train was 50 minutes late, so we did not get in to London until almost one. Found a tall, pale, young man, Prof. Lisle, awaiting us. We took bus to hotel where we left our bags then walked up to Sue Bennett Memorial.[19] Prof. Lewis—a big hale Englishman—met us and we talked in his office until lunch was ready, 1.45. They have about 200 in the school (400 in winter). School support is low and so far they have not been able with unskilled student labor (at 10 cents) to make the farm pay. Shall have to sell it another year. Believes, however, most thoroughly in industrial work—money alone being necessary. They have a broom factory—which pays pretty well. Equipment comparatively inexpensive. Have not raised good broom straw so far and get all supplies from Cincinnati. It is not to teach boys a trade but to give them a means of earning education. Believes thoroughly in domestic science for girls. They have a barn—and president's house beside recitation hall and dormitory—all good buildings. Also have six little cottages where the students board themselves. I judge they make a good deal of music—also have a good straight academic course. Mrs. L. proved to be a sweet faced Englishwoman who did not look as if their ten children were a tremendous care. Their home was pleasant and we had a pleasant conversation on widely separated subjects. Did not seem to know much of sickness, etc. among mountaineers. There is a small Presbyterian school just started in town and also a graded school.

Prof. Lewis called in Henry Probst, who is a Swiss descendent living near a Swiss colony at Abington. Made arrangements to go home with him—and accordingly at 4, we three drove off in a buggy with a gay little horse over a rough road. Found the Probst house large and well built. Very simple inside—and with the usual lack of conveniences—no sink, running water, etc.—but everything clean and nice. A mixed household, the old uncle—his sister—brother and wife with 3 children, nephew Henry and friend. We sat in front of an open stove, played with the baby and talked agriculture. The young husband—a fine looking big fair fellow—seemed to think they hadn't given the soil a fair test—different crops needed. Grapes not successful here—and besides no market. Soil varied much within a few miles—but not good. Thought more could be done with it than was being done. A man could live off it—but would not be comfortable unless he complemented his income with saw mill (as he did) logging, mining, etc. However, he had not given the soil a fair show.

I went out in the kitchen after supper (a hearty one) and talked with the women and helped them wipe dishes. To bed early but up again at 4.30 for an early breakfast chapel where John spoke. Then we saw some classes—a specially good primary, called on Lewises (John drove out to farm with Prof. L.) had a lunch and cordial invitation to come again and spend the night. Off on 12 train and arrived at Berea about 1.30.

NOVEMBER 20th: Were met at Berea by the Secretary, Mr. Gamble, and a nice team. Drove up to President's house, where Mrs. Frost—a very charming woman—met us and ushered us to our room (furnished with homespun).[20] The house was very attractive—especially the big living room, with a sliding door (upper part glass) opening on porch at end—big fireplace—nice pictures, etc., etc. We went over at once however, to some recitations—it being our only chance. The school has a number of model rooms open to inspection—all with a gallery above to observers. Also the older primary classes are separately taught, as needing different treatment from the children. (J.C.C. Take people at highest level and set before them an attainable standard). There are sloyd classes—also painting classes (a preparation for botany in spring). We saw a forestry class (they also have an active forester who attends to their forest land, oversees, etc.). Have a faculty of about 60 (and use best students in winter also). Quite an advanced botany department. Went into little stone museum—and saw likewise collection of "kivers." At four Mrs. Frost found us and we went through their laundry— a big one. Then she took us over to the church (church is Union) which has a unique way of attending to mission barrel clothes. All women of neighborhood (negro too) came in from near and far (120 there that day) and sew—mending, patching, quilting, darning, etc. under voluntary direction of teachers, professor's wives, etc. They each get so many tickets for so many hours' work—and then at the close, go by sections to the selling room and get what they want according to number of tickets they have. No race feeling—and whole affair is a great success. Mrs. F. says some women look forward to it as the big thing of the week—one said she kept "studyin' on it all week till it was time for the next one"—and that it kept her from getting trouble in her head and being sent away (to asylum).

In the morning we drove with Mrs. Frost and Mr. Gamble out to Pig Hollow—so called from the name of the families there. Berea is really the "gate-way to the mountains"—being literally in the bluegrass on one side and the sandstone mountain region on the other. It also lies on the only thoroughfare through from Cumberland Gap. The armies marched over that road. The hills though not high, still are jagged and imposing. The forests are pretty well cut off on many and ploughing has been done where the sides are very steep and washing cannot be prevented. The school owns a whole line of hills which form its water shed and wood supply. These are being carefully forested and ought to eventually make a fine forest. On the way out Mrs. Frost and I stopped at a two-roomed log cabin (climbing over the stile) where an old lady was doing some spinning. Her wheel was out of gear then—but she fixed it up on our return and we saw her spinning goats wool. This she knits into socks (40¢ a pair) and I hope to get some later. The cabin was moderately tidy—though she apologized. Walls pasted up with newspaper—open fireplace. She told of some step children—kinfolk—in the neighborhood—who were badly treated by their step mother—were running wild—didn't know anything, and asked Mrs. F. to have the church interfere. We then drove as far as Pig Hollow where Mrs. F. and I got out and the men went on up to the reservoirs. We called first on Mrs. Pig the elder. She is a fine strong looking old woman—neat as a Quaker—her hair drawn back—apron and kerchief (a colored one). The house too was very neat—a three roomed cabin with a fireplace at either end. In front of each fireplace—a girl was ironing—beds in the room as far as I could see. One girl, "Zilphy," was Mrs. Pig's granddaughter by her son's first wife. She evidently was under her (Mrs. P's especial charge) and Mrs. Pig showed us a great heap of quilts which had been begun by Zilphy's mother and she had finished for her—a sort of wedding chest idea. We were so interested that she brought out heap after heap—such patterns as seven diamond, nine-diamond, dove-in-the-window (the handsomest), rolling pin, etc. Mrs. F. wanted Zilphy to come to school, which the girl was only too anxious to do—but the old grandmother did not want to be separated from her. Finally Mrs. F. suggested that she find a room in Berea—and that Mrs. Pig could come with the girl and keep house for her—perhaps bring the older of the second wife's children. The 3rd wife we did not see—but Mrs. P. said she was a young girl with one or two children of her own. Mrs. P. then told us (having carefully sent out Zilphy) that the girl didn't have much chance to learn. She was the oldest and had to work outside—getting wood—cows, etc. Another time she sent her out to drive away the cow which was trying to eat the clothes off the bushes inside the "palin.'" While we talked, the younger girl set her iron to heat in the ashes—and listened—and three young children hung around the fireplace. Mrs. Pig urged us to stay to dinner—but we said good-bye and moved on to another daughter-in-law who lived a few rods back in a log cabin. This was one of the poorest of the cabins—(the kitchen was so ruined as to be practically useless) and the living was all in the one room. There was the stove—which however they did not seem to use much. Mrs. Pig Jr. said wood was high and so they used the fireplace both to cook and heat. The fireplace—by the bye, was very racketty—the hearthstone broken and sunken. There was a black pot boiling over the low fire. The cabin was dirty and the three young children also. There were two beds in the room. Mrs. P. who was a worn young woman explained that her father had been to see her. She was right proud to see him and it made her feel bad to have him go away. She had not had time to clean up. It appeared also that after the birth of her last baby (which she brought out of the bed for us to see) she had had a fever and even now could not walk without a bad pain in her side. She could not get to next house and did not know what she should have done without Mrs. Pig Sr. "a good woman" and Zilphy. Her husband was right sickly for two years. He had had several hemorrhages (they say "several molasses") and "spit blood." Poor woman! She had a sweet face and pretty eyes. Also urged us to stay till she got us something to eat.

We walked part way back till the carriage caught us. After dinner President Frost arrived and we went out to see _____ room, practical carpentry, telephone exchange (like Portland one); central heating plant; hospital; house where farming tools, overalls etc. were kept and where the boys washed up; cemetery where celebrities are buried; through town and back to house for 5.15 dinner.

I rested Sunday morn—though John visited Sunday Schools. They have a fine system. Have a specialist to teach their teachers and all teachers teach the Sunday School.

In P.M.—Pres. Frost drove us and a Miss Robinson out to the Narrow Gap Sunday School. A Miss Fox who had been one of their teachers and had started a Sunday School in this district which was one of the worst near Berea, had got interested—and backed by Berea, had gone out there to live and teach. They say the community has been revolutionized since her coming though she has had to live down all kinds of slander and opposition. It seems there is great suspicion of a woman working alone in a community. Mountain people do not understand it.[21] Better to have a man. Pres. Frost says they employ no women in extension work—though he thinks a man and wife make the best combination. Miss Fox had a big Sunday School and Pres. Frost gave them a fine talk on principles, as anchors. John said a few words. We then went over to look at Miss Fox's house—a pretty log cabin. The district seemed to be rough still, for she told of some trouble the night before at their social—also of several stills in the region and much drunkenness. She has one girl to live with her—the granddaughter of an old moonshiner's wife— who when her husband died—was caught and brought down from the hills. They said she was the wildest thing they ever saw, brought with her, hidden in the bed clothes, the still her husband had used—always went barefooted, etc. Finally she had decamped, disappeared entirely no one knew where. Miss Fox's mother now lives near her—having come down from Ohio (?)—but for the first time she was entirely alone.

In the eve we went to chapel—a fine sight. Prof. Rain preached a long rather heavy though well-worded sermon.

NOVEMBER 23RD: In the morning John made a *fine* talk at chapel—on better work—right ideas of manliness, etc. Then we started off to McKee at 11 A.M. with Mr. Gamble. Had rough roads the first half—especially over Big Hill which is the steepest drive we have had. It is fearfully rocky—an unsteady crunch and jolt continuously. We stopped and made pea-soup and had luncheon about 1—then on again. The trees were mostly cut off in this part, hills bare, and many, even the very steep ones, were ploughed. We saw teams of mules high up on the hills straining among the corn. Also met teams of oxen drawing sledges laden with corn husks. The houses for the most part were in good shape—painted and often two story—(though we saw one old log house with chinks as wide as several fingers). [Note written on side of page: "Inside property etc. does not correspond to outward," Mrs. F. says.] Of course this is a main thoroughfare. At Clover Bottom we stopped a few minutes at a little school taught by a Berea girl—then hurried on. It was dark long before we reached McKee—though fortunately the road here was good. It was picturesque enough to see the night settle on the mountains—till finally we could only see the high mountain side on our left and a Virginia rail fence so close on the right I could almost touch it. Occasionally a light would glimmer at the foot of a distant hill—or we could see door and window chinked outlined in the flickering light of an open fire. Suddenly we heard hoofs and a horseman galloped down the hill ahead, drew rein and wheeled waiting. I was all expecting a highwayman when he spoke—and it proved to be Mr. Messler, the head of the McKee School.[22] He had come out to make sure we should stay with them instead of at the hotel. We shook hands—then he galloped on ahead for us to follow.

We found a very pleasant home there—and Mr. Messler proved to be a young man of perhaps 40—with hair prematurely grey and a fine rather worn face. He was a minister of the Dutch Reformed Church—a New Yorker by birth and of old Dutch parentage. They had a tall clock in the room which had been in his family for over 200 years. Mrs. Messler came in then and we had a nice supper. They have two children—the younger a boy of 1–2—and a fine little fellow. They gave up big Northern chances to settle here—and have been at McKee three years. Have had much to contend against in prejudice, etc. For instance—as soon as he started working—the Baptists started up—and that is only a small sample. They have no regular church but are building one (to be Union) at Grayhawk—five miles beyond.[23] He felt very much the need of industrial work and is to start some soon at several miles distant from McKee, which is not so desirable (as the county seat). The mountain people do not like to come so well to the county seat.

NOVEMBER 24th: We visited the school in the morning and found it well kept up and attractive. Good work was very evidently being done. John spoke and Mr. Gamble sang. Then we got five horses (Mr. Messler has three himself) and Mr. Gamble rode Rex, one of our horses, who is a fine saddler. John was lent a beautiful Kentucky thorough-bred of pale buff with cream mane and tail—a beauty with his arched neck and pawing feet. We then rode over to Grayhawk (my first experience side-saddle), where there is a sort of mission social settlement? in a small way, with Sunday School work. I certainly enjoyed my gallop and my fine little horse Captain loped like a rocking-chair. I never enjoyed myself more. The two ladies in charge welcomed us (Miss _____) and got us a good dinner. While we were waiting, two mountain women came in to buy mission barrel stuff—one a woman 6–8 months along I should say. They had come two miles. The other one had come for work. There was nothing for either. The ladies told of the sitting custom of mountaineers—and also complained of BBs [bedbugs] and lice. Said they did not dare to call on mountaineers for help. Did all work even to cleaning of privy. Spoke of great amount of tuberculosis and typhoid—also death from measles. The year before they had had small-pox there, and the fumigations had been few and far between. Mountaineers had no idea of contagion and resented and opposed any fumigation or isolating process. Much superstition in doctoring. A woman who had never seen her father (either because of his death before her birth or by blindness)—cured babies of rash in mouth by blowing into mouth.[24]

We had a beautiful ride home in PM—after showers had let up. We took a circuitous route off the road and up a mountain path where we had to lead our horses. Got home about 5 just as darkness had set in.

After supper—had a meeting—where John spoke again most successfully and Mr. Gamble sang. When over, a number lingered and we talked and John and I sang "Adam" and "Pharesee and Sadducee" with great applause. Mr. M. spoke of difficulties of this mission field. Also believed in not hurrying forces—but in slow growth.

NOVEMBER 25th: Started to Berea early in morn—a glorious morning when hills were golden and purple. Stopped again for John to speak and Mr. Gamble to sing at the little one roomed school in Clover Bottom. We heard part of their Thanksgiving exercises—and much lusty singing. One funny little boy, who had part in a primary stunt, looked down on another tot who should have been on the platform, and said, "Don't come up. We can get along without you."

Had an uneventful and pleasant return, arriving about 2 P.M. Mrs. F. greeted us most cordially and gave us a little luncheon. Then John and I went out to try (in vain) to get a tripod and also to order a large number of photographs.

After ordination of a young minister, we went over to a convocation of teachers which the President had called to discuss with us. Had an interesting time—various speakers the substance of which was as follows: "Mountains about as well inhabited now as possible, with support from crops.

Some counties too few—and some too many people. Many leaving and buying bluegrass farms though wished to live in sight of mountains. Natural affection for mountains. Most of Berea students go back. Especially those in shorter courses. When they make their own homes, these are better than the old ones. Great many Berea teachers in the mountains and they all root for college. Sent in constant stream. Berea does not encourage boys to go away for education, North etc. unless they are coming back to teach at Berea. Feel shorter courses and lower grades are most helpful now. College for the next generation."

Some disagreement as to a tenant class in mountains—but strong evidence for it—for renters (two or three) to one man's estate. Perhaps they each own small plot—then help out by renting more on shares. Distinct lines?—(pros and cons).

Berea has found it successful to return educated mountaineers to teach in own section. Does not believe (so Mrs. F. says) in "foreigners." They have just so many new points of view and adjustments to make—while the mountaineer starts in even. She thinks it best then not to start in social settlement work by outside (church) schools. People however to be reached best by schools. (J.C.C. thinks it matter of personality). Mrs. Dinsmore spoke on extension work.[25] Tried to get to a place before school let out. Went first to *the* most prominent man of the town and got the use of best building and got him in sympathy. Then sent home message by children. A series of stereopticon lectures. Lectures on the life of Christ, on alcoholism, great cities of the world, etc., last on Berea. Found it did women good just to see some one from the outside world. Always had full house and were asked eagerly to come again. Some asked her to correspond, and for years after, students came to Berea, whom she could not remember, and who looked on her as their best friend. She always urged a good school attendance but did *not* speak for Berea. She knew from reliable reports that it had an excellent effect on school attendance in districts. People also said it helped them. Always had good order and close attention.

Dr. Cowley spoke of amount of tuberculosis, typhoid and trachoma in mountains. Due he thought to lack of water.[26] Hard—at times—almost impossible to get water. All family used one towel. Barn used as privy and swarming flies bred contagion. No idea of contagion in mountains or what it meant. Disease went right through a family or community. Many deaths from measles. Told of woman who walked three miles to Berea and brought water buckets with her. Said yes—she could get water 1 to 1 1/2 miles on the other side— but she was coming to Berea and thought she'd bring her buckets along.

Nice custom at Berea on Sunday matter—all required to go to morning Sunday school and then might go during rest of day to any service. At eve must be at students chapel. No trouble on sentimental side—calling allowed twice a week and socials several times where could go together. Very sad when boy went back and married uneducated girl. Dragged him down to same level. Same difficulty here as to getting girls. Needed at home, or did not need education, etc. etc. Boys and girls eat together—student waiters. Have red table cloths.

NOVEMBER 26th: Got off between 1 and 2—and had uneventful ride to Winchester.[27] Train 20 minutes late and we had barely 15 minutes to get across the city to L&E. Finally flung bags and selves aboard mail wagon and galloped off. Long freight delayed us 5 minutes, and before we got to the station, train had drawn up. We just made it.

The ride to Jackson is quite impressive—great sandstone

ridges and bluffs. A woman behind me punched me with her fore-finger and wanted to know my county-seat. She proved to be a widow—a mountain girl. Husband died 3 months ago with tuberculosis. She did not wish to be a drain on the family but to pay her way. Had met two old people (who sat behind at snuff and tobacco—he had been drinking) who wished her to go to Cannell City, as Postmistress—and she was on the way, knowing no more than that. Said she was green about such things—but hard to fool, always watched—had been taught to "work, and watch and pray." Didn't like the old man's looks, but reckoned she could go back if it wasn't a good place. Had never heard of a time-table.

It was dark when we arrived, but Mr. Leonard met us and piloted us over the worst streets a half mile (?) to the school.[28] We found it pleasant and his family nice. Talked to Mrs. L. and went to bed while John went to meeting, where they were talking up Civic League. This does not seem much like a missionary home—as the young teachers are great chums with the daughters of the house—and all are bent on a good time. The house seems also–the mecca of all the eligible young men in town. The school has about 150 pupils—drawn practically all from the town—a *few* boarders. There is a public school—but very short in term and poor. Mrs. L. confided to me that she thought there was great need of the three R's—also of simple cooking. There is a good domestic science outfit—and a nice gasoline engine and several lathes at present lying idle—as the last man did not use them. Mr. L. has only been here six months and at present has not money enough to revive the industrial work. They are Bluegrass people and new to mountain ways. Mrs. L. was much distressed over carelessness and slovenliness—lack of stock law, pig pens, etc. etc. Said she thought the mountain people had been so much exploited that they thought themselves IT, and just lay back on their oars and felt it a right to have the church schools educate them. Did not take the trouble to be interested in taxes. Were satisfied in their own conceit. Did not approve of mission barrel scheme—said the lazy good-for-nothing mountain women just came in and expected to be given things. Said one of their mountain girls resented people sending things—and she liked that spirit better than the take-all one. Spoke of the spirit of lawlessness fostered by mountain valleys and roads. Had been allowed to have their way too long. No water works in town and great difficulty in drawing all water for dormitory. No one in town who can fix pumps etc. for them. Three or four churches in town, fairly well attended.

Mr. Kennard seemed to be more onto the situation. Had been around to a number of counties. Was especially impressed by need of hospitals. Great amount of tuberculosis.

Mrs. L. spoke of immodesty brought about by lack of sanitary appliances.

NOVEMBER 28th: Had a very interesting ride from Jackson to Helechawa—in a mangy little car, discolored and patched and smelly—but with a nice young conductor who had been "raised" in Jackson.[29] Said he couldn't see much difference in it from 20 years ago—as mean and meaner than ever. Hargis-Cockerell feud responsible for much—thought feud would end now—with death of Judge Hargis (shot by his own drunken son)—and Cockerells also pretty well shot out.[30] We heard also from other sources that old Judge controlled State elections by same means and simply assassinated every one in his way. Saw bullet-hole in his own store where one bullet, shot by his son, had lodged. Conductor, Mr. Back, also said he bet there were 20 blind tigers in Jackson—moonshine and otherwise. Possible to shut them out if strong man would push it. Afraid of antagonizing. Said his Superintendent would spend $1000 to prevent liquor getting into Morgan County. All conductors had government warrant to search baggage and arrest men carrying more than 1 gallon of liquor with them. Told of one man who had 78 bottles of beer in his trunk. Another, half drunk, slashed him with his knife—but on another occasion, gave him his pistol to keep until he got off. Lots of drinking. Said Superintendent had tried to get Express to promise not to bring in liquor. They refused and he took out all express offices on L&E line. Express re-shipped at Jackson under company care at express rates.

NOVEMBER 29th, Sunday at Helechawa: President Carter, of Hazel Green—a pleasant young man—met us with team and drove us out to school.[31] All the country is suffering with fearful drought. We saw small boys hauling water and at the school, they are having an expensive time hauling water for electric lights. The county—Wolfe County—is not so rough as that around and on the way to Jackson. The hills are lower and more rolling—soil looks better. The school itself is situated in a long valley—though on a little plateau-like rise in it. It is quite surrounded by hills with the little town at its foot. The school has a fine, new boys' dormitory of concrete—a brick recitation building—wooden girl's hall and industrial building (of wood and new) and two or three student cottages. There is a heating plant in the industrial building, and near it the electric light tank. The pumping noise till 10 at night is rather unpleasant. They have from 32 to 33 acres. We were given a pleasant room in the girls dormitory where Prof. and Mrs. Carter live—and a little luncheon in our room. We rested a while—then walked over a swinging bridge (made me sea-sick) between boys dormitory and us to make a call on the former minister's wife Mrs. Derthick. He is out getting help—preaching etc. etc. In the eve we went to a production of one of the literary societies—boys and girls. Mr. Carter has only recently decided to separate them as he thinks it breeds sentimentalism and hinders serious work. He has also cut out all of the societies for which the members were wearing black. The children did well and showed a pleasant spirit throughout the faculty jokes, which I was told, were uncontrolled from headquarters. There is a fine auditorium with circular seats.

Prof. Carter, personally, is much interested in industrial work and anxious to push it, especially to give work to the needy boys from whom he is constantly hearing. His desire was to teach that side, but when Mr. Derthick withdrew, he was obliged to take up, against his will, the principalship. Believed thoroughly in secondary education, and said few boys graduated, and at last he had realized that perhaps this was best at present, as these further advanced boys did not go back to the mountains. Did not know much about sickness though he was anxious for domestic science and nursing for girls. They have a sewing teacher and a laundry room as yet unequipped. The girls, however, do their own washing—also wait on table, sweep dormitories, clean bath-rooms (closed at present from lack of water) etc.

While we were looking over the industrial work and sewing, he spoke to two girls who were quilting, and found one knew how to weave and that her father made looms—and he made arrangements to get one then and there. This girl was also knitting—could do anything.

The faculty was an exceptionally nice one. Miss Hines, (math) from N. C. and Miss Miller (Eng) from Louisville. The latter had taught in Dr. Curry's school (?) Boston. Then there were Mr. and Mrs. Long, Miss Coleman, Miss King—

In the morning, we went to Christian Sunday School— and then to a revival Methodist preaching. I was much pleased with the liberal spirit. It was Communion and "all

who truly repent" were invited to the rail—of whatever denomination and even if they had not joined a church. The
minister then invited the ministers of other denominations
to assist him in dispersing the elements. Mrs. Carter tells me
that the women of all the churches (3 active but no Baptist)
combine in one society which gives a fair, the proceeds of
which are equally divided. Last time they divided with the
Cemetery Improvement Society. It has done more, she says,
to unite the people than anything else. In talking with Mrs.
C. in eve (while others had gone to hear John speak) she said
they had some trouble with the girls but perhaps no more
than in any boarding school. One chief matter was lack of
cleanliness. It was unpleasant to sit beside some of the girls—
and it was a delicate matter to right. Generally left to favorite
teacher. Girls had been taught nothing and she cited an experience of her own. She, poor lady, was having great trouble with her eyes—which no oculist could account for. Miss
Miller spoke with enthusiasm of the children's brightness,
responsiveness and frankness. Only two in school who are
not working their way.

The town has a neat rather progressive look—houses
painted, etc. Most of the women in sunbonnets, though the
well-to-do—wear elaborate ones. Mrs. Niles had on a beautiful black silk one with white ruffling inside. She also has a
beautiful white one, Mrs. C. says. She said too that she felt
they were not reaching the snuff-stick, tobacco-chewing class
(O.D.C. Perhaps not in Kentucky?)—and Mr. Carter said he
felt they were not reaching enough. On the whole thought
this county more prosperous than some. Mr. Mize says it is a
fine fruit country, raise splendid small vegetables—especially
tomatoes—but need to know how. Some people coming in
from back counties, had actually never seen a plow. Considerable sentiment between boys and girls.

NOVEMBER 30th, Monday: Mr. Carter drove us to the station, where we met Mr. Derthick, who turned out to be a young man.[32] He evidently was on to the situation however. Spoke liberally of all denominations. Said they never asked a boy wishing help, to what church he belonged etc. Need of union among churches and education based on strong Christian foundation. No other would succeed. County schools would need 20 years in this county before successful. Failed in teachers, Christian training, etc. Told of one town nearby (about 500 inhabitants). Only 4 men were not drunk at election time. Complete lack of religious life. Liked people however. Hated to give up school. Said Rockefeller Board would give no money to church schools under *Women's* Board—but was planning to give to mountain work. Mrs. Boutelle had evidently written ahead about us, for their Board had given him directions to let them know (by telegraph) when we were to arrive and they would come on.

Talked to Mr. Back on return, arriving about 2–2.30. Went to Imperial of lofty name, found trunk and washed up. Then to the Leonard's for a little call and to get coat and other case. Came back to hotel and Mr. Leonard brought a letter from Miss Pettit saying that her boy would not arrive until Tuesday noon and we had best start early Wednesday morn in order to have a good night's stopping place. To bed early.

3

DECEMBER 1908

KENTUCKY

Hindman was probably the first mountain school to appreciate fully the native culture of the mountains, to use the old handmade things, and to try to preserve the crafts themselves. They also used native shrubs and "pretties," such as gourds, hornets' nests, vines and berries. The "Big House" made a great impression on us, as indeed did the fund of information passed on to us by Miss Pettit and Miss Stone. They were remarkable women with experience and wisdom—Miss Pettit quick and sparkling, Miss Stone balanced and serene. I shall never cease to be grateful to Miss Pettit for opening to me what was to become an absorbing and illuminating interest as the years went on. She asked, that first night, as we sat after supper in the living-room before a huge open fire, if I would like to hear an old ballad. When I politely assented, without too much real enthusiasm, she called on one of the girls— Ada B. Smith, her name was—to sing me "Barbry Allen."

Shall I ever forget it? The blazing fire, the young girl on her low stool before it, the soft strange strumming of the banjo—different from anything I had heard before—and then the song! I had been used to sing "Barbara Allen" as a child, but how far from that gentle tune was this—so strange, so remote, so thrilling. I was lost almost from the first note, and the pleasant room faded from sight; the singer only a voice. I saw again the long road over which we had come, the dark hills, the rocky streams bordered by tall hemlocks and hollies, the lonely cabins distinguishable at night only by the firelight flaring from their chimneys. Then these, too, faded, and I seemed to be borne along into a still more dim and distant past, of which I myself was a part.

Of course, I would not rest until I had learned this new, fascinating "Barbara Allen"—quite an undertaking, I found, for the new intervals were subtle. Later I was to learn much about "gapped scales" and "modal tunes" and the special characteristics of these "old-timey song-ballets or love-songs," the ballet or ballad being the words, the "song," the melody. I was attracted by both words and songs, but it was the melodies that especially intrigued me, and I began at once to pursue them whenever I had an opportunity. The search, continued over the years, has proved one of the most illuminating and rewarding experiences of my life, leading, as it has, into the realms of pure and lasting beauty and opening the way into many related and inexhaustible fields—folk hymns, folk games, folk dances, folk tales, folk arts, folk material in general, here and abroad. At the beginning however, I merely watched for "song-ballets," learned the tunes and wrote down the words, thus adding a new subject to our expanding and deepening inquiry.[1]

DECEMBER 1: Had quite a furious talk at breakfast with a Mr.— who believed that the R.R.s were the only salvation of the mountain people—at least in this section. Said the conditions were not paralleled in any section of the U.S.—marriage and intermarriage, degeneracy, lack of ambition etc. Was didactic and severely hopeless. Insinuated that he could prove point if I were not present. Mr. Kelley, another young man present, differed with him. Said he had seen improvement in time he had been there. Men were up on law etc.

A lovely sunny day after a pouring night.

Had a quiet day sewing, sleeping and reading some new magazines. We took a little stroll up to a coal mine in the morn, where the young engineer was not enthusiastic over the country. Jackson is not a prepossessing place—and I understand there are places in it not safe to visit in daylight. It is small too—streets fearfully irregular—houses at all angles. No pigs loose but sties are in evidence and sad looking cows trip and lumber along the narrow irregular plank walks or lie dejectedly on the bare damp earth. I don't see why they range. There is nothing to eat but paper.

In the eve Mr. Kelley brought in a Mr. Vaughn—Kentucky Supt. of Sabbath School Society (lives at—but was brought up in Laurel Co.) and has spent months and years traveling through the mountains.[2] Has established many Sunday Schools which have been the salvation of his own county. Laurel is now the best county morally—but only 20% of school teachers were Christians or had any connection whatever with church work. Public schools bought and sold, and instruction poor and teachers even immoral at times. Astonishing lack of religion. Churches deserted. Told of spending one night in out of way cabin (on agreement of $1.00). He asked to say grace and then prayed with them. In morn when came to pay, the old mother cried and would take nothing. Thanked him for his prayer and said her boy had said he was never going to swear again.

At another time he met an old mountain negro 70 years old who said he had never been to church—or Sunday School—and to "tell the truf, sonny," he never prayed. Nearest church at Jackson. Mr. Vaughn told him he was concerned about his soul's welfare, reminded him that the time was short and he should use the means of grace. The old man's eyes filled with tears—and he said slowly "Thank you sonny" and five times "Thank you sonny." As Mr. Vaughn turned about a curve in the road, the last he saw was the old negro looking at him and repeating "Thank you, sonny." Spiritual needs very great and better education. Great extremes in Kentucky. The highest (often moonshiners who would shoot, and feudists) and the most degenerate. Along certain remote branches and creeks and coves great degeneracy in places where families had married and intermarried until relationship was lost. Many physical defects—idiocy, lunacy, (he had passed cabins boarded and barred up and heard shrieking and talking) defects in body, lameness, deformation, dwarfishness etc. Only thing to do was to shake them up and drive them out. More eastern counties, the more intelligent and progressive. Felt need of better home making. Much tuberculosis and typhoid. In Paintsville, people had lived on swamp land with shallow wells. No family unbroken—typhoid expected. Now were boring wells and conditions much improved. Same things true in many places—said in a number of counties that assessed value of firearms twice as great as that of farm implements—and also that many did not give in account of firearms. They have the most up to date kind of rifles etc.

Mr. Kinnard came in later and told us of some of his experiences. He spent 4–6 months in one place—a log cabin with two rooms upstairs—one a store room and the other where an old loom stood. This was moved into the store room and a bed was put there for him. The first night the rats made so much noise he couldn't sleep. Beds also full of occupants. The cracks of ceiling were spread above with paper and when he saw a rat weigh it down, he hit up with a stick. Gave up idea of sleep—but killed seven rats in one night. Used to sleep as he could daytimes out in field or mountainside. Was particularly distressed over health conditions—accidents, etc. Had seen a little girl with broken hip which had been roughly set and put in wooden box. Anyone could see it was not done correctly. Some years later, he saw the same girl grown up—and lame. Was eager for hospital at Jackson. Was full of interest and enthusiasm and not afraid of work and obstacles. Intended to stay by until place was in better shape.

DECEMBER 2: A clear but very cold morn. Grover C. Perkins a handsome dark boy of 19—came about 7 and we got off by 7.45. The road began early to be rough—the mud being frozen in heavy ruts. We wound out through peaked hills bared of timber—houses painted and frame. At noon we stopped before a cabin and fed horses and selves. Also took a picture of two sows and little suckers. The road by this time had begun to run in the creek bed and continued to do this with occasional short lapses to the bank the rest of the day. Of course there was little water—the season being so dry—but how we jolted and rattled among rocks and stones, crashing into frozen pools and out! Although the sun was bright and high, the air continued so cold all day that my hands were stiff and tingling when I tried to eat lunch. John and I got out and walked about 5 miles to get warm. The houses grew more and more far apart—their vicinity being heralded by flocks of ducks and geese in the creek and a few hogs rooting on the hillsides. More timber on the hills. It began to get dark by 3–3.20 indeed the sun first dropped out of sight before 2—and only reappeared after at intervals. Fortunately there was a half moon—bright and very cold, which reflected in the creek. I couldn't help thinking, of what the family would say if they could see us crashing through the ice of the creek bed that cold moonlight night—the dark hills high on either side and dark hemlocks close at hand—no houses in sight.

Finally about 5 P.M.—Grover pulled out of the creek and we stopped at a faint light on the left bank. Here proved to be a dark barn and a two story house faintly lighted. Some one hailed us—and there was old Mr. Hayes (a former Confederate soldier) who was to take us in for the night.

We introduced ourselves and were ushered into the room

where there was a brisk soft coal fire. Two girls were sitting by it—pretty, big eyed and shy—"hired girls" Mr. Hayes said—and a small boy of 2–3, whom Mr. Hayes explained, laconically as "said to be my grandson. Hardly think so—but I've got him and mean to keep him." (Miss Pettit told me later that the mother, when asked, said she really didn't know whether it was Tom's child or Ed's or Bill's—one being a nephew).

The girls then went out, and after we were warmed up, were ushered into the cold dining room. Set with a long table, low homemade chairs—oil cloth and slim crockery. Had black coffee without sugar or cream, fried fat pork, corn bread, white butter and sorghum. The girls waited and the men ate.

After supper, we returned to the fire and the older girl (surnamed Fugit) put the small boy into one of the two beds in the room. Then they returned to get our room ready. Presently Mr. Hayes told us we could go up when we were ready and asked if we minded having Grover sleep with us. I bit my lip and John answered with overdone cordiality, "Of course not, be glad to have him. I'm used to sleeping with the whole family."

We then retired to our room which was chill in spite of a fire. I pulled off my boots dress and petticoat and crawled between the one sheet and pile of homespun covers. John followed suit—after putting out the light and spreading my coat over us. Then we waited. There was a great deal of moving about but no Grover—nor did he turn up all night. He had been to the school and was evidently embarrassed. I don't know where he slept. We had a chilly night and were glad to get up at 4 A.M., in spite of the cold. Had a good breakfast of fried chicken and biscuit—and for all 3—8 horses feed, paid $2.30. Mr. Vaughn, by the bye, declared that the old mountain hospitality is a thing of the past. Once a minister or educator could not have paid a cent keep from Lexington on—but commercial spirit had come in. Money made the people mad. I don't wonder.

Got off at 6.30—into the creek bed again and we continued in it all day practically. Troublesome, Town Creek,—Fork—crashing, grinding in and out.[3] We had two mountains to cross, and John and I must have walked a good seven miles. All the cabins practically were log (except a few box cabins). Some of the chimneys were below the roof of the house. I saw many spinning wheels and one loom on a porch. Cabins all roofed with hand split shingles. All creek and valley land seems pretty thickly settled. Hillsides are ploughed high high up. Most of the corn in shocks however. Creeks lined with marked and stranded logs.

At one we drew into Hindman, which we found remarkably neat and prosperous in appearance.[4] It has practically no bottom land, just a rift in the hills by the creek—so that the school itself—a little beyond the town, has to be crowded close to the road. It has a big log house where the girls and teachers live—a small cottage for the boys, a power house and water tank though no water to use in this dry season. They haul all their water and boil that for drinking.

Miss Pettit and Miss Stone ran out to meet us—and took us into a fine big room to warm up over a roaring open fire while dinner was put on the table for us.[5] The house is not sealed inside, just finished carefully with plaster between the chinks. It has quite a charming effect—all the furniture in the house except the mission (a present) in that one room has been made by the students. It is quite charming too—of black walnut, finished dull and on simple old lines.

Our guest room is a big one—with two white iron beds covered with natural color linen spreads and blue kivers— woven rugs on the oiled floors. Electric lights throughout—

run by steam. The school furnishes them to town for a small sum which goes to support a man to run them and watch the buildings. They have had two fires (one incendiary) and now keep watch. House is steam-heated.

There are—teachers, Miss Cobb from Newton, Miss Beasly the housekeeper, Miss Mock the stenographer, Miss Butler the trained nurse. A Miss Breck was visiting here.

We rested in P.M. and in eve all the children came in like a family to sit for an hour over the open fire. Miss Breck got them to singing old ballads, The Swapping Song, Barbara Allen, Brown Girl (Nut Brown Maid) and Barliff of Islington. The tunes were as old as the hills—the real old plaintive folk tunes handed down from mother to daughter—absolutely minor and fascinating—Ada B., one of the girls, accompanied them on the banjo. "Barbra Allen" was quite thrilling—the Barliff Daughter was quite a different version—the girl not recognizing her returned lover.[6] Miss P. showed us a dulcimer, they are even now used occasionally among the hills—and made though at present there was no one in school who could play one.

Spent most of Friday resting—though I had a good talk in the evening with Miss Butler. She has wrought wonders in her 4 years here. Came first in a siege of typhoid and got close to peoples' hearts. Taught them to bathe, which they thought would kill them. Even the doctor (with whom she insists on working) thought it would raise temperature. One girl thought it would kill her but let her do it, because she said afterwards, she looked up into her face and thought she didn't look as if she would kill any one. Fearful conditions at childbirth. No washing for a long time after—child wrapped in dirty rags (responsible for eye trouble etc.) Old birth stool. Woman sits up when she has child and midwife catches child. Woman is no good if she can't walk back to bed. Very lively children here. An old midwife had "catched 50." Great feeling here of having women nurses and midwives for women and men for men. Inherent modesty always maintained even with 12+ in cabins. Miss B. told how one girl always took her bath on the porch even in winter (Miss B. insists on baths). Said she had to as she was never alone in the (one roomed) house. Moral feeling however weak. Women frequently had children before marriage. Might or might not marry the man and man did not seem averse to taking such a woman and marrying her and taking child. Some cases of child desertion. Little Goldie 7+ in the house here was "bastard" and could remember when her mother "threw her away." Went to school and told her father to take his child. She had kept her long enough.

Fearful condition of sanitation—no idea of infection—Miss B. told us of one woman "spittin' blood" and with a cancer on her nose, who was incensed because Miss B. would not allow the household to buy her milk and butter. Houses dirty and careless beyond mention. Immense improvement now. When first came, she was called to woman with miscarriage. Woman had been in bed over a week and nothing had been washed and changed about her—absolutely nothing. The bed was in a fearful condition—dirty clothes dropped around it—and plates of food of all kinds were set about. She was most grateful on being cleaned up—had never seen such a thing. Now Miss B. says she thinks it would be impossible for such a thing to be in this community. Neighbors would know how and she is trying to foster a community spirit. Miss Pettit told of a woman who said "You women have come to larn us a better way. I always knowed thar was a better way, but I never knowed what it was."[7] She lowed she was too old now to learn but her children must know and she is sacrificing everything that all of her twelve children may get an education.

Five are in school now and one is in Lexington at College (not an unwise waste in this case, as the girl is a leader and under fine care).

Lots of eye trouble in mountains—must be treated constantly and bad cases sent to Lexington and Louisville. Miss Butler's idea is for a hospital at Jackson and here a district nurses association. Believes it would reach people and home life better. Doctors eager for it. Hopes to have here for school a model home at head of which is trained nurse. A few girls in ideal home life—with nursing. Rooms in cottage for sick boys and sick girls of the school. She is planning this summer a model tuberculosis cabin. Will explain to doctors and all visitors and distribute pictures and literature where it can be read.

SATURDAY MORN, DECEMBER 5th: Miss Pettit took me horseback up Perkins Branch. The branch was the road and a very wet and poor one—closely set between hills and gray beeches and mossy green rocks. Hemlocks here and there—several times we had to squeeze against a hillside to let by oxen drawing sledges with corn husks (fodder). The branch is set along quite closely with little log cabins—(150 to 200 children in 2 miles) mostly one roomed in two sections formed by the fire place. At two we called—one at the head of the branch—where a pretty young tobacco chewing woman wanted us to sit down before the fire. There was a baby of 1–2 on the bed and a little thin wizened new one in her arms—10 in all and all present. Older ones go to school—and will allow none of children to chew tobacco. Mother may if she wishes. Cabin did not strike me as so fearfully dirty as ones I have seen—but it was no model.

An old woman on the way told us how their landlord(?) had jumped on them and what difficulties she had in getting in the crop—with help of her two small boys. She couldn't spare them for school.

At the next place there were 12 children. The mother had only got out of the branch 2 times in all Miss Pettit's stay here—once to bring her drunken husband home—he laying in bottom of wagon and she standing up and driving up that branch. Five children in school now. Home life seemed happy—but dirt pretty prevalent. A baby in her arms. Houses are fenced in from hogs and cattle, and one generally has to straddle the fence to get in. Convenient however in mounting a horse.

Miss P. and I had a long conversation on needs of secondary and industrial education—lack of understanding in people away from the field—her family etc. She is most eager for a farm—and has one in view. Also needs more bored wells. Sanitary conditions at school not desirable—but no water now to run bathroom. Hard to get good teachers—many fall in love with the boys. Miss Berry has had same trouble.

She told me a most fascinating tale of one woman from a colonial home near Abingdon, Va. Fell in love with her cousin, ran away and married him. She wrote home twice and father said he never wanted to see her again. After baby was born, wrote again with same result. She went to Kentucky, selling everything to get two horses. Carried baby in her arms and at saddle a roll of linsey-woolsey she had spun. As she came to the divide, she looked back at Virginia and the loneliest feeling she had ever had came over her and it had never left her since. Finally came here and settled at the source of this little branch and raised big family of children. Oldest was married before he could read or write. Learned afterwards when teacher came in—and when dying of tuberculosis, made Miss P. promise to see that children should learn. Five in school—but the oldest and most promising (a good nurse) had openly been in love five years with her second cousin whose father had killed her grandfather. One night this fall—school heard pistol shots (brother said any one could have told that they meant a boy was carrying off his girl) and Miss Breck saw a boy riding and leading a horse with side saddle. Next morning boy and girl were gone.

DECEMBER 6th AND 7th: A quiet Sunday. In P.M. went to W.C.T.U. meeting where John talked, and in the evening, climbed flights of high steps to the Methodist church, a bare little barn where John spoke again.[8] Sang all kinds of weird hymns.

Monday morning worked on raffia gourd and napped. In P.M. John and I rode up Elberton's (?) Branch, a very rocky watery way. John took several pictures of the road and beechy hill slopes—lovely. As he was struggling, an old man came up with an axe from the nearby cabin. He guided us a bit further up the branch, but it grew so rough and steep, we turned back. We stopped at his cabin to meet Mrs. Miller and see a huge gourd—lacking three inches of being six feet in circumference. There were two rooms (covered with newspaper and full of cracks), but only one was used to live in. No stove but big fireplace, two beds, few chairs, and spinning wheel. The other room had corn in it and various truck. Mrs. Miller was cooking white stuff (hominy?) in spider over open fire.

DECEMBER 8TH: A splendid bracing morn—which called for my flannel-shirt, vest, sweater and Pontiac coat—tights and woolen stockings. Had a talk with Misses Breck and Stone and at 7 the horses were brought up—two blacks. The younger livelier one belonging to Mr.—was saddled for John, and the other (Mr. Napier's) for me. It proved to have a bad limp and in addition would hardly crawl along the road. We stopped in town to get a pair of woolen socks to draw over my boots—then went to see Mr. Napier.[9] By that time the boy's saddle which John was riding was already becoming pretty uncomfortable and we felt quite a sorry pair—with saddle

bags agape and uneven under my saddle. Mr. Napier said the
horse had just been shod and probably the shoe pinched—
also he was to meet his brother part way and this brother
Callaway would bring an extra saddle which John could take.
So we hied up to the blacksmith's and had the horse's shoe
fixed, also changed horses, giving John the old boy to hike
along with a spur, as Mr. N. said he wouldn't go for ladies.
Then we waited for Mr. N. to catch up. After a good half
hour he appeared galloping along on a white steed. We rode
cheerfully some mile or two, hearing tales of his experiences
as Sheriff—then he rode back a mile or 2 on an errand and
we waited again. Finally he caught up and we rode to the
forks of the creek where his brother was to meet. Examining,
however the unbroken ice, Mr. N. decided that his brother
had not come, so rode on with us another mile or two. After
meeting numerous men and mules, none of which had seen
Callaway, at length a man hove in view who turned out to
be the same. By good luck he had not forgotten the saddle
and at length we were fixed. Off rode the Napiers (Nap-
per pronounced) through to Morgan County to help their
brother get nominated for sheriff and we took our way along
Troublesome at about 10:30. We rode along thus apiece and
turned up Mill Creek—then over the mountain to the head
of Lots Creek.

The first house we came to was that of Reece Young and
we rode up a very wet road to the palings where we tied our
horses (and fed them) and clambered over and up to the
house. A woman with a double harelip welcomed us cordially
and took us in where an old man of 86 was sitting warming
up over a coal grate fire (recently put in by his son to replace
big wood fireplace). He had been husking corn all the morning and felt stiff. He chatted along amiably—said he had never travelled much—born 4 miles from there 86 years before.

Son was up on the mountain getting wood. Miss Y. was much disturbed that she couldn't get us dinner and the old man insisted that John should not pay him for horses feed. He however dropped money in his hand and we left with cordial invitations to come again and spend the night.

From there we rode a mile further, by log cabins on Lots Creek, to Mrs. Alec Young's. She had a good sized house and one daughter, looked quite young, vigorous and intelligent (a widow woman for years which accounts for it perhaps). She welcomed us in to the usual coal grate fire and told us about the process of weaving while two tame gray squirrels climbed all over us. Processes:

1. First plant like wheat—using 1/2 bushel of seed to acre. When seed of plant is yellow, it is ready
2. to pull.
3. Spread on the ground to dry.
4. Tie in bundles,
5. Lay in water or on the ground to rot the bark.
6. Break it up like hemp.
7. Beat it with a flat stick to separate wood fibre—the flax projecting over board or stick and projecting ends beaten. Called to "scutch or swingle."
8. Pulled through a hackle (board with nails driven through to form rough comb then is tow [?].
9. Spin to make linen thread.
10. Weave.

She brought in a hackle for us to see and took us out behind the house where her loom was in the sun (under a roof) with quilts pinned up on either end to keep out the wind. She was weaving some linen curtains for Miss Pettit and gave us an illustration. Were too late to stop at poppet makers—Mrs. Nancy Smith.

We then rode on to the mouth of Lot's Creek. By that time it was quite dark and we were all (people and horses) tired and cold. My saddle had a fearful tilt—forward so that my feet were way up and all the strain was thrown on my back. It was bent like a bow and I couldn't sit up straight. We were glad to be at the mouth of Lot for it empties into the North Fork of the Kentucky, 3 miles from Hazard. We met several groups of people but rode on in the darkness through what appeared to be exceptionally pretty scenery— a full river and peaked hills beyond.

It was fully 5:30 before we dragged into Hazard—my pony sadly relinquishing his proud morning's lead and slowly plodding up the hill behind John's slow but steady old nag.[10] We asked for Mr. Petrey and rode out to his house up a steep hill some 1/4 mile out of town. My poor pony moved most reluctantly and I was too cold and tired to talk. Arrived at the house—a rather slack looking woman was outlined in the doorway—Mrs. P. Mr. Petrey wasn't home—she wished he was. He didn't expect us till Friday. They would have to get us another supper and the barn was small. I was almost ready to cry—but we turned our horses and plodded back to town to D.Y. Comb's Hotel. Had a very decent room and I fairly fell off the pony in John's arms and crawled up to the grate fire where I could bake arms and legs and aching back. The bed was hard and none too clean as to its pillow cases and single sheet—but we turned the former inside out, heaped clothes from the second bed over us, and clad in cambrics and stockings, crawled gladly into bed. We did have a chance to appreciate the moonlight (almost full) that night—for John and I had bad cramp and had to creak down the stairs in the night. Front door and everything was open, and in turn we found one way around the house and to regions beyond. It was almost as light as day.

(Kodaks: 1. Cove, foot of mountain, near Lot's Creek,
2. Top of Mountain,
3. O. on Horseback.)

DECEMBER 9th: Up at 6:30—feeling more encouraged in spirit, though I, at least, felt pretty stiff and lame. Made ready for a prompt start—feeling none too enthusiastic toward Mr. Petrey, but about 7.30 he showed up—a pleasant man of 40— with clean cut features and English cut of hair and cheekers. Had not known we were in town until too late. Evidently was cut up at our reception. He insisted on paying our bill and urged us to stay over. Then he took us up over the buildings (two) which had a truly beautiful site on a knoll overlooking the town and surrounded by cedars. The morning was perfect—warmer. A white frost like snow on the ground, and on beeches, and cedars outlined against them—hills above. The buildings were of brick and good but very dirty inside, as the school building is leased to town up to Xmas (keeping teachers employed by board, and paying enough to pay janitor— but no good janitor now—hence dirt). There seemed to be some quarreling going on and unsatisfactory conditions. Mr. P. does not expect county high-schools to amount to anything for 10 to 20 years. County too poor to support them. Besides politics will be bad for them. State was setting premium for them by granting graduate teacher's license without examination. Idea that county high school is to be only a school for graduates of the grammar department of public school—not to include common public school grades. These students will be few in number for years to come. Didn't think magistrates would want to vote or put before people plans for raising money to put up buildings and supply teachers for the few—especially when there were good buildings and good church schools. He felt they were going to divide up the money raised for the common public schools which would reach further.[11] Told us difference between Primitive or Hardshell Baptists—Old Regulars, Missionary, Predestination—whosoever can will, and whosoever will, can.

Said he would get us a copy of the Sweet Songster and another old one if he can. Spoke of United Baptists which is historical name rather than doctrinal—[illegible phrase follows].

Took us up to his house—pleasanter outside than in, where I froze, and where we stayed till 9:45 and talked to his wife—6 children (and one coming) then to hotel to pack up. Also got another saddle pad to fix my saddle which proved comfortable strapped further back. Mr. P. appeared at 11 with nice box of crackers and fried chicken and we started off in good spirits—our saddle bags pinned up and strapped on. Off at 11.15 but had a series of petty delays which kept us till twelve. Forded North Fork of Kentucky and went over the mountain and down the Curly Fork of Brown's Fork—got off the road up Brown's Fork—then followed it down through two gates, to where it unites with Big Creek. Up Big Creek after luncheon across the mountain and down to M—Creek—up M—Creek and over the mountain to Wooten's (pronounced Ooten) Creek to Felix Farmer's, where we had neat comfortable quarters. A pleasant ride all day with fine scenery. Took three pictures—

Mountain view just out of Hazard;
John coming up Creek (Big) road,
Bend in Big Creek.

Hazard to Felix Farmer's on Wooten Creek—Leslie Co.—12 miles.

Mrs. Napier's—(Mrs. Farmer's mother). Her son died last October was two years ago of "pure corruption." Had just had his funeral preached this fall by Campbellite preacher.

Brother Hoskins, who said in sermon—"Just one thing to which he objected. On his deathbed he (son) prayed and had been a mighty good boy all his life. But preacher said it was too late as he had not been baptized or joined the church."

Because of her "experience"—Mrs. N. is to have funeral repreached next fall by a young preacher. "Ever since her boy died she had been apraying that he might speak to her through a dream—and about two weeks ago, he spoke to me just as clear as you'all. Said that his death due to catching cold while wagonin' in rain and had to go wagonin' because Bud (?) Eversole had called him off (from the race) for sheriff when he had the other fellow clean plum beat." Eversole and his men called him off for a man at the head of the river—Mac Roberts, saying he was a poor man and needed the office. Eversole promised Jo (son) that he and his men would support Jo three years from then for sheriff. He (Jo) was right young and could afford to wait. Mac Roberts was beat because he hadn't so many friends as Jo and was killed accidentally by a bullet (got to quarrelling at the ford). Jo had a right good farm but he could make more by wagonin'—so went wagonin' and took his death from the rain. Son told her in dream that he wasn't goin' to have nary preacher standing over his grave and saying such things. When his soul was shining bright as any star—but to get young minister and tell him to tell his mother's experience at the preachin'. Also said to go to town to Eversole's store and get a $10.00 cloak for she was a weakly woman to go out in the cold (she was crippled with sciatica). Also was to tell Eversole—and to call on Dr. Ray and tell how Eversole had promised to support her son and make him promise to support Jo's half brother for sheriff this next time. In life he had never told her of the promise.

Two days after, a whisper came in her ear—just as you all's voice—"Do you believe on the Lord Jesus Christ? I do. Do you believe on His Spirit? I do. It's His spirit that's a telling you this" Eversole has heart dropsy (Eversole had been thinking of going up to Arkansas Hot Springs). If he goes and has his men support Jo's (half) brother—he will come back cured, but if he stays and fights half brother, his heart dropsy will wear him away "drop by drop—drop by drop—drop by drop—till he's all gone."

French-Eversole feud, Leslie County—32 men killed.[12] Jo Eversole the beginner was Campbell on his mother's side (she said he had some good blood in him. Her mother was a Campbell) and also her husband's brother-in-law. Day he was killed (wife believed in dreams) told him not to go to court at Hyden or he would be killed. Then he told a dream of his own. Dreamed he had gone up Big Creek on his big gray mare—water was at a flood and had to swim. And when he got to the ford below—house, he saw himself floating on his back—and there on that day at that ford he was shot from a blind—and him the brightest lawyer in this mountainous country. Old mother still lived at house, which looks deserted and all dropping to pieces—shiftless family he married into. Men would not work and drank all day and women would not clean up.

DECEMBER 10th: Wooten, Leslie County: Directions for the day—6 miles, to down the road a piece—ford Cutshen 3 times and up Flacky across a right rough little hill to the head of Owls Nest; down Owls Nest to the Middle Fork and up Middle Fork to a "wide place in the road—which is Hyden."[13]

Photos: Three of Rex and Annalea Farmer and grandmother, Mrs. Napier. John crossing ford of Middle Fork just below Hyden.

Up about 6.40. Colored boy had made the fire and we

dressed in luxury. Had a fine breakfast—chicken, sweet potatoes, oatmeal and real cream, coffee, corn flapjacks and hot biscuits—also eggs, jam and sorghum. House was clean and family up. Colored man had to sleep on mattress in Mr. and Mrs. F.'s room—and privy pretty primitive but otherwise good. While we waited for the sun to rise over the mountains and thaw road, we talked to Mrs. F. and Mrs. N. and took pictures. Mrs. F. had been to school at Hyden. Mrs. N. said that a heap of the ladies passed that way—teachers from Hyden, etc., but she hadn't seed such a pretty one. She should think those teachers would feel pretty—to see me. Mr. F. would not take a cent for keep. Said he never took from religious or school people. Thought he'd better sell out if he couldn't do that much towards helping.

Got off about 10. A heavenly morn again—quite warm and springlike, with brooks flowing and wrens singing. Had the roughest road yet of our travel—and the mountain was really quite a stiff one. Even I got off while John's old blacky wheezed and crackled and his poor old nose ran. These beech woods of this country are wonderfully pretty with their fawn colored leaves and pale trunks shaded with black and set with green moss. The steep hill slopes are covered with the fallen leaves and the fallen trunks of old trees lie among them, heavy with rich green moss. Above, the sky is an intense blue and the sparkling air makes it a joy to be alive and riding along. Just below Hyden we had to cross the Middle Fork—quite a deep ford, at least in part—and we started straight across to some old wheel tracks instead of way zigging up to the more beaten track. Got up to bottom of the saddle bags in water (where I took John's picture) and then had to follow up the bank. Got to Hyden about 12–12.15 and found Mr. Lowrie expecting us—our room at the Oakland Hotel and dinner waiting.

Mr. Lowrie proves to be a very young person—only last year graduated from Green-Tusculum. He appeared much astonished and worried at people's indifference to school matters. New this year and did not thoroughly understand last year's plan—but believed it had been arranged for County and Presbyterian Board to build and run public and board school together. Brick building to go up and Board had sold old dormitory on strength of this. Now new school law—and whole thing had fallen through.[14] Teaching two together however this year on same plan. We walked up to the schoolhouse (which has been closed 2–3 weeks on account of scarlet fever and found it a good wooden building somewhat in need of freshening up inside. Met two young women teachers—a Miss—from N. Y.—and a Miss Post from Maryville, who blushed when we talked of Prof. Campbell at Jackson (had been classmates). Then John went down town with Mr. L. and I came back to hotel in time to be ear witness at least to a hog shooting in the back yard.

In the eve we met at table Judge Brown from London, the County Superintendent—who acted scared to pieces.[15] Neither thought the high school law possible to enforce though believed it would work out in a modified form eventually. Young R.C. lawyer Calvert also talked. Compulsory education law no good as it had no penalty attached. Judge B. said wonderful change over country in his time because of schools.

DECEMBER 11th: Hyden: Directions for day: One mile to deep ford of Middle Fork—4 miles from Hyden ford again at Mr. Baker's (bad ford down a log-shoot) 1 1/2 miles ford again—2 two miles to Wilder Branch (Hell for Sartain is 10–12 miles from Hyden in this neighborhood, pretty—got a picture). From Wilder Branch cross mountain to Carnahan's store and get directions. If necessary stop over night at Robt.

Bowlings's store or Robt. Flander's (good place) at mouth of Elkhorn—or further on at Mr. Boger's store.

Hyden–Buckhorn, 22 miles: More specific directions next morn, which we followed. Go down big road and ford Middle Fork below Roberts—a deep ford. Several miles on ford again. Next ford is at mouth of Cutshin and Bulls Creek—dangerous because of shifting quicksand bottom brought in by three creeks. Better to remain on left bank of Middle Fork past mouth of Bulls Creek and ford at Shoals 1/2 mile below. Then keep on right bank of Middle Fork 2 miles past mouth of Hell for Certain to Adam Huff's store. Follow up Wilder Creek 1 mile or more—then take main wagon road across the mountain—down Elkhorn Creek to its mouth. Ford Middle Fork again and go up stream (instead of down) through a lane with two gates to Robert Bowling's house then turn up through Bowling's Holler and down Bowling's Branch to Middle Fork (near Possum Bend and Judas Hill). Ford again at Buckhorn and follow up Squabble Creek to village and college.

We followed these directions above except that we forded quicksand ford at Cutshin, as it seemed safe. Squabble Creek is so called from a squabble or quarrel years ago over a deer. It heads at Whoop-for-Larrie Hill (so called from man who used to get loaded with moonshine and whoop it up). Most names around here have significance. Because of paucity of language—teachers are continually called on to give new names. So many Marys and Marthas—they are degenerated by father's names—Mary Jo—Mary Bell etc. Hell for Certain gets its name from two hunters who got lost in rough county around creek. One said "This is sure Hell"—which being interpreted is "Hell for Certain."

Left at 6.45—horses in fine spirits especially John's with saddle bags rearranged. A gentle rain when we started, settling into heavy pour. Our oilskins stood well however. The best road in the country along the river and pretty scenery. White ghostly sycamores (with mistletoe on some) on banks or outlined against a misty hill back. A regular bridle-path in places—getting squashy as the morning wore on. Wonderfully pretty over the mountain—which reminded us of Indian Grave Gap. Bigger trees than before—chestnuts and oaks—arbutus all along the banks. Passed a house where Mr. Murdock says a democrat (few here) painted high on new white house "Corner Stone of Democracy."[16] He says it is riddled with bullet holes. Man, however, has changed now to republican and is trying to swab over old print—natural aptitude for politics. No interest in election of president. All peaceful—but a week later on, County Judge election, great excitement, drinking etc.

At Bowling's Hollow (or just beyond) we climbed over a high hill and asked at a typical one roomed cabin how far to Buckhorn. A slatternly women with a crowd of children came to the door and said she "reckoned three miles." John asked if she were sure—and she said she had never been there, but she had heered tell it was three miles. (It was seven). She asked us to come by and I should have liked to, but we pushed on and as we went up the hill, we could hear the thump of her loom.

DECEMBER 12th: Forded Middle Fork and got into Buckhorn about 1.15. Mr. and Mrs. Murdock ran out and brought us in out of the rain and we had a fine luncheon of fried chicken, potatoes, baked apples, tea and hot biscuit.

The school has a beautiful situation on the slope of a hill with a broad flat [?] ground at its foot for campus, baseball diamond etc. The buildings are all of logs valued at $18,000. Girls dormitory, boys [dormitory] (where a few boys live and Mr. and Mrs. M. keep house with three girls) a refectory, a school building—a new and exceedingly pretty hospital, primary building. They have only been here 6 years.

Mr. Murdock explained working of the new law which does not allow church and public school to run together. Here for instance—money for next year voted this year but cannot be collected till next November. Public school has no house, no fuel, no books, maps, etc. Result will probably be that some scalawag will open old log building for a few days, close up and draw salary or they will want to rent a room of Mr. M.,[17] which he will not do—as that would bring on the campus boys (perhaps bad) over whom he has no control at all. This is the case at Hazard, he says Mr. Petry has no control over school though he ventures to say that the Baptist Board does not know this. Mr. P. has reputation in the county as the narrowest of all the principals. Ran out Presbyterian preacher at Hazard—opposed even outside school and speaks against Berea. Has few supporters in Hazard—his trustee defeated in election etc etc.

Conditions in Hyden also unsatisfactory. Oneida man original and good. Manchester man, Mr. Miller, a Christian gentleman—but overworked and unequal to the situation. Great mistake of Presbyterian Board to draw out now. County unable to handle situation. Need of church schools for years yet.

Mrs. M. told me of her three girls—Sarah, Martha and Mary—antecedents, etc. Bad mothers. Dances "frolics" in this region very bad—bad women, whiskey etc. Childbirth without birth-stool, woman often sitting on strong man's lap—uncle—husband or friend, and midwife caught baby in her apron. Guessed one old woman here (as bad and mean as she can be) has caught 20 on an average a year. Much intermarriage with resultant deaf-mutes—foolish children—stuttering, etc. Also many illegitimate children. Two girls in family way now by 1st cousins. One family protested and boy mad. Will not marry her. Second is waiting and hoping.

Told interesting and picturesque things—homecoming of a sick and homesick girl from city hospital. Carried on cot by 6 men—crossed by ford and mother by foot-log. As the mother came near again, she heard the girl talking and laughing. Grew better as she approached home. At every little branch or creek, more men came out to change hands on the cot "them Makintoshes." (Every creek has by number of one name) "them Napier's" etc. They sent word from the house to find how many were coming and when they got to the house there were "27 strong men."

She says Mr. M. runs the town—has a powerful way with him. No trouble with discipline. Trouble however with drinking. Cleaned out one set of blind-tigers—but found men he trusted mixed up with the sale—elders of the church, etc. One church elder had several children around the country before he married. Told of one unusual and charming girl 12 years old—at school for a while—devoted to young sister, who died when Mr. M. was away. She wrote Mrs. M of her sorrow, how she wandered round trying to find comfort and some remembrance of sister. Remembered they had buried some apples and went to find them. Her sister was dead— but there were the apples, and near them the little print of her sister's bare foot. Said "I never knowed what trouble was till Mandy died." (They had hilled up six apples apiece in orchard.) She put her foot in the print and found a certain peace at tangible evidence.

Film 8—Buckhorn College from Hill

DECEMBER 13th: Sunday: Buckhorn: I lay abed until 9 and Mrs. M. came in and spoiled me by bringing breakfast and washing my face and hands, and talking to me. Finally got up and went to church, which was held today in school building as the "window lights" were out of church on the hill. The hall was full—many young children. John preached. Saw a number of foolish looking boys—but good attention was paid. In P.M. Mrs. M. and I retired upstairs and lay on the bed and talked and talked of everything. Made a short call on the two young teachers—Miss Taylor and Miss Lanier. Went to bed pretty early.

DECEMBER 14th: Up early and off about 8 o'clock—very sorry to leave the Murdocks. My pony was as gay as a lark and cantered off merrily across the campus—while the black horse pounded behind. The air was fresh and mild—and the sky dimmed slightly by thin clouds. Roads pretty rough where the mud had stiffened. We forded the Middle Fork and followed up the river for a mile or more on our Friday's route—then at the fork of the telephone wires, followed up Gay's (?) Creek to Chavis—about 7 miles. Had to climb a mountain—and stop several times to fix the saddles—but found it pleasant riding. Chavis is only a cluster of houses with a church house and schoolhouse and store. We stopped at the store to get directions and had some trouble rousing any one. Finally a half drunken man told us to keep to the right—across a bridge and ford the river. (Several other men in a numb condition looked out and stared at us.) We followed directions—but could find no ford and the river was flowing deep and swift. So we turned up toward Hazard, instead of fording, and going up Grapevine Creek. The river was full and sycamores with mistletoe and the hemlocks were fine—still we worried a little as to where we were.

We rode 2–3 miles up and down dale till at last we heard a shout and found a small boy driving a yoke of steers. (At every question of John's he roared "Hey?" in a perfectly stupid and exasperating way, but) we finally discovered that he had a grandfather up a little piece, and avoiding the swaying steers, we hurried on. Found the old man, Mr. Napier and his son outside a neat house. Proved to be son of a Campbell and uncle of Mrs. Napier of Wooten Branch. Directed us to a ford at about 1/4 mile—and told us to follow the river down to Jim Campbell's—"Black Jim's"—and get directions there. The ford was deep but we crossed safely and followed up the river about seven miles looking for Black Jim. The road was good but very hilly. It was up and down continually, so we could not make good time. River scenery very pretty (saw a foolish boy behind a tree). At last we arrived at Black Jim's, on Sam Campbell's Creek. The old lady—round and pretty face and smoking a pipe—invited us in where we drew chairs around the grate fire (black kettle boiling on it) took out our lunch and ate (though she offered to feed us) sharing oranges, cookies and candy. Then Black Jim came in and we all claimed kinship. Said his great-great-grandmother came from Scotland. Lived to see five generations and (400?) grandchildren. Said there were 500 or 600 Campbells in Perry County (and as many in Breathitt) and no one had ever been "penitentiaried"—only one indicted for false swearing and he got off. (Didn't know whether he did it or not. Rather thought he did).[18]

John gave them a good list of old Scotch names for boys and girls, which the daughter wrote down. They refused to let us pay for corn. Said they had plenty and couldn't let kin pay. Then we rode up Campbell's Creek and over two mountains to Second Creek, over another to First Creek. Not very thickly populated right here. Saw one entirely isolated and lonely cabin near top of mountain. Many children but no remote possibility that I could see for education. Followed First Creek about 300 yards—then turned to left on main wagon road over small mountain down to North Fork. About two miles from the bridge at mouth of Lots Creek. Passed first house on river—Cranford's (good place to stay). Went up Lot's Creek past Jo Feltner's place (place to stay) and landed at dusk on Trace Fork of Lot's Creek at old man Holliday's.

(Black Jim Campbell—said father was still living—100 years old and came when 9 years from North Carolina. Forty odd families of Campbells in that bend and none had less than 6 children—running up to twelve. In giving account of good Campbells he neglected to say that John Campbell was leader in French-Eversole feud "war" (on the Eversole side). Was killed in the feud. Also neglected to say how many had died with their boots on.)

Two wagons had just come from Jackson and stable was full, but they took us in and gave us a good room, iron bed and two sheets. Cooking was pretty poor and old lady had hair in a wizened pigtail. Has a nice little teacher—Miss Avons—in house and we had a pleasant chat with her. One of the sons—Jim—played the dulcimer, a simple arrangement, I thought, but was too bashful to sing, in spite of urgings to the "Ground Hog" (that, by the way, was the only thing he played, in which I could distinguish any difference of tune). There were two drivers in—Combs by name—one as handsome as possible—18 perhaps—six feet and straight as an arrow, great dark eyes, with heavy fringed lashes. Some of these boys are stunning and one hardly wonders at the troubles in every school, of the N. Y. teachers falling in love with them, marrying them in some cases, to repent at leisure.

The old lady told me her troubles. One of the boys ran for sheriff, mortgaged farm, etc.—a good farm—40 odd bushels to acre of corn. Rented some out, for boys much in Hazard on business(?). Old man had been killed this last summer— mules had run away with him. We paid her (charging 75 cent apiece but no change, and we gave her $1.00) and got off again about 8.

DECEMBER 16TH: Fair again but promising rain, and in fact, splattered a bit toward 12 o'clock. Followed up Trace's Fork and over several mountains to Dwarf (three miles), then down an excellent road along Troublesome, 12 miles, to Hindman. Travelled slowly as we were tired and got in about twelve.

Kodaks: Logs on Troublesome,
Ox being shod on Troublesome,
Gourd and sledge,
Back W.C.T.U. house.

DECEMBER 17TH: Went calling with Miss Pettit. School girls' houses clean—others not so much so. One woman picking geese (every six weeks) to make feather-bed for each of children.

DECEMBER 18TH: FRIDAY: About noon the pouring rain let up and we were ready to start—oilskins and all. Miss S. had Rachel's barrel made up, when just before we started, Mr. Gayheart drove in with a big canvas covered wagon (full) drawn by two teams of mules. No box for Rachel, but by chance Miss P. opened one unmarked, which proved to be hers. Then there was a grand bustle to change—candy-bags, packages, oilcloth, etc. Every one hustled opening boxes and getting us off. We were off by 12:30. All were tired and it was a relief simply to be out in the fresh air without any immediate responsibility. The road lies up Troublesome (left fork) a piece and then over a mountain (where John and I and a young chap, Ed—, walked, while John Everidge drove and Miss Stone rode) to Ball's Creek, over another mountain, to quicksand and the house.

This is a particularly pretty part of the country—beeches and oaks with occasional mistletoe, banks covered with arbutus and partridge berries—great rocks green with moss and fern. We sat with heads hanging back, looking up the steep hillsides for a well shaped hemlock to cut off for our Christmas tree, with many discussions as to the superiority of this or that. The road along Ball is very lovely—the hills being thick with tall rhododendron and hemlocks—to the shaky edge of the narrow winding road. The brake too was out of order, which left one room for thought—especially as it was growing dark. The last mile or two we pitched down the steep incline more or less at a gallop, with darkness ahead. It was entirely dark when we drew up before an old double log house and squashed out through the mud with Rachel Everidge to guide us.

The house consisted of two large square rooms, each with a huge fireplace (good wood fires), and one with two beds and the other three beds. The two bed rooms looked clean and neat—a wonderful change, Miss Stone said, and due undoubtedly to Rachel. Rachel proved to be a pretty dark girl of 18, very enthusiastic. The family with whom she was living consisted of step-father (who had been in Philippines in war) mother—a tall handsome blonde woman (baby coming), two big girls of her own, and a little girl, Viola. That made 11 of us to sleep in two rooms.

We had supper soon—a grand combination of preserves, fried pork, fried potatoes, corn bread and biscuit and coffee, and then told stories a while over the big fireplace. Then the women folks retired to the second bedroom to open the box and sort out and label presents. It proved to be a fine box and with the constant aid of eating candy, we finished up the work early, then for bed. Finally it was decided that all the women should sleep in the third bedroom, and four men in the other (they thus getting the clean room of which I was glad for John). Miss Stone and I crawled into bed together and by her clever forethought, had clean bandages to put under our heads and across the neck where the bed clothes came. The latter were none too fresh in smell, but we didn't notice it except when we turned over. During the night it certainly grew warm in the room, for the fireplace was the only ventilation. There was one window in each room, but closed of course—probably not made to open.

We were up before any sign of light and dressed by the light of the fire. Then Miss Stone washed in her own little wash bowl, which she always carries (I followed suit) and we stole out on the porch to hang over the rail and clean our teeth. This was followed by an excursion into the dark rear of the yard, (where we squatted down as best we might).

Our breakfast was the same as supper—and we started off still in the pale gray dawn to the school house, 2–1/2 miles down the creek. It is right pretty—with the laurel and holly— but a hard winter road.

The school house was a one-roomed, frame building, with a stove in the middle. Three small boys, full of interest, were hanging around outside, but we shooed them off. On either side of the door Rachel had had a lovely holly tree stuck into the earth and the windows and walls within were all decorated with holly—the tree being in the corner (account of stove). We all fell to work—John decorating the house and I the tree, and directing John Everidge, while Rachel and Miss Stone sorted and arranged presents, etc. Before 9:30 a big crowd had assembled, waiting, and I went out to take a picture. At ten we let them in—the children in front of a rope—the elders behind—all standing; packed in 150 to 200 in that one room. Rachel led some singing (Old Ky. Home), then John spoke on Christmas story, and more singing and reciting. Finally we fell to distributing presents. The greatest enthusiasm, however, was when the candy came to be given and left-over presents. One old woman came three times to John—the last time winking prodigiously, saying she had given away the other two bags of candy. Everyone took what he or she could get and there was great excitement. I went out again and John and I took two more pictures of the crowd, which was picturesque enough, with saddled mules and horses tied about—bright colored fascinators and red stockings. The wagon too looked pretty with the holly trees heaped in—boxes of holly and all our traps. Miss Griffith had ridden over on a mule and Mary Everidge on a horse. Rachel rode back double with the latter.

Miss Stone, John and I left the others to go by the road while we walked up Newman's Branch (three miles)—a wild lovely place with much holly and rhododendron. Sat down on a log and ate our lunch; and just before climbing the hill to join the wagon road, stopped in at a little log cabin to call. There proved to be the old woman of the candy bags,—a man who told us of his experiences in jail, a little girl with a bad face, and a girl of 14–15 perhaps (evidently in trouble), a very dull face. The old woman spat continually on the floor where a black pig was comfortably snoozing in front of the fire. There were two beds. (Evidently the moral atmosphere was pretty low.) They gave us a queer gourd for Miss Pettit and some flowers they call blood-drop (?).

At the top of the hill John went on to look up some mistletoe and a hornet's nest (we got two from Rachel), while Miss Stone and I waited on the Virginia Rail. Soon came hoof beats and Miss Griffith and the girls appeared in high spirits,—cheeks red—laughing and talking. They looked picturesque enough. Miss Stone was cool, so walked ahead to meet John, while I waited for the wagon. It was one of those still, over-cast days, when the tree trunks stood dark against the grey sky, and the distances were blue-black between the mountains. At length I heard the wagon creaking and we

went to catch John and Miss Stone. By this time the weather
had turned decidedly chill, but we rode cheerfully on, Miss
Stone telling me of moral conditions, which are bad, but less
so, she thinks, than in the city (one man's wife left him and
he lives with two sisters—children by each. Another brought
in strange women into own one-roomed cabin before own
wife and daughters. Indifferent to such things, and soon forgotten though commented on at time.)

At Ball we stopped for rhododendron, and took two ex-
posures of the wagon. At the foot of the mountain we stopped
to take a picture of a name-sake of Miss Pettit's sister, and got
the whole family and part of the log house in addition. They
gave us another great hornet's nest, and a little further down
the road, a little girl ran out with another one in her hand.
Dark when we got home. Very glad for the rousing open fire,
warm supper and good beds.

* * *

(W. Wade, Oakmont, Penn.—Allegheny Co.—Difference
between Kentucky and N. C. Mountaineers):

"The former seem to me to be criminal but not vicious.
The latter are vicious but not so criminal—crime being what
we make laws against, vice being what we preach sermons
against. The Kentucky mountaineers seem to be a distinct
type not now found elsewhere."

CHRISTMAS EVE: The crowd began to arrive early in the afternoon—children first, who stood playing around the door;
then a gradual gathering of horses and mules with the older
people. At the second ringing of the bell, the crowd poured
in and completely filled the school hall—although before
the exercises, outside, one drunken man had to be removed
and although there was a little drinking and some shooting on the outside, on the whole, the exercises were most
orderly. Several babies were pretty persistent. I noticed one

mother serenely unconscious while the infant shrieked and beat on the chair in anger because he could not share the apple she was eating. Another weeping little girl was picked up by a boy of 10 or 12, with a roguish face, who took her on his knee and proceeded to comfort her in an entirely unconscious fashion.

The recitations were hard to hear, but the songs, especially the one of the younger children, elicited great applause. Three of the boys were dressed in costume and sang "We three kings" very prettily, though they were scared to death. The appearance of Santa and Mrs. Santa was greeted with such roars and shrieks of delighted excitement that the jokes they got off were quite inaudible. Then a series of little fairies helped put on the presents and marched, singing, around the tree.

This preface ended, the great and glorious moment came to distribute. A line was formed to collect and pass the presents to Mr. Day, who called the name and passed it on to some helper to be carried to the person. We timed him and found that it took him 10 names to a minute. He was calling names for two to three hours, so one can get an idea of the number of presents. I had a chance to watch the faces and found that the older boys were just as delighted as the little children, though they made some effort to conceal it. There was an abundance of everything, and a candy poke for each child as it left the room—so that the rejoicing was general.

After supper we all hung stockings around the living room and the children in bed, we elders filled up each with its pile, grabbing at the dolls to choose a particularly pretty one for some favorite. The room was a pretty sight, with the stockings filled and a doll peeping from each girl's and a trumpet over each boy's. Some of the boys asked for dolls.

I went to sleep to pistol shots and my last glimpse out of

the window into the dark showed two muffled figures with a swinging lantern, and accompanied by flashes and reports, past the house and up the road.

While we were waiting for the Christmas stockings, it thundered and lightninged heavily, but just as we were ready, the clouds broke and a shaft of sunlight touched the hills with a brilliant rainbow outlined against the gray. It was wonderfully beautiful.

CHRISTMAS MORNING: My awakening was quite different. We were aroused by singing—first in the distance, then nearer, then passing to every floor of the house. It was the little boys with Miss Furman, singing old Christmas carols. It was wonderfully sweet and pretty. We could hear them down the stairs, then out down the path, disappearing into the town. At length (they had sung a verse at every house), the sound returned again, and as it was beginning to be light, we peeped out to see them, marching along two by two in the rain, singing cheerily, Miss F. ahead leading the chorus.

At the gate, it was too much for the children of the house, who burst out with "Christmas Present," "Christmas Present," which elicited an answering yell from the singers, interrupting the song for the time being, then the little flock was again marshaled and marched to the cottage.

The morning work was put through with a will, while we filled in a few more stockings and took a flashlight of the room. Then Baby Smith, basket and all, was solemnly carried into the room and laid on the big center table. The door opened, the children came crowding in, while the little boys again sang and sang their carol. The stockings were handed out rapidly, but it was pretty to see the children—even the little boys, who seemed most interested, crowd around the baby, ignoring the stockings for the moment.

However, the stockings had plenty of attention—and

such radiant faces over dolls and beads and books. Nelson must show all his possessions to Miss Furman then to the baby—and then must peel his apple with his new knife, although, for a wonder, he said he wasn't hungry. M—hugged her doll, and sat in the corner with it in her arms, absorbed in "Cinderilla." There was a general rejoicing over the football and the baseballs, and the horns made a joyful noise continually. The girls tried on the beads and combs and hair ribbons, compared dolls and other treasures without any apparent dissatisfaction. Every one seemed happy and satisfied.

Then came the parting. There were a dozen or more horses and mules tied outside the paling and every one (going or not) came out to see the home people ride away. Mr. Combs had two mules, one of which he rode, carrying all the presents, while Myrtle rode the other, with Molly sedately pitched behind, unable to conceal all her happiness. Almost every mule had double burden but they splashed cheerily through the mud as if realizing the Christmas season. The house seemed quiet enough when the last one was gone.

Vision of Old Regular Baptist to put an end to Sunday School. Saw a church house with door at either end (like one in question)—at one end a roaring lion and at the other a white figure which drives old lion. Meaning,—the lion (newfangled ideas, such as Sunday Schools) is conquered by old time religion (the white figure).

The same story, apparently only church house is seen with Sunday School filing down on steps and church members in at the other: Baptist revival: Mr. Hicks looks into the faces of an "intelligent ordinance," wants to know what is the meaning of pitch on inside of ark—"Can any poor sinner tell? Just raise your hand to show that you know what pitch means. Brother Combs, can you tell? Now, God bless my soul, there's nary hand, nary one," followed by wild singing—half dance, swaying body. As a conclusion to service, he shakes hands with front row, whereat one women leaps up shrieking, "God be praised," doing a double shuffle, shaking hands, swaying her body, shouting, jumping up on benches, etc. Quite a terrible scene in its emotional waste.

DECEMBER 28TH—30TH: Rode fifteen miles to Sassafras on Carr (Kyarr pronounced) over with Miss Griffith (Willie Hayes and Miss Belle got ahead) and met Mr. Smith at tree, where we arrived a little late. Very peaceful audience.

Then others went home and Mr. Smith, John and I went to near house—Dixon Cornett's, to dinner. The house was a pretty good one, but dirty and confused—five children (a baby in home-made cradle), all dirty and rather forward, though pretty. Mr. Cornett taught public school to help out his farming. Said 100 acres was ample for a family—"one man crop," and, in fact, a man could only work 10 acres off which he could expect to make 200 bushels to carry him through. Said he thought the mountains would hold a lot more people, for soil was good, and as population increased, people would farm more scientifically. Mountain side fields, the first year, would bear 50 bushels to acre and would recover its fertility if left for some years. A man could live easily on three months' work—easy country to live in.

Wife seemed easy-going and shooed chickens and dog out of house every once in a while. Had a pretty good dinner (delicious honey made from some common weed). Mr. Smith said the kitchen and cooking seemed fairly clean to his eye—oilcloth, of course, and iron three-pronged fork and knife. (While the men tried to scare up a rabbit back of the house, I tried to find some privy place—being offered by the hostess either the hen-house or barn—the latter being surrounded by thick mud, I chose the former, which was too low to get in, but offered a shield from the children's eye.

It was not, however, concealed from the hunters, as John later told me. I played with the children a while, who were hilarious over Christmas gifts, then we rode down to Simon and Mary Stacy's.[19] We found a house neat without and within, though oddly assorted as to trimmings, ancient and modern. All sorts of modern trash set in with old fashioned things. One sheet on bed and bright homespun blankets (We bought one for $5.00). Mr. and Mrs. Stacy were about forty, intelligent and progressive—no children. She boasted that he was the only man in the county who had never been drunk. He said he had tried it once to see if it was good and found it wasn't. Had much to say of moonshiners. A good deal made in county. Told how Malcom Holliday, when Sheriff, cleaned up stills. Went with brother Talbot (whom we saw when there and shook hands with) to arrest some moonshiners. A number went with them but waited at gate. Malcom went in front door and Talbot at back. Moonshiner (Cam—father) shot at once. One hit Malcom in right hand but he continued shooting as well as he could with left. Wounded moonshiner, who caught hold of him and hung on, shooting seven shots right into him, one grazing his side. Malcom could see flashes going right into himself and believed self dead. Meanwhile, Talbot was shooting at moonshiner—six shots, and he wouldn't let go then, (said he hated to but had to save brother). Said he went up and hit man over the head with butt of pistol. Malcom's thought was to ride at once, dying, to doctor at Hindman. Jumped on horse and rode ten miles, then had to get off, he felt so weak, and spend the night. It turned out he was only wounded a little.

On another occasion, the sheriff and deputy went to arrest a moonshiner who deliberately stood ground—six of them—and waited, an apple orchard between them. They shot the deputy and shot the sheriff in the arm. He shot one of them, called a truce and agreed to quit. As sheriff mounted horse, they shot him in the back—dead.

A man fined twice, is sentenced to penitentiary third time. One man got off on promise to reform, then skipped the country. (Recall that Virgie Perkins—grand-daughter of the girl who eloped from Virginia—herself eloped with son of man who had killed her father).

Mr. Hilton Smith's father was twice in penitentiary for murder, twice pardoned, and finally killed by Camille's (?) father.

While waiting the other morning to see girls off to tree, a ruddy cheeked, good looking young man came up on a pretty horse. They said afterwards that he had been drinking, but I couldn't see that and he looked attractive. He was Willie Hayes' first cousin, a right-hand man of Judge Hargis—had been in the penitentiary, "I don't know how many times," and a triple murder (at least). Shade does not "aim to rise above his raisin'," in line of dress, collar, etc. Nelson asked, on saying his prayers at Miss F—(?) knee, "How long do you have to do this before it does you any good?" Nelson, "whopped" seven times in a day, is still Miss F's greatest trial and chiefest joy. After two days at home, returned because he is homesick and cries bitterly when Miss F. leaves for two days' vacation. Cries and can eat no dinner.

Mrs. S. told us of old Regular Baptists—many of them in country.

Tuesday morn we were awakened by 4:30, for the Stacys are early risers. Had breakfast (very nice and had a rabbit which Mr. Smith shot the day before) and were sitting in front of the fire again before six A.M. It was a gray morning, fascinating before the dawn, when I could catch the misty mass of the mountains large against the light—the cedar at the fence in black outline. Could not see Carr, but could hear it rushing. After breakfast Mr. Smith and John, accompanied by a small army of men and boys, (9–10) and a number of dogs and guns, set out to hunt rabbits and squirrels (John not too enthusiastic, as he does not enjoy shooting anything). I talked a while with Mrs. Stacy, then she saddled the old gray and I set out across Carr and up Red Oak to see a blanket about which Mrs. Cody had told me, also to see Mrs. Enoch Combs. It was a gray, still morning—the west lined with white clouds along the mountain ridges. I could hear, for a while, the men's voices, barking of dogs and an occasional shot, but soon the hills shut in and I was riding quite alone up the narrow branch. It was very pretty, with trees and rocks thick massed with green—small ferns, green and fresh, vines of patridge berry. The gray walked deliberately and I led him, as the bed of the branch was rocky and slippery. Finally, after passing two empty cabins, I came to a good sized house and barn group, where the branch split. After a long halloing, I finally aroused some children and an old woman, who turned out to be Mrs. Enoch Combs, and directed me to Mrs. Cody's. Mr. Cody met me on the way and asked me about his two cows. Said he supposed I was going to see his woman as I was passing that house. Mrs. Cody is Mrs. Combs' only daughter and the old man—who has $5000 in the bank and owns 600 or more acres of land way back to the head of the two branches—works on the road at 50 cents a day. Later we passed him by the branch—an old man with long white beard. He was cutting down a beech to burn in his fireplace, for his wife will have no modern cookstove or coal grate and he is quite as saving.

At Mrs. Cody's, the family came out to see me. Mrs. C. fastened the horse and ushered me in with the apology that they hadn't cleaned up from Christmas. It looked so too—

four unmade beds in one room—but they make some effort to hustle around with a little broom, Mrs. C. scolding the oldest girl the meanwhile, that she should venture to approach me in sweeping. She had had her share of children, she said—thirteen, six of whom were dead. She gave me the list of names, asking me mine. During this time she bounced a fat baby on her knee, asking him, playfully, every minute of two if he didn't want more "titty"—this cheerily before her son-in-law, who had started shooting but had been called back by a roar from "Iry"—a dirty faced, mean looking little boy. "Tom, there's some one here." Tom was a nice looking boy, possibly 19, and was planning to go to school at Hindman after Christmas (when he would bring the blanket). Mrs. Cody said he was a good boy, and passed the baby for him to dandle. This he did very nicely, and when she wanted it back, it wouldn't come. Then Iry threw himself on her and there was quite a scene. During it, Mrs. C. continued to urge the baby to have "titty," and Tom addressed me on the subject of plenty in squirrels and rabbits. Tom at last started off with his hunting, while Mrs. Cody accompanied me down the branch to her mother's. She wore homespun and strode along like a man. Her conversation was about her bad lung, loss of babies, and change of life, with interjections against Iry—"Get out behind that horse. He'll kick you. There—go on—keep back there—He is the meanest child!" etc.

Mrs. Enoch Combs was a big cheerful looking old lady, dressed in homespun, with a black shawl over her head. Every one—from grandmother to baby—wore red and black striped homespun. The house was log and outside, wood was well piled up. We saw a number of good black walnut stumps and a pile of black walnut kindling. Inside they were burning it in the fireplace, over which a black kettle bubbled.

We sat down socially over the fireplace and talked till I introduced the subject of covers. There were two little black eyed girls living there (Mrs. Cody's children), and Mrs. Combs asked Molly, the elder, if she would give up her "kiver."[20] It presently transpired that Molly had refused to sell it the last year to Miss Stone. The little girl had sold hers and had received a doll for Christmas. Molly had been left out and now was ready to sell hers—with a hope, I suppose, of future poppets. I hastened to promise a poppet and for $7.00 purchased a lovely old indigo cover—"Queen of England" pattern—"Queen's Victory," as Mrs. Combs called it, doubtless meaning Queen Victoria. Then they asked me if I were married; where my man was; to bring him to see them; to stay to dinner—and finally gave me two big apples. Molly came running out with the largest of all, "Had got it on the Christmas tree," and thus escorted by the family to the gate, I gracefully mounted the top rail to my horse and set forth.

The men got back about 11:30 (John looking very blue circled and weary). They had four rabbits and four squirrels. I invited John (to his relief) to come with me that P.M. to see Mrs. Combs' homespun instead of hunting again, so we rode out, to find the homespun was diamond dyed. Got more apples and rode down the creek to L—Stacy's father's—Jim. He was at the sawmill, but we made a little call on the old lady and her pretty daughter. The house was clean and prosperous in appearance. On the way we discovered Mr. Smith's horse, Wade, which had escaped and was ambling on the road. We caught him and brought him back.

Then Mr. Smith, John and I rode down to the Cornett's to call on them. Found the old man (85 years) deaf and almost blind, but full of stories of old days—hunting, finding of Indian graves, etc. They say he plays the dulcimer and sings. His grandfather was born in 1778. Mr. Smith says his desire to get religion and be a Christian is most pathetic. He thinks he must have a big experience, according to the old Baptist idea. He wants to do right, pray, etc., but can't honestly get one of those visions which he has been led to believe necessary all his life.

Mrs. C—was a pretty old lady, who wore a black cap edged with a white frill. She said the children were a great pester, but she cared for the grand-baby very carefully. The son and his wife and four children live with the old folks. I see that so much—the old folks by the fire, and I wonder how this arrangement works in the mountains.

We rode back to Stacy's for the night, while Mr. Smith stayed at Cornett's. Off early in the morning, to pick up Mr. Smith. They had been out the night before and caught a big fat possum, which they displayed to us, holding it by the tail and letting it prance around on the ground. The family all came out to the gate to shake hands and ask us to come again. Then we rode off. Had a pleasant, uneventful ride home. Began to rain the last three miles. We met Miss Pettit on the way to her colored tree, but were glad, on account of weather, that we had returned.

DECEMBER 31ST: Had a pleasant party of town people in to watch the old year out (one old woman, confused on story, told me her grandmother had told her that the bees roared and cattle bowed their heads at midnight of the Old Year— certain thing). We played games, had refreshments and John spoke a few words, with a prayer at midnight.

In the morning we flew about straightening out things, talking with Miss Cobb, Miss S. and Miss P., packing and all. Sorry to leave. I put in the last few minutes getting two or three girls to teach me "Guide me, O Thou Great Jehovah" . . .

1908–1909 Diary Cover. (Southern Historical Collection)

Olive Dame Campbell, circa 1908. (Southern Historical Collection at the University of North Carolina, Chapel Hill)

Captions are drawn from the original photographs in Olive Dame Campbell's album.

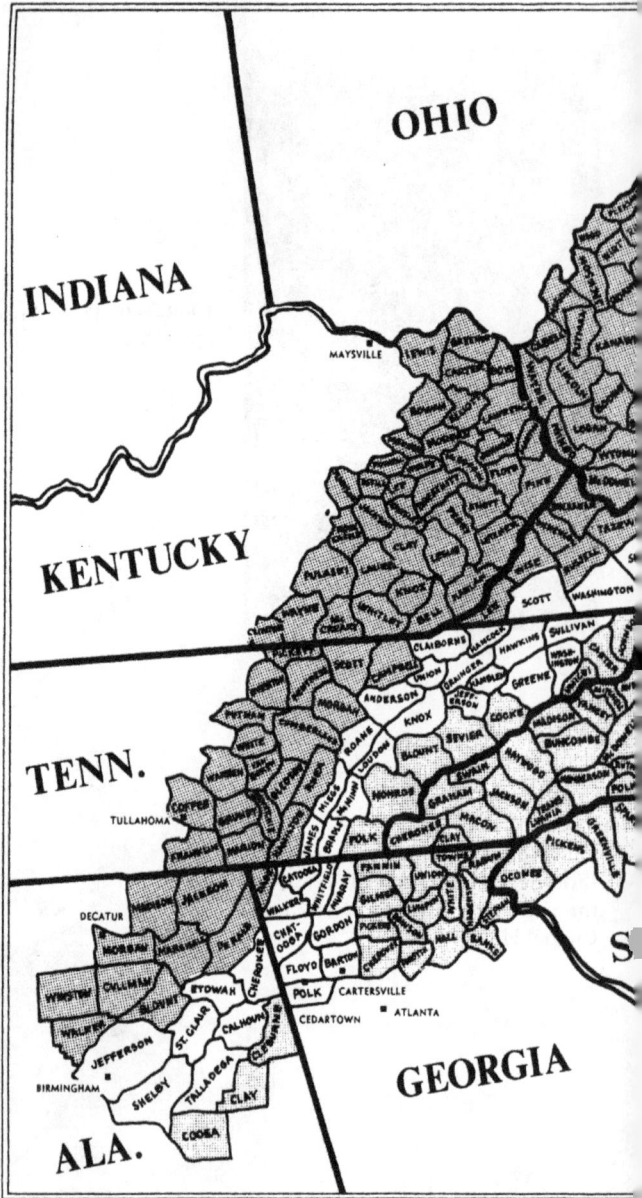

Campbell's Map of Appalachia. (*The Southern Highlander and F land* [Lexington: Univ. Press of Kentucky, 1979, c1921])

NNSYLVANIA

CUMBERLAND

MD.

WASHINGTON

FREDERICK

DEL.

D.C

ROCKINGHAM

AUGUSTA

ALBEMARLE

ROCKBRIDGE NELSON

AMHERST

BEDFORD LYNCHBURG

VIRGINIA

RTH CAROLINA

ROLINA

N

The Southern Highland Region

BLUE RIDGE BELT

GREATER APPALACHIAN VALLEY

ALLEGHENY-CUMBERLAND BELT

Olive and John Campbell at home in Demorest, Georgia. (Southern Historical Collection)

Visiting a Mountain School Sixty Miles from a Railroad. (*The Southern Highlander*)

A Mountain School. (Southern Historical Collection)

"The traveler that follows the trails of this far country." (*The Southern Highlander*)

Fording the Headwaters of the Nolichucky. (*The Southern Highlander*)

A Kentucky Family. (Southern Historical Collection)

Interior of a $20.00 house. (Southern Historical Collection)

The Loafer's Gallery: Ernestville, Tennessee. (From Olive Campbell's photo album in the Southern Historical Collection)

Discontinued Post Office, "Briggs," on Devils Fork in Tennessee. Has been a blind tiger most of the time. (From Olive Campbell's photo album in the Southern Historical Collection)

Levi Hensley's Store—Oneida, Kentucky—Combination Stores and Post Offices—Good Places for the Discussion of Politics and other Things. (From Olive Campbell's photo album in the Southern Historical Collection)

(Above and below) Ballads copied from diary in December, 1908, in Olive Campbell's handwriting. (Southern Historical Collection)

Revolving Table—Upper Troublesome. (From Olive Campbell's photo album in the Southern Historical Collection)

Eating Watermelon—Madison, Kentucky—Thacker's. (From Olive Campbell's photo album in the Southern Historical Collection)

4

JANUARY *1909*

KENTUCKY AND TENNESSEE

Whatever its drawbacks, riding horseback over rough mountain country was usually to be preferred to going by jolt wagon, especially in winter. We had a trunk to transport, however, and so by wagon on a cold but brilliant January 1, 1909, we left Hindman via the regular Eastern route to Beaver Creek on the Chesapeake and Ohio Railroad. . . . Such trips were always harder on John than on me, for everywhere he had to speak, and often, while I snatched a little rest or wrote up my notes, he was interviewing someone, taking outside trips with some eager principal, superintendent or teacher, or roaming about the community in conversation with whomever he might meet. We were glad to move on to Lexington (January 9) and relax a bit in a comfortable hotel—the old Phoenix. A mountain of mail was awaiting us, and we were soon deep in it, interrupted only by the telephone, which began to ring as soon as we arrived.[1]

JANUARY 1st: Hindman: By special message our departure was to be at 11 A.M.—but no team appeared until after 12. Then it appeared in front of the schoolhouse—John's old black horse and the white horse harnessed to our Jackson wagon.[2] The black horse was balking and no amount of coaxing or whipping did any good. Evidently the driver—a big rough man—Bray by name had started them wrong and the black finally ended by kicking the harness to pieces. At length he was replaced by a mule. We said our farewells for the 3rd or 4th time and rolled off in triumph. It was then after one. The team went fairly well during the afternoon with some balking on the part of the white and a resultant seesaw—but the mule was steady. It grew very cold and gray and the roads were fearful—muddy out of the creek—and rocky and beset with logs in the creek. The houses all along seemed very forlorn to me—and I couldn't but wonder whether the people were being reached.

We passed a government distillery—the most progressive looking place around.[3] About 4.30 we came to a stop in a mud hole that swallowed the wheels above the hubs. The horses would not pull together and I danced on a log to keep warm, while first the man tried to combine the seesaw—then John took the reins and the man pried. Finally I took the reins, John the whip, the man pried—and with a rope to mend a broken bolt—we came out. By this time it was quite dark and the moon was shining. The roads were in such fearful condition that we determined to stop at Webb's instead of pushing on to Allen's.[4]

We found a very comfortable place—warmed our toes before the open grate, had supper and piled to bed early—to be up again at 4:30—a chill morning. A little girl brought us a fresh towel and we were electrified next (we in bed) by the entrance of Mr. Bray who came to wipe his hands. John was dressed first and while I was finishing, Mrs. Webb entered and talked and watched me complete my toilette. We had a good breakfast on fried chicken and went out to find the old gray in a balky mood. He was finally started but stopped at every rise of ground—so that our progress was slow. What with bucking and whipping and seesawing, the harness in addition was soon reduced to smithers, and we stopped at every few houses to get a bolt, rope, chain, and finally—a grand climax—the single-tree broke. That was three miles from Beaver.[5] There were two boys watering mules across the creek and we called to them to take us to town. This they agreed to after some dickering or rather hesitation. So we transferred baggage, said farewell to Mr. Bray and gaily trotted off to Beaver behind two willing curly brown mules. Arrived about 4.

Went to Combs Hotel where a stream of people seemed to be circulating—many on the way to Normal School at Richmond.[6] We had an interesting talk with an educated mountaineer of the county (Floyd)—who had received bad treatment at the hands of a Louisa man, Byington—name Allen. He spoke frankly of bad conditions in public schools, lack of good teachers (perhaps two in county with Christian connection), lowness and vulgarity in very little children; necessity of educating parents; old feud feeling which prevented one set of families sending children when other set was sending; no papers except a few low class ones subscribed for; no farm papers (two in his district taken by self and brother). He had been teaching county school and all year had done subscription work on Post, Ladies Home Journal, etc. Was discouraged at outlook with dwindling farms, no mineral rights, lumber gone. Thought mountain people would be pushed to the wall.

We left at about 8.45—a mild night. Walked the platform a while waiting for train and talked with boy who had been at Hindman and had much to say in praise. Got to Pikeville at 10+ and found Dr. Record waiting. He took us up the hill to the grand new dormitory to stay. The scenery looked very pretty at night—mountains somewhat higher than those north and west. Dormitory has fine situation.[7]

131

School registers so far this season about 300—quite strictly a literary affair with training for teachers. They have a good brick school building and an old wooden dormitory for boys—Mr. Carmichael has a printing press and has boys learn to help him. Would like some manual training for boys and domestic science for girls—though does not care for farm training in that place. They have a good music department and the teacher Miss Robertson sings very prettily. I went to Church Sunday and heard an enthusiastic missionary sermon. In P.M. after listening to singing we went to Dr. Record's rooms and while John talked to Dr. Record, I struggled with Mrs. R., who was weak and ill—and deaf besides. Rested a bit—and went to bed early after tea. In the morn we all went to chapel where the town ministers each gave a spiel. Then I had to make a polite evasion for a speech and John gave a talk mostly of jokes with wisdom sandwiched. Much appreciated—got off at 12.30. Had a queer crowd on train—girls evidently much dressed up and attendant inferior swains.

(Property four acres in one piece—two in another—Running expenses—Want to make it a college) Dr. Record told story of Baptist preacher electioneering at funerals in contest with dentist, who could not speak, but pulled teeth at funerals. At one funeral, the dentist (uncle?) saw a man suffering and told him he could relieve him, pulled out forceps, while Baptist preached on, and gave a yank. The sufferer cried "ouch" and jumped up. Tooth came out and preachering kept right on. He ran to branch and washed out mouth—then came back and said, "Friend, I've never voted the democratic ticket in my life—but I'm going to vote for you." Dentist won out.

January 4th: Got into Paintsville about 3—and went to hotel. Very fair.[8] I rested and read, while John called on Prof. [ ]. The Mammoth Hotel proved to be small but pretty good food. A killing funny bus to it like a huge yellow tram on wheels drawn by two horses. A roof of red velvet arched above with a dangling bell rope which I felt ought to be of gold and tasseled. Town is pretty unattractive.

JANUARY 5th: Left Paintsville on early train 7.30—riding once more in the palatial bus. No special adventures except the loss of my sweater. Louisa about ten and found it a very neat nice little town with a very fair hotel (Brunswick.) We deposited our things and went up to the schoolhouse which was dirty and packed. It seems Mr. Byington has a great faculty for drawing students and there are so many they have to use Masonic Hall.

Mr. Byington came suspiciously out, viewing us as book agents—a queer looking dirty man with a dirty shirt and no tie. We listened to his recitation 1/2—3/4 of an hour and then talked with him. He walked to hotel with us. Their work is largely normal.

We came from dinner to find Mr. B. waiting with another teacher and two prominent citizens—a Mr. [ ] and a Mr. Carly—brother of Supt. of O.K.-R.R. He was the most interesting and progressive man we have met—a born mountaineer. Is about the wealthiest and most trusted citizen—editor of "Big Sandy News." Encourages farmers, institutes, exhibits etc. through column in paper. Has asked U.S. Immigration Bureau to send them a colony of Swiss or Germans to show mountaineers how to till land. Says he thinks the difference on creeks of people holding or not holding lumber and mineral rights—tenancy, etc.—is due to remoteness. Those nearer to where RR and centers were coming were the first to sell to prospectors. Others more remote profited by their mistakes, rather than from superior knowledge. He saw us off at train—also real estate man.

Got into Catlettsburg at about 5+ and were met by Mr. Boggs, who took us to his house. It was raining slightly and developed into a pour. Were glad for comfortable quarters. Mrs. B. stout and pleasant, three children there and a mountain boy boarding with them. I stayed over Thursday while John went down Wednesday night to Phelps with Mr. B.—where they have a day school. This by the bye is in Pike County—the Southern Presbyterians thus violating their agreement with Northern branch which has the Pikeville school.[9] Seem to be varying opinions as to new school law, some thinking it will hold and some not—but all agreeing on its lack of feasibility.

Heard several amusing stories also feud accounts in Hatfield-McCoy war.[10] Hatfields surrounded McCoy house having in it 4–5 women and 3 men set fire to house and shot women who tried to put it out. Knocked old woman's head on ground until she was senseless. One man escaped—one was shot through the door, and an old man, taking revolver in either pocket and loading pans of old breech loader with powder, opened door and amid smoke of explosion, run through enemies, firing revolvers—escaping thus through "big old corn field" to woods. Is alive yet. Two McCoys on one side of river and old Hatfield on other. If either should cross boundary, other would kill him. So feud stands.

Several stories of Frank Phillips—a leader on Hatfield side—(some of these given us by old Dr. Condit of Ashland).[11] Phillips was a sheriff once, grew cocky and became worst man in the vicinity. Killed boy—then prayed at his side. Other men did not dare to shoot him. Tried to break up Dr. Boggs' meetings and was finally shot himself by boy (whom he had shot.)

Dr. Condit told us of a young "foreign" doctor in Pikeville who was called out one night to go to a sick boy. As he left town at first cross roads, met 3 armed men. Guide held parley and they said— "Go on, go on, doctor." Next road they met 2 more armed men—same result—till finally they were followed by 25 armed men. Found boy shot in abdomen by Frank Phillips and could not find bullet (boy got well however and was probably the one who killed Frank Phillips). Sat up all night expecting attack and guns were stacked up like kindling wood.

Some while later, the same doctor was called to Frank Phillips.' Found him fearfully wounded in lung, bullet had gone right through, but with gun leaning up against corner of bed—one revolver on bolster and another at other hand—cartridge belt hanging at head of bed. Bed arranged to command entrances. In opposite room same arrangement for other occupant. Told doctor to make himself comfortable—they were expecting an attack. Doctor questioned who to defend and man replied that he and Phillips would fight. Doctor astonished, said Phillips would be a dead man before morning; that he couldn't get up etc. etc.—to all of which the man replied "You don't know Frank." Phillips in spite of all—improved and the doctor left. Every little while he met some one who asked how Phillips was (every one knew doctor to his surprise). When said Phillips was improving, the invariable answer was "Better let him die." On another occasion, he could hire no horse in mountain town because he had been Phillips doctor. Pulled up and left such a barbarous place.

Another story of a man who had grudge vs. another. Walked over to house with young son of 15 (in spite of protests of wife, who knew object) sat down at table at people's invitation, though would eat no breakfast. Rifle across his knees. Woman asked him to go away as she knew what he was after. Two boys armed themselves and went out to evaporate sorghum. To get up a fuss 15 yr old boy stood in front of fireplace and refused to let son put in wood. Son gave him a shove and the boy whipped out a pistol and shot at him. Then all began peppering. Brother shot through head and dropped. Son closed in with old man (poor pistol) and shot him, but found himself covered by boy. Was making for woods when shout came and own father came running. Original two made for woods.

* * *

Story of old Baptist preacher who sold brandied peach stones for $1.00 a piece and was to give $5.00 for every shoot. Same man sold yellow jackets for queen bees at $1.00 a piece.

* * *

At Morehead, Prof. Smith told us answer of pupil to give in own words "one sentence," lesson of 10 foolish virgins—"Lesson is always to be on the watch for a bridegroom and any other necessary thing."[12]

* * *

Asked to speak of Eli-Hatfield feud boy said "He was a pretty old feller but had two no-account sons."

* * *

Samson got stuck on a girl named Delilah.

* * *

Prof. tried to hurry girl in recitation on Abraham's life. She said, "I am not ready to kill off Abraham yet."

* * *

Morehead is the seat of Tolliver-Martin feud. Among Mr. Button's first experiences. While talking to a friend, he was drawn aside and the Tollivers and Martins came rushing through shooting, at each other.[13]

Boone Logan originally was not in the feud, was drawn into it because two of his young cousins were shot in cold blood by Craig Tolliver, just because they had witnessed some of his bad doings. He went to governor and got ammunition and pardon in case of deaths, and came in to get all Tollivers—dead or alive. With 100 picked men, he surrounded the town, closing in and shooting all Tollivers but one (an inoffensive chap) who escaped by hiding under floor. This one is now living—a harmless man. Martins were Republicans and Tollivers Democrats—both families equally bad. No one changed sides in county—fear of leaders and "frying pan into fire."

Mr. Butler (or Dr. Condit?) said he did not believe feuds were a result of war, bushwhacking, etc.—were in existence before the war. Frontier country and justice taken into their own hands, gradual lawlessness, no outside control.

JANUARY 8th, Ashland: We found Dr. Condit a fine old man "a Kentuckian who loves Kentucky yet clings to old assembly." Said Dr. Boggs in Phelps School had violated agreement between Northern and Southern Presbyterian churches as to territory. Considered new school law inapplicable—Crabbe not the author and somewhat broken in health. Had great hope of church union. Said "Perhaps when some of us old fellows get out of the way, the younger ones will fix it up between them." Told us a number of feud experiences—spoke of content of mountaineer.

JANUARY 8th–9th, Morehead: Were met at the station by Prof. Robinson and some students who marched ahead and carried our cases. Lodged in boys' dormitory—very comfortable. President Button came in on P.M. train.

Have a good plant—boys and girls dormitory (electricity from town)—big school building—broom making outfit—also printing outfit. Are beginning to look to farm, domestic science and manual training. Gave a few opinions on school law and general situation.

Country here is more like Demorest—lower rounded hills—pines—rhododendron and laurel. Very pretty. Soil is thin, they say, though the valley has been a famous one in its day. They used to drive through it to market 1000 hogs in the early days. These could not get enough corn here now. Soil exhausted with continuous corn crop. Believed there were, however, great fruit possibilities—peaches especially—and small vegetables. Most of their advanced boys leave the mountains.

Town population is shifting—men moving here from interior making a little more and moving on. Town has 500 (?) inhabitants. Stores open 11 P.M. Many distractions for students. Have about 360 pupils now. John addressed them with great applause at chapel. Found Prof. Smith an entertaining and human sort of person. Mrs. Button gave us a dinner before we left.

Terrified drummer of Frankfort—story.

JANUARY 9-10-11—Lexington: Got in about 4—and after settling at Phoenix (room and bath at 3.50 a day) went to reap a great mail at office—photos poor.[14] Found waiting card from Mrs. Desha Breckenridge (Henry Clay's great granddaughter)—and were hardly through telephoning her and Miss Pettit before Sunday School man came to see John.[15]

Stayed at home Sunday—a gray misty day—and devoted the end of our morning (got up late) to writing an article on Tyndaris.[16] Skipped dinner—almost by necessity for our callers began after church and trod on each other's heels.

First Mrs. Beachamp—thought new law would not interfere with Hindman—other counties?[17] Believed thoroughly in manual training and domestic science. Impossible to consolidate schools—counties very poor. Had ridden into every one in Kentucky—interested in hospitals which thought more needed in Hindman than in Jackson. Said mountaineers did not regard women highly so believed in having women at head of school.

Miss Breck came on her heels and we had a jolly talk—then came Mrs. Harrison of the C.W.B.M.[18] She was very

sweet and intelligent and lady-like. Told her theory of mountain people's origin. Stragglers (left by chance and accident
of travels) of pioneer emigrants moving from Maryland, Virginia and North Carolina over the Wilderness Road (then
preferred according to old manuscripts to river route from
Pittsburg). Did not believe original theory. Good minds and
capable with opportunities of anything—showing good he-
redity. Also believed in manual training etc. Best boys were
leaving the mountains.

Miss Pettit came late.

Hurried off manuscript and letters in morn—between
telephone and callers. At 10.30 Mrs. Breckenridge came with
team (misty and chill) and drove us out to Irishtown—where
they are running a public kindergarten as I understand it
with extra help. Children did various stunts for us—among
them waltzing and dancing Jack Frost to an old folk dance.
They looked very much like Daisy's kids—Irishtown itself is
squalid and low, but not crowded like our city poor quarters.
School buildings are makeshifts—bad floors, chimneys in
the way etc. Then we drove to lot where she proposes to put
up social settlement building to be used as public school in
daytime—shower baths etc. etc.

Then we went out to Ashland (Henry Clay's old house)
where his granddaughter (Mrs. B's mother) still lives. It has
informal grounds with beautiful trees and curving approach.
The house itself is broad and low—Victorian—well placed
and dignified, though not beautiful—red stone or brick.
We met her mother and married sister and were shown over
the lower floor. Then drove back to lunch, where a Mr. P?
(Panie?) came, Miss Pettit and Mr. Breckenridge—a very
nice lunch and merry conversation. John and Miss Pettit had
appointments to make at 2.30—Mr. B. and P. at 3—so they
drove me back to the hotel where I found John busily talk-

ing with Mr. Derthick. Believes cooperation can be brought about in denominations—(Baptists and Christians the narrowest). Believes in neighborhood work—centralizing of denominational work rather than spreading out thin. Farming, etc. Says mountaineers here, either purposely or afterwards get out of the notion, and do not do as they promise. Cannot be depended upon. Believes in schools being out of county seat and away from R.R. on account of bad influences in court—and in late shops.

Told of preaching experiences—one where old Christian was terribly disappointed when he (Mr. D.) having been asked to preach day before, came and gave a broad sermon—tolerant and harmonizing—old man wanted to smash Baptists. Baptists of old sort—united—wanted no education or Sunday Schools etc. Told how he had harmonized things at Hazel Green—once very bitter. Did not hold service when others were holding. Christians went to Methodist service etc. Now all liked it. Refused to start up new Christian Church in place where there was a thriving Methodist church—because community could only support one. In return Methodists did not put one in where he had one. Said Pres. Frost much misunderstood—especially on church matters. He believed in union at expense of not uttering own doctrinal views. Mr. D. could not agree to this—so did not teach at Berea. Gave up his school work this fall to be a sort of travelling harmonizing evangelist. He came back for dinner but both he and John left early on appointments—John to talk with Y.M.C.A. [State] Secretary Mr. Johnston. Believed in county work. Thinks there ought to be a building in county seats.

JANUARY 12th, Tuesday: A pleasant day after a snowy night. Found Prof. (Oneida) Burns in town to see us and made engagement. John off for Frankfort where he interviewed Crabbe and met Governor, Commissioner of Education and others.[19] Crabbe said there would be no backward step in law—was very optimistic as to its effect on denominational schools etc. Would write after next campaign in June and keep John informed of all changes.

Saw Dr. Ramsay—Assistant to President of University—compiling school laws of various states for benefit of Kentucky. Is on Jackson Board and doesn't think much of Leonard.

Saw Commissioner Rankin (Agriculture): believes much could be done with intensive farming. Gave reports and will send more.

I was busy all day writing and straightening up until John returned after a dentist appointment. Went out to get a sweater—with poor success. Met Mrs. Breckenridge and Mrs. Morgan—who wished me to go for a drive. Mrs. B. then took me (late and chill) to several places—State College—Transylvania, Carnegie Library and by several fine old houses, among them the Federal Headquarters in the war.[20]

After dinner—Mr. Walker the Postmaster brought up Mr. Burns of Oneida, and we had a most interesting talk.[21] Mr. B. is of Kentucky parentage and leanings (Clay Co.) though born in West Virginia where his father took him when feud conditions seemed imminent. He has a rugged Scotch face and slow manner with humorous reserve. Persuaded us quite early to go to Oneida with him—as his personality is strong and interesting. We were interrupted and much surprised by the appearance of Mr. Gamble, who was in Lexington on colored school matter. John had phone message from Mr. Dix—State Sec. of Y.M.C.A. who wished to come from Louisville to breakfast with him the next morning.

JANUARY 13th, Lexington: John went down to early 7.30 breakfast with Mr. Dix. He believes county work (Y.M.C.A.) is possible in the mountains. They are best products—better views of life than B.G.??? boys. Thinks $2000 per county a year would start work well. Is going to write a letter. Said considerable friction between International Committee and State Committee.

Later came in Rev. Collis (Christian) of Lexington connected with Midway Orphanage for girls. Orphan girls of mountains could be brought from one school to another and finish with them. Is going to write a letter.

A heavy snowy day, changing into rain. I was busy packing all day—and we were only just ready when Mr. Walker sent the carriage at 4 P.M. Found his house pleasant—Mr. Burns there and a jovial Mr. Carnahan—a mountain man (originally from Oneida) who was to go with us.[22] Another lady—Miss LeClair also there besides Mrs. Walker and two young boys. Had a pleasant dinner and got off at about 8.30 P.M.

Mr. Carnahan was amusing. Told us of his efforts to start first store—annoyed by pistol shots. Mr. Burns tried to act as mediator but Carnahan was furious and would have killed the man if he hadn't apologized (Mr. B's influence) and stayed across the river. Bullets came through doors and windows, once right above his and his wife's bed. Said he wouldn't have a drunken man in the store. Told them to get out and if they didn't, he knocked them out. Said every man was his own protector in the mountains. Had to fight his way. Said men who didn't drink, didn't need pistols, or wear them. Whiskey and pistols went together. Told of hearing drummers talking in train of every mountaineer carrying pistols. He himself was in splendid physical trim—and as a joke jumped out in aisle (L.&E near Jackson)—announced that he was a mountaineer and had no gun nor knife and would fight any man singly in train and knock him down—as lie to drummer's story. Had low opinion of mountain cooking. Is a lumber man.

In the station we met Mr. Vaughn and Mr. Gamble. Trains late but we got off O.K. Had two hours' wait at Winchester—our train late. Got into London at 2.15 A.M. Electric lights off on account of sleet storm damaging wires. Crawled into bed by a feeble Xmas candle of red. Up early to start off—only to find roads flooded and that Mr. Carnahan's team had not come through. A heavy rainy morn with a "tide" which took Mr. C. back to the river to superintend his logs. We waited all day for team, only to find late in P.M. that it was not coming. Decided to go horseback in the morning. Made a short call on Prof. and Mrs. Lewis.

JANUARY 15th, Friday: The mail caught up to us in the way and looked very amusing—a man on a mule laden with mail bags and driving another mule who bulged all over with sacks—quite a terrifying object. We made way for the "U.S. MAIL."

Left London at 7 A.M. after a wait for breakfast and horses. The latter were good, however—and we made good time. Roads were fearfully muddy, always over horses' hoofs—often over hocks and at times above the knees. A fascinating day however, warm gray and still—black trunks rising from flooded meadows—branches interlaced against the gray sky. We were constantly splashing through water—but my little horse was willing and comfortable and I enjoyed every inch of the way. Laurel County is part of the Cumberland Plateau—not mountainous in appearance though one goes downhill all the way to Manchester and Oneida. Many grassy fields and meadows. Open country—and the woods, oddly enough, do not seem to be cut as much as around Knott. Mr. Burns says the road is good in summer. We made the 24 miles in six hours, getting into Manchester about 1.30. Went to Mrs. Lucas' where we had dinner and waited for Mr. Miller—the minister in charge of the Presbyterian work. He proved

to be a youthful person—28—pleasant but not forceful. Left
Mr. B. and went out to dormitory to spend the night.

I rode out sideways on Mr. Miller's saddle (on the wrong
side) much to the amusement of some of the boys. Found
Mrs. Miller the "stronger man of the two"—though with two
young children and one coming. She was very cordial. In the
eve we went over to call on Mr. and Mrs. Walker some fine
young married people near by. She was educated in Penn.
Her father, Dr. Manning, came from North and married a
White (one of feud families)—all vitally interested in school
matters.

Clay County is in good shape financially—$10,000 in
bank—but cannot support a good school. Need not only of
high school—but school which will carry *all* grades. Manchester school has a work [program] but has never been effective as the Presbyterian board has either sent worn out
preachers to school or young ones to practice—not equal to
some of the inhabitants. Great corruption in county schools.
Some districts having none at all. According to new law—the
sheriff collects all taxes—getting 10% on school and other
two (Mrs. Walker said however that even with $2500 net, the
sheriff was not paid for his job.) District no longer managed
own fund. Which was in the hands of the County Superintendent and Board. Co. Supt. was more powerful than ever and
was very often a corrupt man. Good roads a great necessity.
Had tried to get cooperation of Barbourville for half of pike
and Barbourville had gone back on it. This would be one of
the educational solutions. Also needed new life. Thought the
good summer visitors who were coming in of late at Oneida
had done as much as the school for that place. An old aristocracy in the county, former slave owners, who had had big
tracts of land (10,000 acres) and almost a feudal tenantry.[23]
Tenants worked lands and lumber, traded at owner's store

and either came out even or fell short. Often were in debt to start with. Never made anything. Emigrated in every direction. People round Manchester are selling coal rights for from 50 cents to $5.00 an acre. This includes rights to what timber would be needed to work mines. Had been talking R.R. before Mrs. Walker's father's time—but lately had had new boom; Southern expected to come from Knoxville (perhaps a continuation of Tallulah Falls R.R.?)

Said Crabbe had authorized this evasion of new law. Mr. Miller was employed by the Board to preach and oversee—not teach. Could be hired by town to teach public schools. Said Mr. Miller got $50 a month—and two other teachers $28.50 a month. Could not expect competent work on such a pittance. Only two or three Presbyterian families in town—all Baptists. Much liquor bought—especially at election time and Mrs. Miller told me that with the new Judge Lewis, many thought more liquor would come in, resulting in the outbreak again of feud. Mr. Burns said this feud began in 1806 (families had come with hard feeling from Virginia)—included best men in county. Did not mean to get in but were drawn in. Young ones were always the ones to start it afresh. Pistols and moonshine "white lightning" as Mr. B. called it.

JANUARY 16th, Saturday Morning: Mr. Miller drove us down to the hotel—raining again—pouring rather. Spent the morning there, mending John's oilskins, where his horse rubbed him against the barb wire and talking to Mr. Walker and Dr. Manning. The latter seemed vague about sickness in the mountains—a little typhoid—a little small-pox—some tuberculosis and granulated lids.

John and I were much amused listening to the men talking at dinner. We were in the next room and could not help overhearing. A lively discussion seemed to be on about some person of doubtful character who was sparking a certain

145

man's sister. Speaker said he would wear him out if he were in brother's place. Said mountain people ought to have a way of questioning and finding out about people before they took them in, etc. etc. Took strangers in too easily.

I dropped my thread on the floor—and in hunting, looked under bed. There was a nice long rifle. Mr. Burns says you generally find them. One of his great troubles has been to keep his boys from wearing pistols. It is part of their manhood creed.

JANUARY 16th: We got off—about 1.30 to 2.00 P.M.—still raining but not quite so hard. I am always much amused at men's (and women's too) wonder and admiration of my daring. "Not many women could ride that 24 miles in six hours." "Mr. Campbell wants to get rid of his wife to take her out such a day—over such roads, etc. etc." Very amusing.

This part of the country is the prettiest and most fertile we have seen in Ky. Valleys are quite broad and grassy, timber left on the hill tops—brooks from every quarter (of course these must dry up in summer). Our course lay along Big Goose Creek—Big and Little Wildcat—Pinhook Branch, etc. Part of the way Mr. Burns rode ahead, looking like some old Covenanter with his black coat and derby hat and leggings—sitting very erect in his saddle and looking straight ahead. Part of the time he and John talked while my little black trotted me nimbly ahead. We passed J. D. Rockerfeller's pipe line which carried oil in a straight line over hills and valleys from Somerset, Ky—to Parkersburg, W.V.,—400 (?) miles.[24] It was dark when we got in—and it had begun to sprinkle again, though most of the way the rain had ceased to fall. Mr. Burns went home and we went to the dormitory for a good supper, cheerful room and bed.

JANUARY 17th, Oneida:[25] Breakfast at 7:30. We did not go to Sunday School but went over to church at 11—where John made a fine talk—much to the enthusiasm of the people. Talked in P.M. to Mr. B., Prof. Smith and Prof. Santon? and Rev. MacMurray, then walked over muddy road and hill to MacMurray's house.[26] River still high and rafts moored to the bank. They said 11 rafts had gone through the narrows the day before (one being smashed all to pieces.)

The MacMurrays have a small house with a beautiful situation and clean but primitive interior. Eight children—bright looking ones. Mrs. M. looked like a fine impassive pioneer with a baby in her arms. Her people were from New England. Mr. M. took the baby while she piloted us up a hill for the view—followed by three dogs—six children, three calves (part way) and a sheep. The view down the river is beautiful and one gets a great sweep for Goose Creek and Redbird and Bullskin come together at Oneida. They swim, canoe, etc. in summer. Natives cannot get used to the former—especially the women going in with the men. One woman said her only objection to Mrs. Santon (matron) was that "she goes washing with the men."

We then went down to Mr. Burns' house for supper. It is a very simple frame affair—3–4 rooms. He has five bright looking children who delight in Kipling, Joel Chandler Harris and Fairy Tales of all kinds. We had delicious fried chicken, biscuits, butter, milk, jam, etc.—all of their own making. Prof. Smith was there and Mr. and Mrs. Santon and little girl. Went to evening service, where Mr. Burns preached an impassioned sermon on God's love. Went to bed early.

JANUARY 18th, Oneida: Early breakfast and a springlike day—with clear skies and warm winds. John spoke at chapel—and then we visited a number of recitations. Eight teachers—one of whom was a woman (primary). They have 138 pupils now. Buildings 3—a good brick school—and girls' dormitory and a very poor boys' dormitory (abandoned).

Boys board and room in town. Grounds generally were clean. The school is on a high hill—with a beautiful view, and they are trying to start grass and trees. Great desire to build up an agricultural school, for land is good—and in the end, Mr. Burns says people must come to that and wishes, too, sloyd and domestic science. They have just built a little laundry, simple but sufficient for the girls. Have not yet put all things on desired basis. Hope to have girls before long, attend to cleaning of building, etc. etc. Hope for farm to enable boys to work way through. At present boys and girls do not work much—though are helped through.

The beginnings of the school are most interesting. Mr. B. was mountain boy, born and brought up in a one-roomed log cabin—cooking over wood fire, etc. Said his right shoulder was higher than left because he carried wood so much as a boy (joke?). His father was a Ky Baptist preacher from Oneida—leaving for West Virginia because he foresaw a feud beginning (Burns-Combs).[27] Mr. B. born there and brought up in a community practically Northern in spirit and sentiment. Most of W.V., Mr. B. says, is a northern state—thrifty and clean. Before 17—Mr. B. had only seen one man who had been in penitentiary, and murderers were practically unknown. Father, however, brought boys up anti-Unionists and fiery Democrats. Mr. B. said he actually thought when a boy that a man from South hurt in the North would perish from neglect—no one would look to him. Hated Yankees and says many many people do now. Some of the best work Northerners can do is to come down and let Southern people see what they are really like. Said incidentally that he used to study history, why South ever tried to stand North—forlorn hope. When he had been in mountains awhile, he understood—when he had seen one man—all alone—take forlorn hope and fight many. A characteristic of people—great pride. Said also that one trouble with South was that spirit was broken. Told of Virginia trip, where he talked with many. Sentiment seemed to be, "If I can't do my way I won't do anything." Agreed with me when I said that South was cherishing an ideal which would not have survived if there had never been any war.

Kentucky was a revelation to him when he came back to it as a boy—feuds, killings and all. Was pretty wild and fell in with his people's ways. Used to carry on his raft, a box of weapons to be used against Combs. Used to go down river on rafts and said they could tell, as far as a raft could be seen, from where it came, North Middle or South Fork—such a difference in people.[28] North Fork people most degenerate—descendants of Virginia folk who came through Big Stone, Pennington Gap etc. Many of them were escaped indentured servants, tenantry etc., poorer stuff.[29] The Middle Fork drew some of these people and some of those who settled on South Fork—that is, North Carolina people coming through Cumberland Gap and the Wilderness Road. Some West Virginians later drifted down by Pennsylvania. These people were hardier, bolder and less degenerate—also were and are the most desperate of all. As an example, the big loggers have to have detectives on North and Middle Fork to protect floating lumber, to keep people from sawing off the ends and re-branding it. None of these necessary on the South Fork.

He says feuds did not originate with war—as early as 1806, and grew out of character and descent of the people. He went in for a while, but found he was getting in too deep and went back to W. Virginia. Told us at another time how he was "killed" in a scrimmage, hit on the head with a gunstock and thrown over the fence into a brambly field—supposedly dead. The young fellows had been drinking moonshine. His supporters went off, and as he began to show signs of life, his enemies took him in cabin and kept him and nursed him at night. In the morning, being not badly hurt, he walked home. Took him all day. Stole into cousin's cabin, where he was living, for the night, and before people were awake, stole out into the woods and brooded all day. Back again at night and out same way for three days—brooding. The first two days he spent thinking over what step of redress he could take—what men he could enlist—what to do and not possible to do—a new kind of gun to buy etc. But the process of being "killed" was not pleasant—and at the end of the 3rd day, he came back with an "ironclad resolution" never to have any more feuds.

While in W.V.—he became converted and felt he owed something to his Ky people. Came back and taught summer school in the mountains and winter school at Manchester. This was the time of the famous White-Garrard feud, which grew into Baker-Howard.[30] This was a feud originated in Virginia, no one knows just how. Killed fifteen men in second feud. A number of incidents—I remember.

A young Baker had shot several Howards, and an old Baker had tried to stop him and smooth over matters. He was an inoffensive old man, but Jim Howard met him and shot him dead in highway. White was sheriff and a friend of Jim Howard. Came by one of Bakers, and asked if the old man had come home. Boy answered, "You know he hasn't and know why." White answered "Yes, I know why, but I thought I'd ask you, to see what you'd say." Boy saddled his horse and rode down and told his sister what White had said. She saddled her horse and rode to Tom Baker's and told him. He took his big dynamite gun, met White in road and blew him to pieces. Mr. B. was a cousin of Tom Baker's and said he would have known that Tom would kill White, if he knew what White said.

There was another complication (I've forgotten what) between John White and Tom Harker (we saw the latter). There had been several killings and John White was suspected. He knew Harker would kill him if he got the chance, and Harker knew he knew it, and knew White would kill him. White was coming home from meeting (horseback) and saw a man driving alone ahead of him and when he got near, saw it was Tom Harker, loaded up with pistols. His first impulse was to shoot him in the back—then he was unwilling to take him that way. But he knew that if he rode on, Harker would shoot him. So he rode along for several hundred yards behind the wagon debating. Should he turn back, should he shoot Harker, or should he go ahead and risk it. He finally decided on the last course. As he came to the wagon, he saw Harker turn, recognize [him] and put his hand to the pistol. White made no sign, kept straight ahead, passed him and rode out of sight, feeling, he said, a ball coming through his back every moment. As it happened, Harker says, his first impulse was to shoot White. Then he began to think that White had had him at his mercy for some time and had not shot. So he put his pistol away and resolved never to shoot White unless it was absolutely necessary. So the two men kept a truce, though they never spoke to each other. This went on for years, till both in office as Sheriff and Judge _____, and worked harmoniously now.

Finally Principal [of] Berea told Mr. B. that he would do more good to the mountaineers by teaching at Berea the young normal teachers, than keeping at that work. So he went to Berea and there met MacMurray (then young with only one child). They became great friends and studied together. MacMurray was preaching for $75 a month and became immensely interested in mountains (came from Kansas himself), because there were so many mountaineers in the parish. They were talking over Berea complications one night, negroes, etc.—and MacMurray said, "Brother Burns—Let's go up into the mountains and found a Baptist mountain school." Mr. B. said his heart leaped, but he hid his heart as he wanted to test MacMurray so told only difficulties in the way. But a little later, MacMurray said the same thing and then Mr. B. said "Brother MacMurray, I'll go whenever you are ready." McM. immediately resigned his position—and mounting his wife (baby in arms) behind him on a little Western pony, they set out—Mr. B. with them. The Baptist Board fretted and scolded—said their Board's work was not secular but spiritual, and they need never expect one cent of help from the Board.

Mr. B. made his own tools, hewed and quarried rock in hot August sun and began on the foundation. People thought him crazy but inside a year the school had begun with 100 pupils. He never exploits people for money, but trusts. Speaks at churches—and is now thinking of trip North. Told of meeting with Dr. Butterick but says if his work has a place, it will endure.[31] A wonderful personality. The people all over the country swear by him.

Has little use for mission boards. (Southern Baptist Convention has recently come around and fairly begged him to let the work under its care). He thinks the State has failed. Says the new law will not be really effective for 100 years. Is eager for every improvement—sanitation (taking it up in Oneida and just recently had every man out cleaning up the streets) hospitals, intensive farming. Is eager to give the people an appreciation of the beautiful. Says they haven't enough culture to see anything in the trees, woods, flowers etc. Wishes our New England mission boards would send down a few young married couples to live in the country and show the people how to live. Is hoping to have locks in the river—a new one promised at Beattyville would throw water 12 miles up into South Fork. More would make all Forks navigable—and would be quicker and cheaper than new roads and far cheaper than R.R.—L & N. is regular robber to poor man.

Gets $35 a month (also MacMurray) and all teachers put back good share into the work. The school has done wonders in bringing people together. White and Baker children in school together. Big Tom Burns and __ Combs were on the first Board of Trustees though neither knew what a Board of Trustees was.[32] Wanted to back Brother Burns in his enterprise. Combs had been all cut up by Big Tom Burns and one day Combs in retaliation (feud between these families and personal grudge as well in consequence of fight) took a shot at Big Tom as he was coming along the river bank on his mule. Bullet hit the mule in the head and killed it, and it fell into the river with Tom. But Tom disentangled himself from the stirrups and escaped by swimming.

Mr. Burns is a liberal minded Baptist—would take any one at communion and any kind of Baptism. Some of Mission Baptists have withdrawn fellowship from him on account of missionary views of his school. So there is now the anomaly of a Missionary Baptist Association—Armenian in theology but anti-mission in practice—opposed to the Association which Brother B. has been compelled to form and which is in keeping with the liberal Baptists over the country.

Before arriving at Oneida, we came to the __ Baptist Meeting House which crowned hill overlooking valley to the north—a fine new church of 20 members. On the opposite side of the short valley is the old Missionary Baptist Churchhouse, which withdrew fellowship from these 20 members because they subscribed to the Philadelphia creed which is a restatement of the London creed (look up in church

153

history)—a creed practically like the Westminster Catechism with differences only on church polity and baptism—a statement of belief which Mr. B. says almost brought about a Union of Baptists and Presbyterians lacking but one vote of the Presbyterian Synod, at Geneva (he thinks).

This creedal objection was only a pretext on part of old Baptists to get rid of a young minister who had been trained in Bro. Burns' school. Burns says there is more hope for Hardshells with new young preachers that are coming in, than for many of so-called mission Baptists churches with anti-mission practices.

(Look up Spencer's History of Baptists, of Ky) Old Regulars? Hardshells? or Primitives?—Missionary, Free Will, United.[33] (When Tom Baker was summoned to court, he refused to come unless a guard was sent for him. This was done—but as he was standing in the courthouse door, his wife's hand on his shoulder, some one (not known) shot him from a window opposite. As he fell—all his wife said was, "I hope my unborn child will be a boy.")

[Here at the end of the first part of the diary, there is a list of names and addresses and miles travelled.]

JANUARY 18th, 1909: Oneida, Clay County, Ky: We got off about 1.30—Mr. Burns, John and I and had a beautiful ride down the river, fording at the mouth of Laurel Creek. The air was like spring—full of bird notes and red birds fluttered to and fro. There are some fine mountain sides of uncut timber and good stretches of bottom land. Elms along the river and white sycamores. Mr. B. told us many feud stories. Got in a little before 5 and had supper. We three talked over the fire for a while.

JANUARY 19th, Manchester: Got up about 5—and were ready to start by six—saying a reluctant good-bye to Mr. Burns who seems like an old friend. A beautiful morning—

ground stiffened by frost which silvered the country. A little new moon shone up over the mountain, and a bright star just below. Gradually a pink glow came in the east, but the sun did not rise over the mountain tops for an hour or two. Bluebirds and yellow hammers were about. We had a splendid invigorating ride, though the roads were hard for the horses and kept growing worse as we approached London. We fell in with two young fellows on mules. They lived in Barbourville—but had been mending telephone wires and poles broken by sleet storm. We fell into the companionship of the road and chatted till they swung off south.

We got into London at 12.15—a few minutes behind the mail. Found the train schedule had been changed—so possessed our souls in patience—wrote, etc. and slept until ready to take 2 A.M. train to Hagan.

JANUARY 20th: Got the 1.48 train O.K.—and slept by fits and starts all the way. Many miners and loggers on the car, freely passing around moonshine—which scared man near us very much. Got in to Hagan at 6.10 A.M.—dim and misty. Got breakfast at little hotel and sat round fire while people discussed the murder at Harlan, whether Harlan people would lynch murderers etc. A young fellow of Irish countenance but related in Harlan got off the train and went along with us. My nag was stiff of knee and reared dangerously without apparent cause. I got him over one mountain—a high one (Cumberland)—and enjoyed myself in spite of feeling that I might be pitched off any moment. The road is very curving—in loop on itself—and the wood growth is heavy—not much cut. We wound up between great oaks and beeches whose trunks were outlined black against blue haze of ridges and hills beyond. Down in the valleys lay heavy clouds of mist through which the river gleamed. As we turned the top of the mountain into shadow, we could look back and up where the sun struck across and illumined great shoulders of slanting rock. Lower down we ran into beautiful fresh rock ferns, moss rhododendron, holly and hemlocks. At the 2nd mountain my horse balked and refused to continue. Finally I got off and removal and exchange of saddles showed that all three had raw sores on their backs. By padding we fixed up, and although my new mount moved slowly and walked down hill sideways in evident pain, we got along. We kept meeting wagons on very narrow roads, and had some difficulty in passing. Road was in fearful shape—rocky or heavily rutted and still in curves and loops. The cabins were more primitive in general than any we have seen—much isolated, log and one roomed. In one I heard a banjo going and wished I could stop off.

The rest of the way we followed creek beds and river bottom, winding along half asleep in the sun. The day was as warm as summer, birds singing and men ploughing some rich looking bottom land. A good 16 miles it seemed but we finally made Harlan near one. We were taken into Teachers Home, and spent rest of P.M. reading mail. Got to bed early.

JANUARY 21st, Harlan: The Academy here has 7 teachers (one music) and a resident preacher.[34] There is a girls' dormitory where 20 girls live (turned away 50 this year) a teachers home and a good though crowded brick schoolhouse. We went to chapel and heard a number of recitations. Everyone here almost is new to the work and could tell little. In the afternoon we mounted two stout white horses and rode the eight miles to Evarts along Clover Fork. Still warm and springlike, and the road is especially [pretty]—the creek, clear and rippling like a broad northern brook—on one side, and on the other steep warm sunny hill slopes well forested. We poked along enjoying the ride and got into Evarts about 4.[35] Felt pretty tired but talked to teachers awhile and to Rev. Mr.

Burkman of Williamsburg who was here giving some meetings. John went out to a meeting but I crawled into bed.

JANUARY 22nd: Springlike with gathering clouds. Talked to Mrs. Wood before school. There is no doctor here and they have to do their own doctoring. About 200 enrolled in school—none walking much over 1–1/2 miles. Says Friday does not amount to anything—either here or in county schools, as washing is done then, and besides it is the end of the week. Good feeling and no opposition with illiterate Baptist preachers—even exchange of pulpits. A little learning they find more troublesome. Pennington Gap School got away one Baptist boy by convincing him that it was wrong for him to go to Congregational school. Less damp here than at Harlan—less fog though people seemed to have colds—perhaps on account of the warm weather. They say there is less sickness here as well. I noticed some bad looking heads and necks—scabs etc. A good deal of killing here—this year very bad (on account of election?) 11 killings since August. The accounts I hear sound brutal and worse than in other counties—combined with stealing in a number (3) of instances (liquor stealing). Heard of several cases of men carrying brass knuckles (knucks). I wonder if it is at all common here. Pistols seem common enough. Mrs. Wood said some of the boys carry them—though not in school she thinks. Good farming country. We saw a number of fine bottom land farms along Clover Fork on our way up and Martins Fork has more. Plenty of coal here. Iron on the Virginia side of the mountains.

Visited school for a while (5 teachers)—then called on Mrs. Dean—a friend of Miss King's. Wrote a letter to Miss King and read "Judith of the Cumberlands." After dinner John and I both slept for a couple of hours—talked and finally went over to supper at Mr. and Mrs. Turner's—pork and all the rest. John preached in the eve—but I stayed in and waited till the service was over.

We then went over to Mr. and Mrs. Woods' and talked a while to teachers. Woods are eager for industrial work in school. Mr. W. does not like pastoral work—is not fitted for it and has too much to do anyway. The teachers confided in me that they felt they were losing along church lines in community. Many people also thought that a man should be principal of school, though Mrs. W. was a good teacher.

JANUARY 23rd: A very promising day for rain but it only showered on us a little. We got off early and rode back to Harlan with a Mr. Johnston Smith who introduced himself to us. Were very tired on arrival, but decided to go over to trial a few minutes. Henry Carter the murderer was on the stand—a strong looking man of 30 odd with fair hair, hard brown eyes and retreating forehead—mouth concealed by mustache. He seemed cool and hard. He was followed by Sidney Pope—the 2nd accused—a young man of 20 (wife 15 years old)—with a weak face and under lip receding. Room had a number of women and a crowd of men, the latter standing crowded down front or sitting on window sills and backs of seats. There was a steady pattering of spit on the floor. Yesterday, they said every one who came in was examined for concealed weapons. The story seemed to be—though this did not come out in the evidence while I was there: The murdered man—a boy of twenty—Tolby Howard and a friend were wagonning (friend ahead) from Hagans to Harlan—bringing in a load of whiskey for some of prominent citizens (a Kentenia promoter).[36] The whiskey was in the front of the wagon. Both had been drinking and stopped at Pansy for more. At Pansy they met Sidney Pope and Henry Carter also drinking. These two wanting more whiskey went out, took out whiskey from Howard's wagon and hid it under the house. Friend found it and put it back in Howard's wagon. Result an altercation, with threats from Carter. Another man in the store—Bob Osburne had some brass knuckles and seems to have given them to Carter (Osburne was dismissed at trial, perhaps to turn State's evidence). Carter and Pope wanted whiskey and started after wagons which had gone ahead. Now dark and cold. Went through field and branch—presumably to hide tracks. Evidently came up and hit Howard in head with brass knuckles, perhaps not intending to kill him—but did so. Dragged body some distance and hid it in small place. Then ran up the road to kill friend. Friend had supposed Howard to be close behind in dark but after calling several times and getting no answer became alarmed. Then he heard whispering behind and getting no response to calls, jumped out of wagon and ran for life to house near by. Howard's wagon stood all night in the same spot—but in morning his body was not to be found. Carter and Pope got up about 4 A.M. and came in to pay for whiskey. Town alarmed and stirred up, began search for body. Pretty well known from evidence that Carter and Pope had killed him. Carter a desperate man. Shortly before had killed brother-in-law. Shot him through and through again and again, when he was already down. Prisoners had consultation with friends, evidently resulting in body being brought from hiding place and put in creek as if drowned (no water found in lungs). Town ready to lynch but lacked leader and danger passed.

John went over in P.M. and heard decision. Carter held without bail and Pope bailed for $5000. I stayed at the house and rested. In eve Mr. Michael sang and Miss Henge played for us. In the morn John preached and in P.M. went out to a little chapel with Mr. Snodgrass. Chapel had an interesting origin. Stands in a place where there was a Sunday baseball field. Mr. Smith went out one day, and asked why they didn't go to church or Sunday School. Found there was none—and town too distant. Got players interested to subscribe—raised chapel, built bridge across the creek and now has a fine church there.

Went over to Christian Endeavor in the eve—a great crowd—and came back to talk a while. Alters eager for industrial work. Discussed possibility of farm work—a hill top farm in neighborhood which brings in fine vegetables etc. A good fruit country but orchards badly placed and neglected. Need of home nursing etc.

We had Saturday night also (January 23rd) a meeting with a roomful of prominent citizens at Judge Lewis' house. Four or five judges present. No valuable information. They were indifferent to county high school law—no idea of enforcing and little knowledge of it. Wanted big church schools and general boom. Seemed to think most of mountain people would eventually get out of country.

Monday morning we talked to Mrs. Osburne who has been in Harlan eighteen years—was here when feuds were at height; when they shut blinds and hid in houses and one time put women and children in Court house. Said children needed culture—love of beautiful. Her girls were ready to go back to dirt floor log cabins and would as lief eat from oil cloth as white tablecloth—or said so anyway. Thought dormitory should be made as attractive as possible. She put us up a nice lunch and with aid of Mr. Snodgrass (from whom we got some pictures as well as from Mrs. Lewis) Mr. Michel and Mr. Alter, we mounted our white steeds and got off about 10.30 A.M.

The weather was threatening when we started in our rainclothes, but cleared bright and cooler and we had a good ride—and leisurely—over to Hagan. Had to pass the place of the murder opposite a sulphur spring near Pansy. Part of the way, the country is beautiful—especially over the 2nd mountain and I enjoyed it to the full again—though I couldn't help thinking how bad a road it must be for the wagoners to keep travelling. They cannot cover it in a day at this season, and one can not wonder at the drinking, especially with a government distillery on Clover Fork and several moonshine stills. We met six or seven wagons rumbling and crawling up the mountain—all the drivers but one mere boys.

It was growing dark when we got into Hagan. Found 2 girls and boys who had passed us on road in hotel. Situation seemed sentimental. We decided we couldn't go a meal at the hotel—especially after seeing the old man with sore eyes. Took 6.10 to Hubbard Springs, where we found comfortable place and fair dinner at Mrs. Noe's. Raining outside—but we went down to 8.45 train. Got into Cumberland Gap at about 10 and tumbled dead tired into bed.

JANUARY 26th: Up again at 5, to catch 6.10 train. Clear and cold. Got into Knoxville at 8–9 A.M. and went to Colonial. Had an uneventful time in Knoxville, getting washed, shampooed, face massaged etc., and going into a few cinematographs. Got off to Maryville on afternoon train. President Wilson met us at station and piloted us to the house—a brick one and rather cheerless. Mrs. W. was not very well and the 6+ children absorbed. We got in some rest however and found the college atmosphere very pleasant.

JANUARY 28th: Maryville has quite a plant—fine new chapel, seating 1000, big hall, President's house, Y.M.C.A. buildings, girls' and boys' dormitories (both inferior wooden buildings but well kept) Memorial Library and new hospital just to go up. They have a big piece of land—partly in forest. Sherman camped on main hill in war—also Confederates. Hill covered with fine old cedars—one full still of bullets. Situation is something like Demorest though mountains are nearer. The great Smokies form a beautiful irregular shaded ridge of blue off to the East.[37]

Spirit of the college is good—majority mountain students but a number from states all around (150 perhaps). Registration is about 630—fairly even—divided between boys and girls, I should say, judging by appearance in chapel. Most of these are in Academy—comparatively few in college. High school course is now four years and college course, they try to base on Williams, Amherst etc. No industrial work so far—though students wait on table and take charge of rooms. Grounds are naturally beautiful but are disorderly with scattered bits of paper. Board is down to a fine point—7-1/2 cents a meal. Help is given in small amounts to students—just enough to eke out what they can supply. Boys work some on college grounds. Desire now domestic science for girls.

We came in moment of rejoicing, Pres. Wilson having just completed his endowment fund, $200,000—getting indeed $226,000. This was announced in morning chapel and greeted by cheers. All faculty made speeches of thanksgiving, and compliment to President. He gave long talk, telling some of suffering and outcome—whole talk religious in feeling, and frankly stating dependence on God's mercy. Students enthusiastic and tearful. Prof. Lyle (originally at Grassy Cove) showed us over the buildings and we met a Miss Greene—a Woburn girl in Josie Stevens' class at Smith. Knew her well.

At noon we went to dinner at the dormitory—a huge room where 332 ? eat. Sat at teachers table. Girls and boys allowed a good deal of freedom. May walk around campus together at noon hour—call Saturday P.M. and go to entertainments together. Have no special trouble with co-education though I could see plenty of budding sentiment. Said there were some marriages. Also boys who went through college, did not go back to mountains. Farming good in mountain coves. Many coves of limestone fertility. Believe that establishment of little summer schools (like Miss Henry's) leads to boys and girls coming to larger schools and then going back. Pres. Wilson says that he does not say they are making good stuff out of poor material. What he emphasizes is that it is so easy to make fine strong men and women from these mountain children. Only need a little chance.

There were basket ball games in P.M. and in the eve a general complimentary speech making. Singing was not up to Demorest in my opinion. We went out to the huge bonfire—1200 there I suppose—quite a sight. The boys took the professors, Pres. W. at head, on their shoulders and carried them round and round the blaze. It looked odd enough—as if they were riding tall horses. Pres. W. said it broke his back.

JANUARY 29th: John spoke at morning chapel and received great applause. Then we went down to Mr. Webb's (Flag Pond Webb's brother) and got some photos. Visited two good classes—English one of Prof. Lyon and Bible of Prof. Lyle. In P.M. called on Dr. Ellis—a business like young man who was much delighted in our interest in health conditions. Medical standard low in Tennessee colleges—great ignorance all around—especially in regard to contagion. Hard to get scarlet fever etc. posted even in cities—seems to be regarded as disgrace. No conception of infection of typhoid and tuberculosis. Will not disinfect and disease spreads rapidly. Tuberculosis—fearfully prevalent and measles often run into that and into pneumonia through neglect. Next comes typhoid—then measles. Anemia common in the mountains—poor food. A good deal of insanity due to isolation and monotony. He himself has been amazed at the extent of venereal diseases even in very remote places. Low moral tone. Loggers come to cities and return. Rapid spread of disease. Told of some bad cases of syphilis—thinks lectures ought to be given in schools. Problems best reached through schools. A trained nurse best perhaps—as she gets into homes—and rural doctors often inefficient. Need to teach nursing, domestic science etc. more than higher branches of learning. Criticized Maryville for her lack—at least suggested a criticism. Said people moved often and went into houses infected with tuberculosis—indifferently. Appalling lack of knowledge.

John talked in P.M. with Prof. Lyle and Dr. Wilson and I finished some writing. Mrs. Wilson was sick—so I got off by my lonesome—meeting John at the office. Dr. W. went to train with us. A heavy wind, cold and snowing a little. Got into Knoxville about 6—got supper out, went to two cinematographs and to bed. Remembered story Dr. Wilson told of incident in cove near Maryville during Civil War. Union sympathizers in cove and mountains had made great flag—woven and dyed with home things and put at mouth of valley. One of few Confederate companies recruited here, was sent to coves to collect arms left there. Warned by old man in Maryville not to touch flag or would be killed. So passed flag with a salute—fortunately for them—as woods to right and left were lined with concealed armed men. These were mollified by respect to flag and sent word over country to entertain Confederates. So the Confederates were royally entertained everywhere—but never found a gun.

JANUARY 30th: Cold and blowy. Spent most of my time getting my clothes in order and letters written. In the eve went to "Polly of the Circus" and found it good.

JANUARY 31st: Sunday gray and chill. Had a late breakfast and wrote up diary. Kept all day at writing and packing—with a nap to ease off.

5

FEBRUARY *1909*

TENNESSEE

*The next day [February 3] we visited the school, about forty pupils pres-
ent, with an enrollment of under fifty. The public school was now closed; it
had a six month term and enrollment of sixty. The Webbs and the teachers
had quite different ideas as to the work, and there was no real cooperation
between them—partly a matter of point of view, partly temperament, and
partly seeming unwisdom in the organization set up by the Board. During
our 3 weeks' stay in and around Flag Pond, we had plenty of opportunity
to talk this over with the Webbs, along with a good many other things—denominational friction, health conditions, local mores, etc. For example, the
teachers disapproved of the health work; they felt the Webbs gave too much
time to what was outside the minister's special province and not enough
to the church's real interests. Church work was made more difficult by the
opposition offered by the Baptists, many of whom seemed to think the Presbyterians were a sort of political organization, trying to get possession of the
whole country and centralize power.*[1]

FEBRUARY 1st: Left Knoxville about 7.35 (or rather delayed 1/2
hour)—and got to Jefferson City along 9 o'clock—John feeling desperately tired and both of us indifferent. We walked

up to Carson-Newman [Baptist College] which is quite an imposing group of buildings on a hill. Had an interview with Dr. Jeffries, who likewise showed us about.[2] They have about 500 students (Baptist)—a big recitation building and four dormitories—2 boys' and 2 girls'—(2 on the straight boardinghouse plan and 2 with boys and girls working and dividing expense—that is cooperative). Buildings were good looking and brick, I think. No industrial work is being done except as a start in direction of cooking for girls. Miss Henderson the matron, proved to be from Boston—a former worker in Ruggles St. Church. She had many plans for combining cooking with a nursing course—a model hospital room etc. At present she is confined to practical work and has had to give up cooking classes. Matron left and the work fell on her—but she tried to give a practical training to girls. Girls come on by 10's every week and do all work under supervision so they can learn. Is quite a prejudice against domestic science—as being merely "dishwashing" of which they have plenty at home. Miss Henderson's horror and surprise at conditions amused me. Much disturbed because things were not finished and kept up; buildings badly kept; girls ignorant of contagion, diet etc.—the same old story of smuggling in to sick ones things to eat, etc. etc. She felt she would not come back again. Cost about $35,000 (?) to run school.

We were dead tired, so refused invitation to dinner and went down to hunt up a hotel. There seemed to be only one—a very unattractive one near the station. We went in and sat a while before a dead fire and dropping grate, dingy bed and cracked bureau—until darkey got fire started in sitting room. Then we sat there till 3.30 (with an interim in dining room over pork) writing and viewing the lithographs of dead relatives. Train left about 4.15—late an hour. Crowds of cheap youths bustling about station. These small southern R.R. towns are certainly unattractive. Little pickaninny amused us—picking off the dirty polka-dotted platform scraps of peanuts fallen from the slot machine. Mother much disgusted with "dat trash."

We got into Greenville between 6–7 and were met by Dr. Gray—who had a team ready to drive us to the college—4 miles.[3] He himself scooted off on Dixie—a fine little horse once owned by Vanderbilt and brought from England. It was moonlight and cold—the drive very pretty though carriage curtains cut off view.

Greenville seemed to have some quite prepossessing looking houses. We got to Tusculum—O.K.—and were taken to Virginia Hall [at the Presbyterian College] where Dr. Gray [the President of Greeneville-Tusculum] and family are living while their house is being finished. It had a fine big open fire in living room—most grateful and we had a good supper. (Their meals average five ¢ apiece). Talked a while to Miss Alexander (sister of Mrs. Boole) and two other teachers— a Miss Johnston, who knew Leslie Hayford of Tufts (taught there last year) and domestic science teacher, Miss Gash, who comes from North Carolina. Mrs. Gray has three boys—8— 12—14—the latter two upon six feet in height.

In the morning we went to morning chapel and heard some unusually good singing by the Boys Glee Club (Mrs. Gray thinks there is more musical feeling in Tenn. than in N.C.(?)) John led exercises but did not give a talk. There are about 250 (?) students—nice looking and really picked as they are the selected ones who come up via day schools— Home Industrial etc. Of course some come from the town. All looked pretty well dressed, and acted self-possessed.

There are three buildings and the campus is naturally very pretty. Buildings are of brick and Virginia Hall and Academy building are good. Boys' hall is out of shape. There is no industrial work for boys—but the girls have a four years course in both sewing and cooking. In the latter a little is done in dietary work. Practical work (?) Miss Gash gave us a nice little meal in P.M.—done by girls of one class—corn soup—corn-pone—Hamburg steak coffee charlotte—all good. The girls do some work in the house, waiting on tables etc.—but the work is not yet on the basis Dr. Gray wishes. They are putting in a water system and have had to buy a small farm which they planned for a big vegetable garden. There is an old brick building—Old College—on the grounds—now used for girls to board themselves.

Say people in immediate country are not in such poor condition as in mountains. Country not so mountainous. Mountains near at hand however, and looked gorgeous in the P.M. light—all purple and snow ridges. Of course their conditions are the same. A man who drove us to station, said that Greenville-Tusculum represented 1000 children their only chance for education. Washington College is supposed to be joined with G-T as preparatory school—but at present is not especially satisfied with arrangement.

Mrs. Gray told me confidentially about their troubles at Marshall with Baptists and some Methodists—also Woman's Board. Says Presbyterians are losing great ground in every school they give up.

We went down to see some old people who live opposite the original school building (a log cabin). Mrs. __ was setting butter in the springhouse, but came in and showed us some lovely old furniture, desk, tall clock and sideboard—small tables.

After supper—the carriage came and we drove—Dr. Gray with us over to Afton Station—2 miles. It was brilliant moonlight and the road ran literally among the tree trunks—lovely. The driver had brought his team way from State of

Washington. We had to wait a while in office of station and got into Johnson City about 10 P.M. Went at once to hotel (Dr. Gray to a friends) and piled in for the night at the Arlington House—fairly comfortable quarters. In the morning Dr. Gray brought Mr. Brading down for 6.30 breakfast. We left on 7.10 train for Loves and got there about 8.

FEBRUARY 3rd, Wednesday: Loves is nothing but a station and couple of houses. We hung about the station and changed our clothes in freight room, but no word from Mr. Webb.[4] Finally telephone operator said postboy had gone by with Mr. W.'s horse and two saddles. We hung about till the fried tobacco-juice was too much—then prowled outside to find the weather had warmed up and the mountains were very lovely—higher and ridged like geography pictures and snow lying on the shady side. Along near 10.30 the postboy arrived with the horse, but had been unable to get the mule (which Mr. W. promised in letter brought by boy) as said mule had followed some one off. So John and I mounted double and started off down the creek. All went very well till I slipped off going up a steep hill and then John mounted me and he walked the rest of the way to Fordville. It is steep country and beautiful, with white pine, hemlock, laurel, etc. Brooks are clear and rushing. The ice had melted a good deal and roads were muddy in places and ice cracked through in other places. Half way over we met Fox—the lost mule and he meekly turned in after Dale (Mr. W.'s horse) and so we drove him to Fordville. There we got him bridled and saddled with a man's saddle, which the loafers presented somewhat apologetically to me—and we were off again. Lost the mail boy after a bit and got into Flag Pond alone 2–3 P.M. Mr. Webb ran out to meet us and Mrs. W. had a fine steaming dinner ready—tomato-bisque soup, roast 'possum (possum had been skinned and parboiled and wasn't greasy at all) and ice-cream. Had a long talk and tumbled to bed satisfied.

Mr. Webb had to go over to Rocky Fork to Prayer meeting—but got back about 8 P.M. before we turned in.

Flag Pond is a little settlement where once was a flag pond—now drained.[5] It has a pretty situation right in among the hills which are ribbed and clustered with pine groups. The teachers have a little home in connection with the school—and the Webbs have a pretty new house near by. Mrs. W. has had medical training and she is a trained nurse. Both came originally from Ohio.

FEBRUARY 4th, Thursday: I helped Mrs. W. in the morning, while John went on an errand with Mr. Webb. In the P.M. we mounted double on Dale and Old Fox and rode down to Rocky Fork where there is a day school under Miss Moore. Miss M. has been there for six years—raised her own salary etc. before the Board would accept the school. Also has to raise her assistant's salary. Painted house with her own hands.

Miss Moore and her assistant walked back with us to Devils Fork which is a narrow cut between the hills where a lively branch drops down in a tall icy waterfall—very lovely. The cleft was as green as summer with tall hemlocks and rhododendron—moss and fern. We walked along on a wooden tram way (built on trestles) used for logging. The trucks are drawn by mules. Then we came back. All this country seems full of water-power, rushing streams and a score of pretty grist mills, picturesque enough with the overshot wheels. The mountains are distinctly the highest we have yet seen,—Bald being about 6000 feet. They are the Unakas.

The Webbs are great observers and have had a various experience. Are much upset with the Woman's Board (Junks Mr. Webb calls them)—also have met with Baptist opposition and lack of cooperation. Mrs. Webb told me of many cases of dishonesty in dealings with people—short wood—poor wood—two prices on all commodities—shifting and scheming for a few more pennies. One man would not sell his chickens for 40¢ because he would go down to Mr. Webb's and sell them for 60¢. Could not buy corn because people were holding it for $1.00 a bushel—etc. etc. Seemed to have no sense of fair play or gratitude. People take what they can get and do not repay. This true in medical work. Women much neglected. So many have female troubles (remember the Clay County woman who had been pregnant 25 times.) Have little attention at time of children's births. Even doctor's wife had only what help she could get from woman who was doing all the work. Mrs. W. offered to instruct and oversee special girl—but doctor hardly thought her strong enough to do *all* the work. Mrs. W. told of experience with woman living in little shack. Woman's husband was away and she expecting baby—showed strong tubercular tendencies. Mrs. W. did not wish to take responsibility. When she and doctor went up found the woman in bed and bed soaked through (other children in room) baby was born already. Mother so badly off she could only nurse on one side and baby grew one-sided—told Mrs. Webb that when she had had her other babies she had lain on the floor until baby came so as to leave the "mess" on the floor and get clean into bed. She later went to N.C. and died (baby too) of tuberculosis. Mrs. Webb told me of another case where doctor had nothing to help woman and just let her suffer until Mrs. W. sent for chloroform by Mr. Webb (no chloroform used in country) and doctor knew it was a breech-presentation. Said nothing about it at all to Mrs. W. A great deal of tuberculosis here—not so much typhoid—and heaps of venereal diseases—scrofula etc. etc. Moral standard very low—illegitimacy "in almost every family." Talked about at the time but girls continue to go with same people and marry different men who take the children too. Mrs. W. says—in her observation, it is the duller girls who get into this fix (?)—taken advantage of. The first time she cannot blame them—they say "He said he would marry me." Boys handle the girls too freely and girls provoke and allow it. Steal boys cap etc. and thrust into front of waist, and boy has to explore to find it. Of course none can be innocent where everything is seen in the one-roomed cabins. Many mountain girls have been "bid off" by this proposal—"How would you like to put your shoes under my bed?" Man spoke of "theological surveyors" instead of "geological" and "distill right principles into them" and "Solicitous liquors" instead of "illicit." Hills are so steep that they have to shoot in their corn with a gun and bring it down in a jug. At one store here—they buy every 70–80 days $200 of a certain brand of tobacco—exclusive of all other brands and snuff—making $400 every 2 months for snuff and tobacco.

Mr. Webb says the educated Baptist ministry have no more prestige here than Presbyterians. Told case of native who had had college and seminary training. Had never been asked to preach here except by an old uncle—which he did not come. Young man told Mr. W. that he had no more influence than he. Many people think Presbyterians are sort of political organization (like Catholic middle ages) trying to get possession of all country and centralize power.

FEBRUARY 5th, Friday: In the afternoon, I mounted the mule Rhody—behind John—while Mr. and Mrs. W. started on Dale. Warm and pleasant though we could see a threatening thickness gathering in the mountains ahead. Had to follow part of the road to Loves—then turned off to the right up Spivey Creek. As we crossed the rocky creek bottom, we met a woman with a baby in her arms—and mounted on a horse. She had a dark full blooded face—on the tramway walked a man carrying another baby. Mr. W. saluted him as Lehan Shelton. They said they had come over from North Carolina. Mr. Webb says they are the digger Indian type—the lowest of mountaineers. Live in wretched shack which we saw.[6] When wife was very sick one time, Lehan cried and told doctor what a religious Christian woman she was. Doctor reminded him that a short while before, when wife was lying dead drunk by road, he offered $20 to any one who would take her home. Some one offered Mr. Webb $40 if he would spend the night at Lehan's. Lehan told Mr. Webb that he could say something that many men couldn't say—he had 7 brothers shot and had seen 4 of them killed.

They passed out of sight—Lehan holding the baby awkwardly and staring backward at us. We kept on up the creek—going over a mountain with creek below. It is a very beautiful region, with the rushing creek and steep green hillsides.[7] There are a great number of little overshot wheels all along—most picturesque. Mr. W. pointed us out a number of pine trees in which knots had been tied—some grown, now, large and explained that these were lovers' knots. A young man (or girl) tied a knot in end of twig and if it stayed and grew—all would be well. But if unknotted or dead, all off. We picked several on the way back.

At the Falls Gap churchhouse—we dismounted and went down a steep slippery path to the creek where we found a magnificent ice incrusted water fall—70–80 feet high—a wonderful sight. Logs at the bottom green with moss. It was sprinkling a little when we got back so pushed along and before dark, crossed a deep mill dam and came in at an old log house—belonging to John Butler Hensley—where we were to spend the night.

Mr. Webb and I dismounted and went in. Mrs. Hensley proved to be a youngish woman and quite handsome though unkempt. The kitchen was in great disorder—things lying all around. A table set in the middle. I took my seat between a cook-stove and the open fire while Mrs. H. dandled the baby—Edward Lee—a nondescript infant in a long dirty brown woolen dress, its head incrusted with dirt and covered with a grimy cap. Mrs. H. said it seemed like he was more company than all the rest put together. Mrs. W. says she nurses him constantly. Says she can't bear to hear him cry—when he wants the breast. Finally she sat him down among a wallow of ancient brown comforters in a home made crib before the fire and set about supper. Mrs. W. inquired casually if she had been giving him his baths—Mrs. H. said—not for sometime—as the second boy (?) had had a breaking out and she was afraid Edward Lee might catch it. Mrs. W. made a few mild suggestions—but at this point, Edward Lee began to roar—having had enough of lying down. He was evidently not suffering—but in a rage and thrashed about furiously. I couldn't help being amused by Mrs. W.'s tactful suggestions—that baby was O.K. and should be taught that he could not have his way always—and Mrs. H.'s laconic rejoinders, which ended in her calling to the smaller boy to come in and nurse the baby. So he soon appeared—round and red cheeked—with round brown eyes and a round black hat on his round head. He picked up the baby, which promptly ceased its roars—and rocked it by thumping his chair back and forth, first on the front legs—then on the back. During all this time, Mrs. H. was making hoe cake (baking in the spider) biscuit, frying pork and boiling coffee—all at my left elbow and not greatly to my appetite.

There were two other rooms in the house—lengthwise—the one next to the kitchen having three unmade beds in it—and the front room having but one. Mrs. H. said [she] was keeping the saw mill hands (no one else to do it)—and they made the linen so dirty. It certainly was dirty—no mistake. The saw mill hands proved to be four big young men and all very hungry. One apologized for his appearance and roughness. Said he would come to the evening meeting however.

Before we finished supper—it had begun to pour—with a high wind, which drove the embers way out into the room. We adjourned to the front room—while the family ate. Mrs. H. fished out a lamp with a chimney which she set on the organ. Every time one of the doors was opened, out went the lamp in a rush of wind.

Finally the storm grew so heavy—thunder and lightning, that we decided not to walk the 1+ mile to the churchhouse but gather the few people into the house. So I took to the organ and we had our little congregation before the big fireplace—both John and Mr. W. speaking. The saw mill hands sat on the bed and all spat speculatively into the fire.

Mrs. W. and I slept together—cannily covering the dirty clothes with a blanket and our pillow with towels from our saddlebags. The six men slept in the next room—all shut up tight from the night air. John said they didn't wait for the light to go out before they began to spit—a regular patter on the floor.

In the morning—we walked over to Big Cornelius Hensley's—(after an outdoor wash)—and found him a bluff old fellow, equally pleased with his own and others' jokes. His wife was not well—but his daughters were on hand—one the common-school teacher—an awkward [looking] girl, who tried vainly to be at ease and gracious. Her hair tied up in a knot and skirt pinned together behind with yawning safety pins. The mother weaves beautifully—linen as well as linsey.

Had a peaceful pleasant ride home and got back about noon. Late in the afternoon Mr. Gillis—a man who is collecting some data for Mr. Webb appeared. He is the tax assessor. He is a large, pleasant faced man with much beard, speaks fairly good English and seems honest and intelligent. Had on his Sunday best. Said forest grew quickly in this country. All you had to do—was to fence in a piece of land from the stock, and in years you had timber to clear. Walnut grew readily—pine and chestnut. Accounted for late failure of peaches (used to be fine never-failing orchards) by the cutting out of timber. Sun gets in now and opens buds prematurely. Used to be many killings about here. Told of 19–20 years' experience of Unicoi boy—a deputy sheriff—who was trying to arrest a man for _____. Went with warrant and man skipped—Sheriff had boy with him, sitting on woodpile—man told him to keep quiet. Sheriff however headed him off and got him. Took away pistol and passed it into the house—where were the father and a S. Carolina man. As Sheriff was mounting horse he was shot. Turned around and saw S. C. man in doorway with smoking gun barrel—Sheriff shot him and he dropped. At this the father came around the corner and shot twice into sheriff. Sheriff emptied gun into him and he dropped. By this time someone had passed gun to prisoner who shot sheriff twice more. Sheriff shot him and then mounted and rode away. Lived several days. Was a good chap and entirely unsuspecting of any treachery.

Much illegitimacy—did not farm land properly—great deal of venereal diseases—sturdy stock being run out. Thinks disease came in after Civil War. Thinks illegitimacy comes from wickedness rather than environment. Says Baptists are narrow ones.

FEBRUARY 7th, Sunday: Started in raining early. I watched from the window—the snow flakes on the top of the hills gradually creeping down till it was snowing with us. Then snow and rain alternated—fortunately the snow keeping up while we made our 4 mile ride to Devils Fork (Sweetwater Hollow as the people are trying to call it).[8] The mountains are very high that way—and the wood growth to the top was distinct in branch and twig snowladen. The mist and cloud drifted low and sometimes hid the summit completely—then swept aside to show a shaft of sunlight and glint of blue sky before swallowing the peak again. The road was so uphill that I was sitting most of the way on Dale's tail (Mr. and Mrs. W. rode the somewhat cranky mule)—but I had to admire the country in spite of my tired arm which clutched John's coat in frantic efforts to keep on (big saddle took up room). Much of the road lay between heavy growths of pine and hemlock laden with snow which brushed off and fell on the [ponchos] which I tried to hold over my skirt. The holly trees were particularly lovely with the red berries peeping through the snow.

There was a very small congregation at the chapel, but John spoke his best and with effect. The day had partially cleared on our return and we got in about noon. Had a lunch—and John and I rested until 3 while Mr. and Mrs. W. went to Sunday School. There was still a very small audience and John spoke again—after which we went down to the teachers' cottage with Mrs. Webb and talked to Miss Olson and Miss Renich. Came home and had hot tea and dough-nuts and later grape juice, Roquefort cheese and crackers—all very convivial in appearance. Had a gay talk.

Monday—Mr. Webb was off early on an errand in A.M.—but John stayed abed most of morning while I worked and visited with Mrs. W. When John got up we walked over to the school and visited for an hour—small attendance—about 40 (enrollment under 50). There is a public school here (now closed) with a 6 mos term and enrollment of about 60.

FEBRUARY 9th, Tuesday: Mr. and Mrs. Webb went off early

to assist at an appendicitis operation. Were gone all day and came home drenched and tired, for it was a pouring storm. John and I had a peaceful day in the house making out accounts and writing letters.

FEBRUARY 10th, Wednesday, Flag Pond: A glorious clear morning with every branch and creek rushing full of water. Before getting up, I could hear the dam roaring down the road—up pretty early—but had a busy time of preparation before starting off at 8.45 A.M.

I rode Dale, who felt exceedingly lively and gay, and though I did not use my spur, he cut up along Higgins Creek in great shape. The creek rushed in among the rhododendron. Two mill-wheels we passed—but they were quiet with the water shooting out the flume. Half way up Unaka Mountain or Divide Mountain—Mr. Webb stopped and took pictures of us. Then we wound up slowly to the top—beautiful views of the mountains all along. At the top, as we turned down the N.C. side—a cold wind struck us. The ground was frozen and snow lay high up in the hollows of cornfield or ridge. The road followed Puncheon Fork to Dr. English—then swung up over Wolf-pen Gap to the waters of Big Laurel. There was laurel sure enough—in great high masses—a wonderful sight it must be in the spring. We stopped at a nice looking white house with a yard green and smooth and big barn to feed our horses and eat our luncheon. A boy on the road said it was the widow English's house—but that he was not her nephew—but her brother's wife's boy. She proved to be a nice looking woman—very pleasant. Brought us apples from the apple house—which we munched while warming our cold toes over the open fire. She had twins at Mars Hill but spoke well of Burnesville Presbyterian School. We stayed about an hour.

We crossed Windy Gap there and came down onto Ball

Creek—also heavily massed with rhododendron. At near the Swiss post office we fell in with the Star Route Mail Carrier. We stopped at the office and store to buy more spurs, and the carrier went on with us and took us across the bad ford on the Cane River. We zigzagged over single file in his wake—and could not see anything very bad about the ford, although the current was swift. Forded three times and Mr. W. took some pictures. Here was where we had our first really big sweep of the mountains ahead and behind—all purple and clear cut. Here also the wind struck us with a more biting chill and whistled around the rest of the way. It fairly cut us through and the road grew muddier and muddier as we plodded along ankle deep and half way up to the knees. Country was beautiful especially the last 3 of those 27 miles. The mountains were purple where the sun caught them, and black where night had begun to fall. Puffs of pink and windy cloud swept through the cold blue above them and the sun sank brilliant yellow behind. We were tired and chilled when at last we drew up at the school. Mr. Hubbard ran down to meet and took us to the manse where Mr. Taylor came out and helped us fall off our horses.[9] Mrs. W. and I were so stiff we could hardly stand. We went in and hung over the open fire—changed our clothes and then went over to the dormitory to dinner. We had a grand meal—roast chicken, salad and snow pudding. Very dead tired and came home to crawl into bed joyfully.

Thursday—Another glorious day—John and Mr. Webb went over to speak at chapel while Mrs. W. and I hung over fire. Talked to Mrs. Taylor and Mrs. Hubbard.

About 160 registered in school—tuition $50—($3000–3500 a year to run school—$1500 to $1600 in tuitions.) Attendance 130 or more. Fine girls' dormitory and good building for school. Boys room in cottages but will have dormitory next year—sewing and domestic science for girls (our dinner was cooked by department) no manual training for boys.

Too many women teachers—outside Presbyterian schools ought to be centralized under this school or discontinued and money put here. Negro teacher came a short time ago—wanted H. to teach him as he couldn't get higher education round here. H. told him he would be glad to but it would go all over the country that they were teaching negros. Understood negro had been sent to him through Baptists. Had to be very careful what you said—even people who joined church couldn't always be relied on as to what they said. Couldn't make them over. Believed in having a good public school here and Presbyterians going into some other activity—higher education or something else, Baptists have good opportunity here. E. E. Hawkins principal.

Dr. Robinson and Mr. Bailey went up with John and others. Students had somewhat different appearance—not so up and coming. Teachers less high type. Building (a good one) being finished piecemeal as they get the money. Boys and girls dormitories of wood. Hawkins argued for church school—no public as public did not amount to anything and weren't Christian; said they enrolled 150—but not nearly that there. Said were doing good work—Mr. Taylor thinks there are more pupils coming to town and in both schools—because of the two schools—than there would be in either all Baptist or one Presbyterian.

In the afternoon we saddled—and the five of us (Mr. Taylor the 5th) started for Low Gap (or Lower Pensacola). The weather had moderated considerably though the air was brisk. Our way lay much between the mountains, so we found the riding very comfortable. Followed Bowlin's Creek and at about 3 miles from Burnsville pulled up at a store kept by Uncle Josh Young. While the men were trying to get some specimens of mica, I gave Dale the rein and he amused himself by climbing up into the yard and wandering round over the green grass and under the grape vines. Finally John and Mr. Webb decided to go out to the mine and we to continue on to the school.

The mountains were hazy but beautiful—roads muddy but we enjoyed it. Found the school a neat building (2 teachers living in 4 rooms above—Miss O. Hazlett and Miss Bangle). This building and that at Banks Creek—is so arranged because the special building fund allowed only for school building but few extras could be added.

The teachers ran down to meet us and we were soon comfortably ensconced in a warm room. The men appeared after an hour or two—in high spirits. They had been up to the mine and had not only persuaded Uncle Josh out of mica specimens, but had each gathered a heap of beryl—all in rough crystal form—some imbedded in feldspar. Mr. Webb has part of the copper worm of a moonshine still—and he plans to have a jeweler friend make us belt buckles from it set with the rough green beryl. John and I made a design for it—Maltese Cross in a circle.[10]

We had a very nice supper—broiled chicken beans potatoes—cake and pie and all grew very hilarious over it. Talked a while afterward and then the men started down the road to their domicile. We washed dishes and were ready for bed—but got to talking about conditions—and hung over fire discussing and roasting marshmallows (on our hat pins) till nearly 11 P.M. Miss Hazlett says illegitimacy is very common. One case in almost every family—sometimes more—much talk at the time—but afterward girl marries. Skin diseases of all kinds— scrofula common. Suspects venereal diseases in many cases where she cannot tell. Tuberculosis in almost every family. Some typhoid but not so much. A great deal of pneumonia. No privy in the community. Boys coming there to Sunday school, rarely go to closets—but to barn. Cases of vulgarity among children. Discovered picture drawn by one of boys—very low. Took it to mother who said boy must have been told. Teacher said he had evidently seen it and tackled the question of so many sleeping in one room. Boys and girls of all ages sleeping together—3 beds usually—4 common. (John saw 5 at Egypt Bill's) and sometimes 6 in one room. Thinks moral conditions cannot improve much till there are fewer beds in one room.

Mrs. Webb said she had engaged a girl to work for her—but girl gave out because she was afraid to sleep alone. Said that if she could have slept with Mr. and Mrs. W. that would have been O.K. Miss H. told of a night experience, where she slept in same bed with two girls—14 years and 11 years. Before she could get up—the door opened in morning and five men walked in—3 strangers and 2 brothers of the girls. They sat down around the fire and talked comfortably while the 3 girls lay there in bed. Finally the mother came in and Miss H. called her over and explained that she wanted to dress. Old woman seemed to think her odd and fussy but went out and presently called "Tom" and Tom stalked out. "Latte" and Latte went out and so on—till all were out. She hustled into her clothes and stepped out. When she came back the five men were all in the room and the girls were calmly sitting up in bed putting out their clothes.

Considerable friction between Burnsville doctors and Miss H. People impose on Miss H. and feel she is taking away trade. Mrs. Webb says there is need of greatest care, in not running into doctors. Nurses should be strictly "professional" and only work under doctor's orders. Doctors do not use chloroform and let women suffer and die in childbirth. Some birthstool delivery here—but done mostly by old Baptist preacher doctor (no real medical training.)

The teachers put us to bed in great shape—made us undress in the warm room—warmed our bed-room slippers, ironed the bed, put in hotwater bags, tucked us in and kissed us goodnight. We certainly slept the sleep of the just.

Got up late and were eating breakfast when the men came in. They were in high feather—as regard secret allusions to snoring. B.B's. etc; spoke about a night ride. Bed was a little buggy and they had fastened a night mare to it. Both John and Mr. Webb accused Mr. Taylor of tremendous snoring.

We went down to the school about 10 A.M. and the three men spoke. There were about 19 pupils (I don't know enrollment) some as high as 7th grade—legitimate and illegitimate all in together.

Found the road to Bank's Creek (10 mi.) very fascinating—along creek and up through wood paths over mountains. Beautiful views and heaps of rhododendron. Saw one good farm with new brick apple house and triangular roofed structure which we understand to be watchman's lookout. Have a ginseng farm—surrounded by double pickets. Have a watchman constantly and at night turn bull dog (which man has allowed boys to torment all day) out between the pickets. Also saw hillsides being set out with orchards and nurseries.

Our cross-saddle riding caused considerable interest and some amusement. Roads very muddy as we came down near Bank's Creek. We cut up over ridge—fine woodland path with heavenly mountain view—through bars again and over a hill to the school. Some fine farming country there—high up but well placed and raising in places 60 bushels of wheat to the acre.

The school has a beautiful situation on a hill with pine woods to one side and great reaches of blue mountains in front—wooded ridge behind. Miss Gray the B. R.—hung out the window and called us up.

We had a delicious dinner—more chicken, preserves—pie, etc. Talked with Miss G., who had been there 3 years but evidently had not got whole inwardness of the situation. Said tuberculosis not common (denied by Mr. T. later on)—etc. Said these people harder to teach than melungeons who were docile. Miss Mitchell, the teacher, who is a mountain girl from Sneedville, living right near melungeons says she thinks they are a combine of Portuguese and Indian. Miss G. said chief fault of Melungeons was drunkenness. Mountain people here very jealous—had told her so and her experience confirmed it. About 15 in school when we went down to room below. All men spoke again—it being Lincoln's birthday—then they set about to capture the mule which had got loose. Tried chasing, toling with corn but Kate merely sallied down the lane toward town. Mr. W. jumped two fences and headed her off—then the sagacious Mrs. W. let Dale down to the barn, while I threw stones at Kate. Kate fell in behind Dale, went into the barn and so was caught.

Ride back to town was pretty muddy. Found Mr. and Mrs. Hubbard here for dinner. Had a nice dinner and pleasant talk. Went to bed early.

FEBRUARY 13th, Saturday, Burnesville: John had a talk with Mr. Hubbard and at 10 we started for Jack's Creek—6–1/2 miles (Mrs. W. tired and did not go—so Jennie Taylor went with us). The first two miles—powerful long ones—commanded the best views we have had yet—a height of 3000 feet. The day was threatening and distances hazy—but we could see Mt. Mitchell's top towering off on the horizon. The rest of the road was fearfully muddy and not especially beautiful—in and out the creek bottom. Passed several mica mines.

Jack's Creek school (two buildings) is near the creek between low hills that shut out the view. The teachers were not expecting us and were deep [in] preparation for a combination quilting and apple planting party for the P.M. They were cordial however and insisted on getting us a little cold lunch—nice sandwiches, delicious apple and walnut salad and Lady Baltimore Cake—fine! A girl from the neighborhood was there most of the time, so rather hindered free questioning. When she left we asked a few questions. Education not desired much in country. Had to fairly beg parents to send children—school about 15 in number.

Rode back quick time. Roads had dried up a little. Were all tired—got back about 5–6—and had good dinner. John off to bed almost at once.

FEBRUARY 14th, Sunday: John off to preach with Mr. Taylor at Banks Creek—and Mr. Webb with Mr. Bailey to Low Gap. Mrs. W. and I went over to Sunday School and then came home to rest (Baptist service in town). Mrs. W. says, Mr. Bailey yesterday spoke of desirability of industrial work. Only profession in town—lawyers. Good farm land. Need of trained farmers, carpenters etc.

A showery day—with distant mountains dim and nearer peaks hung with cloud masses now and again lit with sunshine.

Mr. Webb came back in the afternoon with more chips of beryl and some rough garnets. Had had a conversation with Uncle Josh who set the tuberculosis rate at about 20%. Mr. Taylor says this is far too low. He would make it easily 50% and in places where they have schools, by actual count it is 60%. He says Miss Gray's statement that only 8 people have died in that community of tuberculosis, becomes significant when you realize that only 12 adults have died any way in the 3 years. Says he knows a family on Jacks Creek he suspects of clay eating.

John had an interesting experience with a man who was

much touched by his talk. Said he had been just that sort of man John described. Thought he ought to carry pistol—got into quarrel and shot his man because he would have been shot if he hadn't. Told of his sufferings in chain gang and attempt to escape with comrade. Comrade escaped but he was shot 4 times—one shot half paralyzing side and other taking out chunk of brain (has epilepsy now). Said he could hear doctor cursing him as he worked over him—saying such as he ought to be killed etc. New evidence came up later and he was pardoned after 2 years—although he was sentenced for 20.

FEBRUARY 15th, Monday, Burnsville: Started off about 7.30 up to the town to see Mr. Ray's museum. He is an old man 86, been through the Civil War in N. C. regiment (Confederate). He owns mica mine the men visited on way to Low Gap. Has made $80,000 in cash out of it. Mine is as good as ever but needs $2000 to put it in shape—and he doesn't bother. Some beautiful specimens in museum— aquamarines as brilliant as diamonds ($5.00 a carat)—garnets all from Yancey County. Beryls of course and mica—smoky quartz cut and looking like cairngorms—Amethysts (from Arizona) and emeralds from Mitchell—and a fine collection of Indian relics.

Got off between 9–10, and made good time the 7 miles to Bald Creek where we stopped to shoe the horses. A showery morning—with fine cloud effects and not enough rain to wet. Dale in high spirits and we cantered along. Fed horses and ate our lunch while the six shoes were being put on. Men amused themselves by pitching quoits with the old horseshoes over a stick. Loafers much interested.

It was between 1–2 when we left for McKinney Gap. Road narrow, stony and winding. Surprising number of houses. Dale picked his way stumblingly and Mrs. W.—coming up behind, discovered that one of the new hind shoes was lost.

The rain began to fall smartly—as we wound up through mud and stones to the top of the Gap. There the road fell steeply down with a purple loom of mountains beyond—the top hidden in cloud. The timber had been cut off all round, and as we got lower, the hillsides looked quite desolate. After a bit we could distinguish Bucktown in the hollow. This is a deserted lumber camp—having once a steam railway on wooden rails. The wooden track still stands partially ruined. It was a most dismal looking spot—box shacks, hogs—and children—scattering corn fields and bare hills all under a drizzling rain. Found a man who could—but did not like to—shoe horses and carried Dale off. Fed the mule again the meanwhile and threw the scatterings to a lively black hog who stood near. Dale limped some on return—but soon limbered up and we left town in good spirits. Passed new house of Mr. Buck—an elaborate one with plate glass front door and city veranda—the only house in town—wound along old tramway to left across the creek, and then began to climb trail up the mountain.

The trail was very rough, round stumps and over logs, now pitching down, now up. In one place where a great log was too high for the horses to cross, we had to drop down a steep place—and at the foot pass under a fallen tree. I was the last, and calculated the height of the tree wrong—and as a result was nearly mashed and knocked off between pommel and log. Fortunately Dale stopped and at the 2nd try, I swung off the stirrup and with John leading, got through. We took the path along the creek—though several led off it, and finally came to a place where an old logging road, choked by fallen trees led up to the left—and a vague rough trail to the right. We decided on the right—and for about a mile struggled up the path—now on slick mud and again over the rough rocks of the creek bottom. It was raining the meantime fitfully, and the clouds rolled down on us, so that when we got to an opened cleared field at the top, we could see neither to right nor left—just vague outlines of what might be mountains ahead. We meditated some while, and Mr. Webb concluded that the path—a new one to him—must bring up between Big and Little Bald. As we wanted to go over Big Bald, we swung to the left and were immediately in a rough timber growth. We pushed ahead—the growth growing heavier and heavier and the little trail more and more crossed by fallen trees. The clouds clung in a thick fog about us and the rain increased until it was a heavy downpour driven hard by the wind. Still no Bald Mountain appeared. We were evidently on the top of a ridge and the trail swung up close to a high new rail fence. All along, were the trunks of the felled trees that had been used for the fence, the big upper branches were thrown all along the way, and our advance was a series of in and outs and "surroundings." Dale with his tender foot and new shoes, moved slowly along 3rd in the file—and going round a tree, where a heavy low twig branched out stumbled, broke the twig and pitched forward. I flew off and by some instinct loosened my feet from the stirrups and rolled to one side before Dale turned over. He was up in a minute, and before I could move, John was off his horse and at my side. I found myself O.K. with exception of a numb leg and wrenched ankle. Dale also, so we mounted again and continued. We must have gone two miles with the rain pouring, wind howling and clouds thick about us before we came to a final decision that we were off our trail. It was growing gray and a night on the mountain stared us in the face. About this time we came to a split in the path—all along the ridge—all down. John called out and we stopped to consult. Then someone remembered my compass. And we found our direction was just away from Flag Pond. The path down—being nearer right, we turned downward—the horses slipping and sliding on the deep soft black earth and stumbling over fallen trees. It was growing dark and Dale's legs trembled at the strain. At John's suggestion—I got down and fairly pulled the baulking [sic] Dale over some great trees. I slipped myself, and fell more than once—stepping on my dress—while the rain continued to drive in sheets. All along Mr. Webb had kept calling and whistling back to be sure we were safe, for it was too thick for him to see us. Now he shouted and in a few minutes we could see smoke and we came out on a little shack—near a saw-mill and in the midst of stacks of lumber. It was a miserable shack but we never were so glad to see any dwelling. An open fire was blazing inside and a big group of men, women and children, gathered at the door to peep out at our bedraggled, dripping figures. The light glistened on our rubber coats. Mr. Webb's question was "We've come to find out where we are."

It appeared that we were on Bruce's sawmill at the foot of Haw Ridge, 3–3 1/2 miles from Streets Gap, which is 5 miles from Flag Pond—and were near 3–3 1/2 miles from Dr. Fate English's at Faust P.O.

There was no hesitation and we decided to strike for Dr. English's for the night. The rain still [ ] down, night was already on us and we were drenching wet. Beside that my ankle pained me. One of the men—Frank Rich then said he would take us across the ridge. He took a lantern and we followed along—by another shack, where the blazing fire mocked at us, through some bars onto a road, then off to the left down another trail, which soon began to mount. We all stuck to our horses (except John at the end, who got off Old Jo—quite fortunately as Jo fell twice), although the hill was pretty nearly vertical and the soil was so deep and slick that I wondered how we could do it. At the top we could see that we were in an old corn field—high up with a steep slope leading down—unmarked by any trail we could see. Then we began to pitch down. I must confess that I expected any moment to pitch over Dales's head or have him fall with me under him. But down we moved—inch by inch—sidling along. I could hear the bleating of lambs about me and as we passed a big log, could just distinguish two baby white fellows trying to seek protection below it. They were bleating in chorus, and I was glad to hear an old sheep answering not far away. By the time we struck Puncheon Fork, it was black, and we could see nothing. Occasionally we passed the lights of a house and once Buckner's saw-mill—but I had no idea how we were going. At length we forded a creek and Rich told us we were on the way to the main road. He went back and we pushed on alone single file. Our only guide was Mr. W.'s white horse, of whose back we could distinguish a patch. Every few minutes he would halloo and we answering splashed on again. It was raining a little less—but black and dreary enough. The cabins we passed—distinguishable only by the flicker of the open fires—seemed as unattainable as if we were outlawed.

Suddenly we came out on the big road and all the horses plucked up new spirit and pushed ahead. Uphill or downhill—we could not tell. We trotted swiftly ahead hallooing back and forth, splashing through fords—spattering through mud, stumbling over rocks and stones. It was only three miles—but it seemed a good five. Once all the horses bolted off sharply to the right—to a familiar house. How Mr. W. knew they were wrong and turned back, I don't know, but we swung about and somehow got back in the right road.

All was dark at Dr. English's house. Not a sign of life. Mr. W. hallooed—with a final response. It was only 8 o'clock—but the good doctor had gone to bed (been out the night before delivering a 16 year girl of an illegitimate child. Had

had old woman trying for 12 hours and girl was fearfully lacerated) and his wife too. He rose nobly to the occasion however and soon came out. Mr. W. and John pulled me off the horse and I staggered with Mrs. W. into the house.

Mrs. English had got up and was throwing wood on the fire so that we had a great blaze. We pulled off what damp things we could and spread them around to dry, while the men put up the horses. Mrs. English the meanwhile went out and got us hot coffee, hot biscuits, fried pork and preserves, which we did justice to. Mrs. W. used some of our lemons bought in Burnsville for hot lemonade, which threw us into good perspiration.

We had good feather beds and John undressed me and washed my feet. Mrs. W. came in and massaged my ankle with liniment and Mr. Webb put on a tight bandage. My! But we were glad to roll into that bed and to sleep!

I couldn't step on my foot without pain in the morning—but we were all cheerful. Our clothes were almost dry and the day was fair. Mrs. E. had a good breakfast and all was well. Neither the Dr. or his wife would take anything—and Mrs. English waited to do our dishes until we were off.

Got off about 9 A.M. The day was not sunny but clear until the clouds began to roll swiftly down the mountain side. After we crossed Streets Gap into Tennessee, it grew chill too. We rode in the clouds until well into Flag Pond—when the sun began to peep through. Had a good [ ] of mail to read—my foot soaked in water and rebandaged—and a general peaceful P.M. to conclude our adventures.

FEBRUARY 17th, Flag Pond: A gray morning with a sprinkling of snow but a glorious clearing before we started out. In spite of the cold night, the day was brilliant—enough crispness in the air to bring the blood to one's cheeks. Dale trotted swiftly along and we pressed behind. Followed the road to Devils Fork and then over mountains to Shelton Laurel. Mountains were magnificent—the cloud fog in which we had ridden the day before—had crystallized on every twig and the mountain tops were glistening and spangled—every twig distinct. I never saw anything more beautiful—especially with the contrast below the frost line of the rich laurel greens. Enjoyed every minute of the ride and my foot gave me little trouble.[11]

Found Dr. Bissell to be the sister of the Miss Bissell at Brooks Hall—whom we met when dining with Mabel Weeks. Got warmed up over fine open fire and had a jolly chicken dinner. Stayed till Miss Ballad, the teacher, came over, a pretty, dignified woman of perhaps 30. (Many illegitimate children in school), Says girls give her more trouble than boys, get mad and sullen—won't speak. Also says girls are crazy over boys—animal seems to be as strong (stronger?) than boys when young.

Madison County, Township #2, District #8:
104 children school age; 72 enrolled:—21 illegitimate
13 Sheltons,
6 Hensleys,
5 married.
One woman of 20 married, and her child of six come to school—both of school age.

[Drawings of house interiors here with comments:]

Heaps of people in this house—Couldn't even estimate number.
Three in a bed usual at least.
Exceptionally poor household.
Room 10 feet square—no porch—father, mother and nine children.
All the cooking outfit: pot, one bread pan, 1 big spoon—

Does not find children or grown-ups feeble or sickly, and not such a great amount of tuberculosis in this particular region—couldn't say what counted majority of cases. Hadn't met much venereal disease. One case of appendicitis. Several miscarriage and obstetric cases. Two cases meningitis. At first had trouble in getting pay—coming better now—also people used to calling on Miss Goodrich and Miss Fish. Moral conditions very bad—about 1/2 children illegitimate. Some regular street walkers—but women more often settled in home. Told of 2 women who had large families—several sets by different men—each set going by father's name. One man has sets by both women. One woman finally married by man she had nursed in sickness. The girl became [pregnant] and came to have baby at father's house. For a wonder, father turned her out and she had baby on big road.

Told of man (Champ Briggs) who had nice wife. Runs now still—(?) gets drunk but has a very charming personality. Before she (Dr. B)—came he got to running with another woman—who became jealous of wife. Came over and fought wife, pulled clothing nearly off. Wife left with children and is now living with another man. Second woman now lives with Champ as wife. Has a lot of nice looking children who come to school. I saw one. Same man got drunk and fell off horse last winter in crossing mountain. Bitter night and half froze both feet; would not have [them] amputated and they rotted off.

Another case of man who was running with two women (this also happened before her time). Second woman jealous, loaded up on whiskey, came down to 1st woman's cabin. No. 1 retired and shut door. No. 2 shot through 4–5 times, finally wounding No. 1 in neck. Bullet passed down above heart. Dr. Hensley could not find in probing. Mrs. Webb assisted at operation. The woman lived and is now married.

Sometimes women seem to live with one for a time and then swap off. Little if any sentiment on the subject. Children seem to be well and strong. Could not see that mountain people were feeble. Of 27 women in house at meeting—only one with clear reputation—something out of the way in every other case or in family.

About four P.M. we mounted and rode down the Shelton Laurel to the Allegheny House. It is a beautiful path between high hedges of rhododendron—fording the creek often—a fascinating creek—clear and swift—with big footlogs. (Above the upper house). There are places where the sun never reaches in winter or summer—deep dark cool places—green with rhododendron and sheltered by high cliffs. The Allegheny House is very prettily situated—and has a little cottage behind. All these schools here are run with the public school (4 months). In some cases the Board owns the school building and some places the county.

Found the teacher Miss Smith, a pleasant young girl—just graduated from the [Asheville] Normal. Miss Fish (Miss Goodrich's trusty lieutenant) made herself very pleasant. Showed us some homespun at 1.50 a yard—to the price of which Mr. Webb objected. Had a rather brisk discussion but otherwise Mr. W. was elaborately polite—John rather silent. Got to bed early—had Miss S. room—a very pleasant one.

FEBRUARY 18th: Much amused and irritated in A.M. John and I were downstairs 2 minutes after bell rang—and found Miss F. seated and serving. She made no apologies and so we didn't. Found later that this is one of her peculiarities.

While the men were harnessing etc. talked with Miss F. She spoke very reasonably but from a pinnacle of self-satisfaction. Did not find much sickness—tuberculosis etc. Moral conditions were different from our standards. People lived together without marriage many times. Often man would have a number of children (who were known as his and so called in various communities) and then marry and settle down O.K. No sentiment [ ] in community. She thought the greatest going wrong for girls—came through saw-mill hands, who went from community to community without settling down. Girls waited on them (where they boarded)—several beds in room etc. etc. Result natural and inevitable. Girls—some of them—regularly went wrong—street walkers? Others because "he said he was going to marry me." Seemed to think this freed them from blame. Told of young man going with two girls. Finally he married one and no. 2 began to appear in cheap finery—was living with sister—who was not married to man she lived with. Transpired later that this girl (No. 2) was living way up the mountain at head of creek with young man—in his father's cabin. Father also living with woman to whom he was not married. (Had a sister the same kind). Miss F. had had no chance to speak to girl—but one night—when they were having a box-party at the school, she found her sitting outside in the laurel. Asked her why she was there. Girl said she was "waiting for Kit." He was inside as large as life. Miss F. said she then asked her if she was married and why not? Girl said she had not wanted to be—till just now (enceinte) and Kit was ashamed to go and get the license. Finally through Miss F's help and perseverance and some one talking to Kit, the license was got and all fixed up happy and serene. O.K. now.

Only glanced in at school. About 30 in attendance. Miss F. says she finds people honest but with a different conception of what—for instance—a cord of wood is. Dr. B. says people say that Miss F. pays just what they ask.

The morning was warm and beautiful. Had a lovely ride to Allanstand—uneventful. Found Mr. Carmichel (new baby in house) pleasant but new to the game, and evidently uninitiated. There is a school building and good sized teachers house (where Carmichels live) and across the road—a two-room log cabin (one room for minister) the seat of the famous Allanstand industries. No loom in room now—just a collection of odds and ends—few baskets, rolls of wool, etc. Mr. C. said industries had gone down and were now reviving. We saw a Louise Payne weaving a carpet (cover pattern) in a cabin 1/4 mile away. Perhaps there are 3–4 women around who are weaving for Miss Goodrich. There are several, I understand, in another county. A great question as to whether total profit would be $1000 a year. Miss G. pays women $1.50 a yard for linsey—which can be bought at Flag Pond for 50 cents a yard. A questionable jump in price? Louise Payne weaves carpet at 50 cents a yard. Can do housework and weave one yard a day. Miss G. furnished wool. Can weave 4 or 5 yards of linsey a day. Takes three days to set up web—warping, etc.[12]

We had already eaten our lunch on a log, but Mr. Carmichel insisted on our sitting down to the table. Were invited to see the baby—but thought it best not to go up. Left about 3 and rode back to Carmen stopping at Allegheny to get our saddle bags and say goodbye to Miss Smith. Found we had just missed Dr. Boyd, who is inspecting schools for Womans Board. He has been on John's and my heels ever since we left Ky. Met Miss Fish on the way and said our adieus.

Had a jolly eve with Dr. Bissell and Miss Ballad. Sang Williams songs (I played!) and talked till quite late over open fire. Cracked jokes!

FEBRUARY 19th: Had a good night in Miss Ballad's pretty room and awoke to a pouring morning. Fortunately, it cleared about 9.30, and after writing and singing, we started home. Warm and gray. Got back about 12.30 and got our mail.

At Allandstand, teacher—Miss Schartle.

Enrollment, 15 attendance 10.

FEBRUARY 23rd, Tuesday, Flag Pond: Mrs. Webb and I made an expedition this P.M. on weaving matters. A windy afternoon with clouds piling up. I rode Dale astride, with Mrs. W. behind. Went up Rice Creek—a very pretty and well populated way. Called first on Mrs. Blankenship—in a small house to the right of the road. On the opposite side lower down an old house was evident—loom up on porch, a good-sized barn and several out buildings, a good deal of stock. The Blankenships have the reputation of being great workers. Mr. B. buys and sells stock, works on farm—8 children—2 at Farm and Home Industrial at Asheville.[13] Mrs. B. is great-grand-daughter of John Sevier—quite a fine looking dark woman—with pleasant brown eyes and cordial manner.[14] Looked to me as if she had goiter. Two beds in room and open fire.

Statistics are so—

1 lb. wool= .25

5 lb. warp= 1.25 (weaves 30 yards)

1 lb. wool= ? (depends on waste)

6 lb. wool= probably weave enough for 13 yards cloth

Little over 2 lb. yarn weaves five yards. Has woven 12
yards for $1.00—but thought it hardly paid; 10 yards
for $1.00 fairer.

Says she is not a fast weaver—especially now with so much housework, field work, and is not well. Says a good fast weaver like Mrs. Profitt can weave five or six yards a day. Woman can hardly spin 2 yds a day, except with help. (Mrs. Profitt's daughter does her carding). Weaving is comparatively easy when wool is cleaned, walnut roots dug (1 day) and wool dyed. Warping and spinning is very tedious work—(Mrs. P's conversation).

Mrs. B. told us how she used to make indigo dye—boiled it up with the madder etc. It certainly makes the finest dark blue—never faded. Told of her first weaving. Spoke with warmth of her work. Said she was mighty fussy about having no roughness or knots in her cloth. All her girls can spin and weave. Her girl in the Home Industrial wrote home that a good loom they had there made her want to weave.

Mrs. Proffitt's house is quite picturesque. Stands back at end of long lane. Hung on one stirrup while I unfastened and opened gate. Log house (recently sheathed) and 2 roomed. Recess between two, with spinning wheel tucked in and big basket. Vines in front. In showing us some weaving slays (?) she pulled them out from under roof of porch.

Room we sat in had four regular beds—one makeshift on long window box—trunk: [Drawing of room]

Mrs. Profitt has worn but sweet face—10 children. Mrs. P. however is considered even over careful with her girls. When men spend the night there, her girls sleep in the kitchen and men do not go in till girls are up and dressed. Mrs. P. has tried to get in, in morn, (men sleep in room with her and "old man") and found big table jammed up vs. [against] the door. This she told us the other day. Also told of a niece who got into trouble. Sister died and husband and children came to live at father-in-law's house. Girl frequently up with children and sleeping in room with man. Old folks go off for days and weeks together and leave girl with brother-in-law. Inevitable re-sult—but old people did not discover matter till night of birth of child. Thought girl sick and doctored her for consumption. And all the time, Mrs. P. said the girl was red and hearty. When girl began to be sick—man arose and called old people, and then vamoosed with house deeds and property. Old people astonished and angry—threatened to turn children onto big road. Man came back at that and wedding was fixed up.

Told of another girl who slept with saw-mill hands and got into trouble.

Mrs. P. said she would just love to get hold of some indigo and fuss with it. It was a heap of trouble—but—it certainly made a pretty color and it never faded. She corroborated Mrs. Blankenship's statement, that to make a pretty gray, one must have good rich colors—a rich black and clear white. Her least one—a pretty girl of 4—Eunice—already helps to card a little.

Mrs. Webb made good arrangement for Mr. W.'s suit but I had to give up mine at present—as women must soon go into field and garden to work. Mrs. P. said some people didn't want to pay .50 for linsey—she reckoned if they made it, they'd be willing.

FEBRUARY 26th: Got off from Flag Pond about noon—laden with baggage. John rode the white (suitcase strapped behind and saddlebags as usual) and Mrs. W. and I rode Dale and carried saddlebags. Had a pleasant, uneventful ride. Creeks much swollen and water rushing in places into my stirrup-hoods. Ate lunch as we went along. Made Loves in the region of 4 and found train 1.20 hours late. Mrs. Webb decided to take Dale through to Erwin, while John and I repacked trunk and waited for train. Mrs. W. met us with Miss Wintzar—one of the teachers.

Erwin: Found that our arrival had been anticipated by Baptists who are eager to start opposition school. However, we got safely up to Presbyterian school and had good supper. Talked in eve with Miss Wyeth (Park College) and Miss Wintzar who is from West Grove, near Mendenhall, Pa. Her father is a florist (French)—famous for roses and hybridizing cannas. Knows Mr. Kelsey. Old story of small Presbyterian congregation in church and Baptist opposition. School draws city aristocracy (enrolls over 100—about 60 in attendance which wanes with year). Railroad shops are to be put in here and all is on the boom. Miss Wyeth thinks outlook dull for school. Does not wish to conflict with public school (present one very bad—no desks—no discipline—children on streets). Possibly new engineers etc. will demand good public school. Doubtful. Says they need a man for principal—thinks people neither "strong—honest or eager for education." Property—good brick school and wood cottage.

FEBRUARY 27th: Left Erwin about 9 A.M.—the teachers walking to the train with us. Met Mr. Bailey, of Burnsville there also two Baptist brethren who tackled John on matter of school. Our reputation was of millionaires who were looking for places to throw their money. Mr. Bailey went up on train with us and regaled us all the way by tales of shooting etc.—especially of the times when he was putting through this road (the old 4 C's), in 1869 ? (89?). Lots of whiskey and lots of shooting. It being Saturday—pay day—we saw plenty of the former—in express bundles at the stations. Stations also lined with workmen. Fare is 4¢ a mile in Tennessee, and 2–1/2¢ in N.C.—and every one buys a ticket to Camp Bottom—the border—a place of shacks, whiskey and shooting. Man shot there the other day. Told how once he was called at midnight to get doctor for shot man. Rode along in dark and just as they came into light from cabin door—a revolver was stuck up into faces. Man loaded with moonshine, wanted to see who they were. Revenue officers? Wounded man was shot right through abdomen, but men would not let the doctor touch him—so the ride was for nothing. Went home disgusted.

Ride is really beautiful—gorge very narrow in places—Nolichucky River very swift and rushing—then up along the Cane proper and North Cane Fork. If the curves had not been so sharp, and my breakfast more settled, I should have delighted in every inch of the ride. As it was, we were both glad to get off at Penland.[15]

Found it a mere cluster of houses about a mica mill. Mr. Bailey who seemed to be general manager (125 families in employ) station-agent and store keeper (also arranged land rent, etc.) directed us up to his house where Miss H. is staying at present. She was not there, but Mrs. Bailey received us cordially and ushered us into room where little sick girl was lying with five cats and 2 dogs. They are Knoxville people (Mr. B. originally from near Bakersville). House crowded (some boarders) but a new little room—built of porch was being concocted for us. In the meanwhile we had dinner, and waited for Miss H. who came in about 3 P.M.—after night with woman whom she delivered of child (dead 6–8 weeks before birth). Says she has had 200 cases of childbirth since coming (7 yrs ago) and has never lost child or mother. At first tried to work with doctors but they preferred her to take own cases. A good deal of opposition on doctors' part and suspicion (now overcome) on part of people. Doctors very poor—no degree. Women especially are sacrificed in childbirth. Men marry many times. Wives simply drudges and servants of men's desires. Doctor never sent for till last moment. Generally, Miss H. says, she gets paid somehow—though people prefer to pay in anything else than money, (Mr. B. says people don't want to pay in anything—will get out of it every time). Miss H. says doctors will not look at case unless $5.00 is sure either in money—or mortgage. Will mortgage man's last sheep, cow etc. (I remember Mr. and Mrs. Webb think nurse should only work with doctor. Doctor knows best what people can pay and may seem cruel—but are right in exacting so much payment before coming).[16]

At Low Gap also, Miss Hazlett spoke of doctors refusing to come on bad nights to people who cannot pay etc. and

Mrs. Webb criticized her (to me) for going where doctor would not go. Said people worked it on her—saved money, etc. Miss Holman says she gives much advice gratis—which irritates doctors. Tells rheumatic people not to eat so much meat (tells them that this advice is on patent medicine bottle—which they believe)—and to drink lots of water. Has been reported to Judge—who however could find nothing against her. New man (doctor) organized medical society to shut her out. (She was not asked to join). Reported her as practicing illegally. She went to lawyer who said this doctor had not had training himself. Had been member of legislature (shady reputation) and put through a law which enabled him to practice.

Does not think people immoral in our accepted city point of view. It is rather animalism. So much sleeping together, 5 etc. in bed—brother and sister-in-laws, strangers etc. At big meetings everyone crowds into near-by houses. There are cases of bad women—but she only knows two. Told of conversation with old Baptist preacher, who said he didn't believe his name was Duncan. Great-grand parents had not been married. Father came in from nowhere and when two babies had come, built wife (?) cabin and up and left. Rode off on his horse no one knew where. Woman then had 5 children (by whom?) and finally married one of best families. Preacher himself said "yes" when some one said "And you are a baseborn child."

Disease however exceedingly common. Got all her experience here (though had seven (?) years of city practice in N.Y. and Philadelphia), Women suffering from diseased husbands etc. etc. Men take no care. As example cited case of that night where she told husband to go for surgical case in Ledger.[17] A little later he appeared and asked what she wanted to have her horse fed with. Said horse didn't need feeding—and remarked she thought she had asked him to go for case. Yes—but thought he would feed horse first. Miss H. told him to go at once and that when they (the men) learned to put their wives above animals, they might be able to keep wives longer with them. "Lordy—Miss Holman—she ain't dangerous, is she?" "Yes—she is dangerous—and you go and get the case just as fast as you can." He disappeared and didn't reappear till he had case—though he sent someone for it and waited outside himself. When she left, he said, "I reckon you'll teach us dumb fellows something sometime." Said woman would probably get well unless she continued to feel so well she would get up and go to cooking etc. according to general mountain practice.

A great deal of intermarriage. In one settlement—people degenerated to nothing practically. Much insanity (most of imbecility, insanity and epilepsy in the men). Many men go all to pieces in religious meetings and have to be shut up a while—too weak in mind to endure emotional strain. Jail is terrible place as insane are shut up here as well as prisoners. Told of preacher—sick with a dozen ailments (for which wife recommended whiskey. He was a reformed drunkard). When analyzed, case appeared to be that when preacher came home from long meetings, he was all used up. Not surprising. Miss H. says she had found in jail—all together—two idiot epileptics, one raving insane—one murderer (two the next week)—three moonshiners. Insane had cell but bars opened into main hall. Murderer in iron cage in middle of room. Was also an insane girl (less so than man) who had torn off shoes and burned them up (stone floor)—and pulled off most of her clothes. Her cell opened by grates into same hall above. She was taken half clothed to asylum by the sheriff—though Miss H. had clothes ready for her. Jailer's wife offended at her for offering them.[18]

Women deaths average higher than men's—so many die at childbirth—in child with fever (often caused by men)—or neglect afterwards. One case in neighborhood—children were 9 months and 10 days apart. After birth of child, has had to tell husband that bed was wife's *alone* for 2 weeks. Incest and abortion both are *not* uncommon. Cited two cases of former. Said she did not believe it at first. Doctors quite generally immoral and have children all around the country. Miss H. said the only one in county from whom she would take orders—was an inebriate and then only when he was sober. Doctors in it for gain. Told of case where she and another doctor were sent for. She came first and when other doctor came and found he was not needed, he sat down outside. The moment he heard her say, "All right—the baby has come" (girl was 14—) he collected $5.00 and went. She told me two unbelievably horrible stories of doctor's brutality. Said that ethically and professionally, she did not approve of herself at all—for practicing, but practically, it was the only thing she could do. Tuberculosis most common, often result of neglected pneumonia. Says typhoid is mild. "mountain fever." Contagious diseases not especially common.

FEBRUARY 28th: Talked most of A.M. and in P.M. rode over to Ledger. John had Mr. Bailey's horse—a magnificent black—while I rode gentle Dan with a comfortable gait. Had a lovely ride. The mountains are very wild about here (altitude 2400 and peaks 5–6000 feet). Followed up the creek, which glittered with mica—and by Keohie Mills—3 miles to Ledger. Looked over good little library (cottage for librarian) school (manual—T. equipment for boys) and teachers cottage. The school part can be bought for $1200—half of which could be raised by the people. People would also tax themselves for school—raising about $800 a year. Looked over Miss H.'s prospective home built by Mrs. Ervine, former president of Wellesley.[19] Then we trotted up to Prof. Wing's (once of Tech-Boston) former home—now owned by a friend of Miss Holman—a very charming log house with all sorts of outside accessories—dark room—smoke house—power house—work-shop, smithy etc. Played with the pretty 6 mos. colt of Miss H.'s mare Dorothy, who was fearfully jealous. John let his big black out on the road and had a great gallop.

We had a wonderful ride home. Took a different way—up a rough creek and over a mountain—taking down bars and picking our way across gulleys and down along a scratch in the mountain side. It was entirely dark, except for a half moon, and the most brilliant starry sky. One great luminous star in particular hung low over the mountain tops in the east. Could just distinguish a few puffs of cloud—all that was left of the fluffy masses and detached puffs that were so beautiful against the clear cold blue at sunset time. Air was cold—my feet got quite stiff—but the night was too wonderful to mind it. When we finally crawled down the mountain side, we found a better road and went along a ridge between black trunks and tall bushes. Long tree shadows lay across the road. Part of the time I was behind—and was amused at the romantic picture, presented by John and Miss H., who rode along side-by-side in the moonlight—talking. Near home we left my horse and John put me on his big black which bolted for home—a fine great creature. John walked up. Mrs. Bailey had supper kept for us and we did it justice.

6

MARCH 1909

NORTH CAROLINA

Full of information we got off on Monday, March 15th, with the affectionate farewells of all the household, the girls waving from the windows. Even at the station John had a hasty last interview with the Superintendent of Southern Presbyterian work, Mr. P. S. Smith. Then Dr. Winston joined us just in time to catch the 3:35 P.M. train to Waynesville, where, talking interestingly all the way, he drove us up to see the magnificent view at Eagles' Nest. We parted with him at Dillsboro, he returning to Asheville, we continuing by buggy—John driving, and the driver following us on horseback—to Franklin, the northern terminus of the little railroad which passed through Demorest. At the Demorest station, Miss Sheak, Miss Rawn, and Jessie were awaiting us with a joyful welcome. The house was ready; supper was all but on the table. And so we returned from our wanderings—as my Line-A-Day put it, "a jolly homecoming."[1]

MARCH 1st: A lovely sunny morn which we idled away—making telephone connections—talking and cracking walnuts with the Bailey children. Miss Holman and Miss Jones saw us off at the train about eleven.

At Spruce Pine we got dinner and after a wait, our ponderous hack drove up. Both felt tired and lumbered slowly along over the bad roads. Arrived at Plumtree about 5.30, to find Mr. Hall away and all in confusion—owing to the December fire.[2] A few boys—in uniform were playing ball outside—cots on the piazza unpacked etc. etc. Mr. Hall's mother—an old lady, came down—much flurried and took us to her room, where we had a most disconnected talk with Joe, her son—as theme, her adventures during the war as refugees from Petersburg, and her losses during the fire (15 half gallon jars cherries, 5 new pairs blankets and a box of letters). She was a nice old lady—but could not give much information about the school, except that it was for poor boys, and that they all wanted to go into the ministry. Later we met several teachers and the doctor (whose wife is also a doctor I understand). They didn't invite us to stay in the infirmary so we went on (6.30 P.M.) to a house a few steps below for the night.

Evidently the old man was in a gloomy frame of mind. He was picking up wood as we came along—and as John called out—cheerily—asking if he would take in some strangers, he hardly looked up and simply answered gruffly, "No—I reckon not tonight." So we drove on. The horses were tired and it was almost dark—the road rough and no near houses. Finally we came to a cabin—and asked where we could "get to stay." He said at "West Franklin" (3–1/2 miles from Plumtree). So we pushed on in the dark. It was cloudy—but fortunately the moon (at half) gave light enough to watch bridges and bad turns.

About 8 P.M.—we made Franklin Store, and the driver, going up the lane to ask, returned with affirmative answer. We found an old two story house—and were ushered into a room with big wood fire and two beds (with woven kivers.) The old man was sitting by the fire with his two sons (one in Plumtree.) Said he had raised 4 boys but couldn't keep them at home—all crazy for an education. Barney was a nice looking chap—and the 2nd (helping at home) also had a good face. The old man had a pleasant ruddy face, grey eyes and bushy beard. Finally Mrs. F. came to bid us to supper—a (strange looking) little bent dark woman—with round too-brilliant eyes, and wrinkled face. Kitchen and food appeared clean. I sat and talked to her after John went back with men. Room had two beds (boy of 2–3 asleep in one)— cookstove and open fire—table in middle. Around the fire sat three little girls—the oldest, Ina, 15—dark and bent like the mother. Mrs. F. informed me that "Iny" had the most terrible cough—had had it since 1 yr old and coughed up pure corruption that smelt the most awful you ever smelt; that the doctors couldn't do anything for her but said she would outgrow it. She reckoned, however, that they only said that to encourage her. (We heard the poor child hacking and hacking away the next morning. She was evidently on the porch outside the kitchen door—spitting on the ground). The second child had had a stroke of paralysis—but was well now, though she couldn't use her right hand much. The youngest Americy—was a pretty shy little thing. Mrs. F. had had 12 children—3 dead.

Seeing Americy yawn, I suggested she looked sleepy— whereupon the mother said it was past their bed time. "Pull off your stockings—children, and jump into bed." This being literally obeyed, we adjourned to the front room for bed. Mrs. Franklin appointed our bed and got off the cover to the other—evidently preparatory for Mr. Ray our driver— but was circumvented by Barney, the school boy, who said he would take Mr. Ray upstairs.

I asked Mrs. F. if she had heard of Miss Holman, and she said she had—that she was the one that rode around just like a man. Evidently the report was good—for at our solicitation, she reckoned she'd take Iny over to Spruce Pine to see her. I couldn't much enjoy my breakfast with Iny coughing at the door and reports of typhoid near at hand—but we did eat something. Barney was off to school on horseback at 7 and we were off by 7.30.

The morn—after a rainy night, was damp and chill. I was much distressed all the way to Montezuma by the deadenings—such a wasteful unsystematic scheme—killing shade trees by the road, which did not interfere at all with the clearings. Saw a number of good-sized apple orchards—simply massed with lichens.

We made Montezuma near ten—a scattered group of buildings, through which the narrow-gauge puffed—laden with timber—at the rate of 8 miles in 2 hours. We drove up to the Methodist preacher's house—to ask about the school and found him a new young Alabaman (Mr. Jackson—looked like Hugh Bissell)—and didn't know much about the school. A good building from outside. Poor teachers had brought about small attendance, but church was planning to build it up. Had only run till November that year. His wife, in dressing jacket, played with the baby. Had come from Mississippi and wasn't much pleased with the mountains. We got new directions at Mr. Banner's store and started on to Linville.[3]

The country grew steadily more beautiful—trees preserved—the great hemlocks banked with rhododendron. The Linville (creek) proved to be a charming, rushing creek—clear and sparkling (and fish, we were told, everywhere with fish). The Linville Improvement Co. owns a great tract of land there (some MacRaes—mill owners in Wilmington, N.C. are kingpins)—and regulate the town. There is a grand big summer hotel—some cottages—golf links etc. Visitors pay 50¢ a day to fish in creek or lake.

We were told we could reach Blowing Rock so pushed on

up famous made road—20 miles between Linville and Blowing Rock. Found beautiful views and fine rugged woodland. At about two we stopped up at the house of Alexander MacRae—on the highest point of the road 5000 feet.

Mrs. MacRae—a fine looking old Scotchwoman ushered us in and said she would get us dinner, and soon Alexander—a fine strong old man came in. Both were full of delight to have a Scotch descendent—and company anyway and the old man said we could not make Blowing Rock that night. So we joyfully piled in before the open fire—while Mrs. MacRae made us Scotch oatcake and the old man told us how he had come to this country 24 years ago—of the Inverness county where he was born, land and rent laws and opinions of America.

After dinner, it seemed so warm and lovely that Mr. MacRae took us up on the Grandfather. A well graded road runs up some 1-1/2 miles beyond the house—beautiful all the way, but with a superb view at the top where a group of boulders jut out some. Above rose two great crags, 600–700 feet above us, their bases swathed in a thick growth of fir balsam. Below lay blue swales of woodland and distant rugged peaks outlined against the sky—now masses of cloud swept over them, changing them to purple or ending them in mist—and against the sun glittered over them. We stood fastened to the rock—till old Alexander declared we would catch cold. Reluctantly we turned away and the enchanted Mr. Ray—who had never seen such a sight before—dug up some little balsam trees to take home. We found later that he had likewise cut some sticks of mountain birch—for he informed us—on the way to Valle Crucis—that he had picked some "tooth-brushes for my wife" up on Grandfather, and also that she was "a dear lover of snuff." It struck me as a tender husbandly remembrance. I suppose they have sociable times—he chewing and she dipping (a practice which old Alexander dubbed "filthy.") The wind was rising higher as we went down and light showers began to fall. We had a good dinner and in the eve sang to the old people, and played on the piano while Alexander regaled us with the bagpipe—and we talked more Scotland. They were exceedingly loath to let us go off to bed—but we tumbled in near 10 P.M.

We awoke to a blinding snow storm, which however (after we had unharnessed and prepared to wait) fell off about 10 and we started out. The first few miles were truly wonderful—with every twig snow-laden and outlined against blue distances. To our left, the side of old Grandfather was hung with constant drifting masses of cloud from the blue—and sadly enough, as we got out of the shelter, these began to descend on us with a heavy cold wind—which pursued us all the 17 miles to Blowing Rock. The blue clouded over, constant driving snow flurries overtook us and the drive was raw and bitter—although the views were continually wonderful with mountains and drifting cloud and storm.

We were glad enough to pass the fine Cone estate (with landscape—garden and apple orchards) and pull into the settlement.[4] Found it quite a pleasant little place—and went to the Watauga Inn for dinner and horse feed. Sent a note to Miss [Par???] Saying we had decided to spend the night at the hotel, but she wrote us that she should be much disappointed if we did not come there. So after dinner (Mr. Ray suggested that it was powerful cold and that if we were going we had better go early)—we started off again—the 3/4 mile to Skyland.[5] Mr. Ray drove back to stay at the hotel (and the wind rose so that it tipped over the hack on the return.)

We found the school chilly but cordial. Two sisters were running it on trial—with a young girl as assistant. Had only 7 boarders—all girls (but one boy for wood, chores etc) who did the housework. It seems there is a 7 months good public school here—as well as one for Mr. Cone's tenants and near-by children, and although the feeling is good, there seems to be considerable doubt as to advisability and necessity of keeping up the school. Sisters were from near Rochester, N.Y. One had been at Saluda and one at Joppa, Ala. (Latter said everyone still spoke of John there as the only real thing)— were new to work in Blowing Rock and doubtful themselves. Did not know a great deal of conditions. We had a good time talking however—until almost 11 P.M. [Note in margin: Good saleable property—fine view and situation. Dormitory and school building would make good house.]

The wind blew tremendously all night and we awoke to sunny skies, but a drifted world. Mr. Ray walked out and said that all said it would be impossible to make Valle Crucis till the wind went down. Narrow cuts would be drifted 10 feet deep (not much snow but all there is, drifts) and wagon would blow over. So we spent a peaceful morn. In P.M.—John and I wrapped up and struggled down to the town to call on the Episcopal minister, Mr. Savage. Found him a gentle pleasant rather melancholy man much interested in sailors. Finds climate very trying at B.R. Seemed liberal—allowing and calling for extempore prayer ("as reading-room where service is held in winter, is not consecrated"). Also had had other men preach there. Said mountaineers thought the Episcopalians were Catholics—so got few converts. Nothing else especially important. Got back to early dinner and had early bed.

MARCH 5TH: Awoke to a still morning—cold air and brilliant sun. Got off about 9 A.M. and had cold rough drive to Valle Crucis. Roads were pretty well drifted and mountains were covered with snow. Looked very beautiful. Mr. Ray felt deject-ed—especially as the Watauga Inn people had put him in cold room where snow blew in. Had to sweep it out, make own bed and own fire. Had never known such weather before.

Got into Valle Crucis a little before one, and found two imposing looking buildings (one of concrete not finished) up on the hillside overlooking a level valley.[6] We climbed the slippery slope and Miss Tongue came out to meet us. Met the two deacons—Mr. Seagle and Mr. Dobbs—and various teachers—among them a Mrs. _____ from N.C. The kitchen-dining-room and school are in one building (a few rooms above). So after dinner we went back to concrete building and I spent most of P.M. talking to Miss Tongue, Mrs. _____, and Mrs. Randall especially. She thinks need of highlands is greater than lowlands (people could take care of poor whites if they were roused to interest—and thinks they morally are not bad)—the mountaineers, on the contrary.

Blowing Rock where she has summer home, is vastly improved from what was 10 years ago, when she couldn't go out on street alone in the evening on account of drunken men. Saturday P.M. you could see people coming in everywhere with tin pails for Sunday moonshine. Schools have done some—but prohibition more. Prohibition has undoubtedly been a success (this was confirmed by Mr. Seagle—who asserted emphatically that the change was due to prohibition rather than schools, although latter of course trained people to see advantage of former.) Morally Blowing Rock is better than Valle Crucis—illegitimacy in almost every family in V.C. Cited one woman with 7 children—all by different fathers. Some in school. Great vulgarity among boys and girls—marriage only regarded in animal light. Said Bishop wanted boys and girls together, but they had found it impracticable in this region.

John visited blacksmith shop and wagon factory—also hen affair. Here they originally raised fancy breed of chick-

ens and made money, but Bishop wanted it to help people—
so shut down and started up with breeds which the people
can own.

We had a very pleasant time sitting about the fire in the
eve talking. Laundry in building and room is planned upstairs for dispensary with trained nurse. At meals—small tables instead of usual long fashion.

MARCH 6th, Saturday: Awoke to pouring rain. John spoke
at chapel and after a look over buildings—Mr. Ray drove up
the hack and off we went—rattling along between closed curtains. Were both tired and sleepy so rumbled along indifferently. Rain let up toward noon and we pulled into Banner
Elk, driving up to Dr. Reed's house.[7] Had a most cordial reception—finding both Dr. and Mrs. Reed alert and pleasant.
Four attractive children. Had a delicious dinner and talked
two hours. Dr. R. was urged to come by Mr. Tufts. Given land
and house which is both dwelling and hospital when finished.
Promised money gave out in panic. Dr. R. has no salary, but
supports family on what he earns. Mrs. R. said she hoped
they could stay—but work precarious. Sometimes he did not
see $5.00 in a month. She herself had to do own washing and
housekeeping. Could get no help. Was ready, however, and
eager to teach in school next year, a class in invalid cookery. Dr. R. has only had a year's experience here—so spoke
guardedly, though along same lines as Miss Holman.

One thing of value he has instituted. Found boys had
nothing to do for amusement, so sat every night in store
and chewed and swapped bad stories. He set aside Thursday evening, got out all sorts of games, and put out papers
and magazines and invited boys in. Told them to bring pipes
and tobacco—and when in—told them to light up, or if they
chewed, to use the fireplace. Now you cannot keep them
away Thursdays and girls are interested.

School is doing fine work. Summer scheme is successful and few drop out for field work. Course in law so far. Great desire for industrial work. Teachers hard to procure and subjects have to be regulated by teachers procurable!

The children brought in their cats and dogs to show us. Dr. R. says he is example of what the climate and proper care can do for tuberculosis. Told of diet when they first came accounts for conditions. But hospital will have to grow slowly, as people are suspicious and slow to convince.

We got off about 3. Rain had stopped, so we viewed landscape. Snow still on mountains behind us, but it disappeared as we descended to Cranberry.[8] Much mud! A mile or two out of Cranberry, we met a little girl carrying a big heavy tin pail. Took her in to ride. Said she walked 3 miles. She however got out at Cranberry without a thank you.

I went in while John went out to interview the mine Superintendent, Mr. _____ a Scotchman. He said mountaineers made good miners though hampered by lack of education. When he first came, mines did not pay, but now paid and men earned $3.00 a day. Had difficulty in finding men well enough educated (and trustworthy?) to keep time (on piece jobs?). Had worked men up to subscribing for pay school.

The town was simply a group of mill shacks—many neatly painted and heaps and heaps of lumber piled about the terminus of the narrow-gauge to Johnson City.

[Note in margin: Saw long rattle-snake hide hanging on porch.]

MARCH 7th, Sunday: Off again at 8. A milder day with promise of rain. Had an interesting though depressing drive in some ways. Country less pretty. Came to one group of shacks where Mr. Ray said one insane family lived—all insane but one. As we came near, we saw three grown men and one boy running around outside, playing and shouting. One ran out to us and asked for a nickel which John gave him. These people look after themselves. Near this we met a crippled man, one with club feet—a woman with harelip and later two children who looked, but may not have been, foolish. Evidently a degenerate community.

Mr. Ray regaled our way with spasmodic conversation. Told us of a man (with whom he had worked) who had been raised in Massachusetts. This man had told him that the women up there never set foot out of the house to work, that is they never milked the cows. (He had never seen a woman in Mass. milk cows) and never went out for anything—to draw water for instance, even if it were a long way off.

Roads very muddy—but we made a short feed by the road. John and I walked a piece. Met several Plumtree boys who had been holding Sunday School down the road. Also met a negro funeral (body in open farm wagon). There were several white mourners.

Got into Spruce Pine about 4.30 and found Miss Holman waiting. At our solicitation she stayed over night—and we talked much. Told of girl (mother in insane asylum) who went to live with insane aunt and was going to marry son (her 1st cousin) of aunt. She and a doctor were trying to break off the match.

MARCH 8th, Monday: In the morning—which turned from gray to shower and later to pouring rain, we walked across river to where a friend of Miss Holman—a Miss Smith—has a summer shack. Saw some fine horses and dogs and then Mr. John English, the care-taker—a high type mountaineer—quite the English gentleman in appearance—(aristocracy) talked to us and popped corn for us and fed us on candy. Had a very jolly time before the big fire. Mr. E. says mountains are best for grass and stock. Had done some little mining in this region and in Georgia. We stopped at his store on the way back and saw some lovely cut aquamarines and garnets.

Took 11.00 train—Miss Holman with us—to Marion—a wonderful looping road around a shoulder of the Blueridge. The best train scenery we have had—truly beautiful in its mountain sweep and marvelous in engineering.

Said goodbye to Miss H. at Marion and started to drive the 2 miles to the Southern Station in 10 minutes over a very muddy road. We stepped along—but as we were coming into the main town, we saw the train approaching. We whipped up and hustled. Fortunately the train was late and had much baggage to load. We threw ourselves out of the surrey and tumbled aboard to the cry of "All aboard."

A pretty ride to Asheville. Got in about 5 and went to Berkley Hotel—which was dingy and smelt like a ship—but endurable. Had two busy days getting clothes, letters etc. John got hold of a nice stenographer. Also had a call from Miss Stephenson and Miss Johns.[9] Dr. Lawrence, who organized Normal & Collegiate, also came in. Wednesday eve we went out to the Home Industrial for dinner and future headquarters. Comfortable quarters and delicious food—the first that has tasted good since our arrival.

Ran over to Pease House for a few minutes in eve.[10] Saw the little chickabiddies sleeping upstairs and missionary meeting of older girls. Had prayer-meeting of older folks at Home Industrial later.

MARCH 11th, Thursday: My birthday! John got off at 6—to catch the early train to Marshall. I spent an extremely busy morning—under Miss Stephenson's laying out, inspecting work at the Normal and Industrial, (Miss Robinson as guide)—the Pease Memorial House and the Home Industrial itself. The first is quite a separate organization—with Dr. Childs at its head. Has its laundry (girls may hire theirs done if they wish), kitchen, dining room (teachers eat with pupils at breakfast and lunch and have dinner alone) etc. We went into a number of the normal classes in model teaching and glanced in at regular work. Miss Robinson is a N.Y. woman, has taught in N.Y. schools. Says, in many ways this is far more interesting. Girls very reserved and shy but blossom out and tell everything. Are like children.

At the Home Industrial, the girls do everything—going on by six weeks shifts. I followed them from bread-making, dish-washing, cooking—to sweeping, dusting and finally studies. Also went to chapel. Girls have regular studies in A.M. but in P.M. have industrial classes. For practical cooking, they cook teachers dinner (teachers dine alone). Have also scientific instruction. Also have class in practical home hints, signs of disease—contagion—nursing—care of children and sick etc. What impressed me was the power of Miss Stephenson's personality. She is keen, executive, and has power of organization (Miss Johns does the close finer work, attends to detail—the two dovetail) and yet is as sweet, tender and spiritual as any woman I have met. It is a pleasure to look at her eyes, which are big and dark, and they shine, too, with a delicate delightful appreciation of the humor of a situation. Has a decided social gift. The girls love her.

Tuition at the Home Industrial is $75—but few pay it all ($25 up). Miss Stephenson writes for scholarships (transacting all business carefully through the Board. Defended Board and its trials.) Miss Johns told me she (Miss S.) writes very well.

No distinction is made between scholarship pupils and those paying full tuition. Miss Johns told me needs of the place. The main building is old—full of dark corners. Much of the work must be done in basement under uninspiring conditions. Need of separate toilet arrangement to induce modesty in the girls. Girls came, irregular in all habits. Need to have watching and high ideals. Far too many sleep in same room—7 and 8. Miss Stephenson says that when factory girls come who have been put to work young, they have literally to be made over from scalp to toe-nails—are in bad physical condition. When they go in older, however, they do acquire a discipline and industry which makes them better pupils than those in small towns—who are left to own devices. Does not think them better than mountain girls.

In P.M. we gave a further look at the Pease House, which is for the young children (one 5 yrs) some of them orphans or dependents—or "too much parent." This department is run much as the Home Industrial—except of course the younger ones have washing done for them. They wash dishes, however, sweep, and do most of the work. We visited some cooking and sewing classes and a kitchen garden class. Mrs. Byers (Miss S.'s sister) is in charge of the little ones.

At 3.30, Miss Stephenson—by a carefully laid out plan, took me down town. Called first on Dr. Ambler—a man of 40—rather English looking and quite belligerent in defense of the people. Has tramped all over mountain region and resented their peculiar cases being represented as entirely typical.[11] Walked out of church the Sunday before (Episcopalian) when a missionary put this forth. Calmed down after a bit and we had a short chat on the unmoral aspect, tuberculosis and typhoid. Was approaching subject of venereal disease when we had to go. He wanted to see John.

Then we called on Dr. Fletcher, whose father doctored in mountains for years—around Waynesville. Was short pleasant and chatty but we did not get much down to business in our short call. Said there had always been tuberculosis in the mountains—due to living. Typhoid not so serious.

Next up to call on Mrs. (Bishop) Horner (the Bishop

being north), and found her awaiting us with Secretary, Mr. Stubbs and Dr. and Mrs. Winston.[12] Had a pleasant call and drank chocolate, but discussion was social—rather on picturesque aspect of the work. Mrs. Horner is a jolly, very executive (I should imagine) cheerful fashionable sort of person. Invited me to drive over Biltmore Estate with her, as she had special passes.

After dinner, we sallied forth again (Miss S. & I) to interview Dr. Swope (Epis. rector of Vanderbilt's church), at Biltmore.[13] Were ushered into a modern inartistic, though luxurious room, much besprinkled with rolls of wall paper. Shortly Mrs. Swope rolled in in elaborate silk gown and exchanged a few condescending words before sailing out again. Next followed the worthy Doctor. Much impressed with his relation to Vanderbilt. Without much greeting he sunk into chair and with a pom-pom air, asked "Did you want to interview me?" I stated my business and asked a few questions— whereat he gave me an account of Industrial Club of Biltmore and work at Arden. The former is in Mrs. Vanderbilt's care. She rides around in her carriage—and gets the women to weave, sells for them and rolls around to pay again. Woodwork, weaving and basketry are taught on the estate—about 150 being employed.

The Arden school is an independent organization begun by Mr. and Mrs. Wetmore. He died and she kept on the work. Dr. Swope informed us—rather unnecessarily I thought— that the Bishop (Chairman of Board of Directors) and Mrs. Wetmore did not agree, but "we" (pom-pom) adjusted the differences. Great difficulty in getting teachers. Original idea was to have buildings etc. no better than what people could have themselves—even fetched water from spring. This is changed now. "Teachers endure many inconveniences etc." Said that "we" (including self and _____) were skeptical as to

Valle Crucis. Bishop had sunk a good deal of money there. Wanted to know my opinion. He warmed up a little at the last, but I was glad to get away. We dropped in at the church a few minutes to an organ recital. Good organ, pretty well played. Got back about 9:30 P.M.

MARCH 12th, Friday: Father's birthday—Miss Bagwell here at 8 and I got a long letter off home. At nine our carriage drove up—and Mrs. Lawrence arrived to go with Miss Stephenson and me to the Farm School. The day was gray and chill, but we had a very pretty drive along the Swannannoa River and 8 miles over to the school. Maple trees in blossom and the bushes bursting into leaf. A very lovely country backed by Blueridge and Great Smokies. Red clay and green pines like Georgia.

Got out about 11—and I spent an interesting hour talking to Dr. Roger.[14] He was brought up on a farm, has a college and medical training (practiced a number of years in Canada)—also industrial training. Is a pleasant shy man who talks much and feels much. Said he could earn far more practicing and would never stay here—but that he saw such great results and possibilities. Has been there three years. Has little trouble with discipline on the whole, though boys find it hard at first—to learn that they must do certain things at certain hours. Says he tried to find common ground with each boy (and each case has its peculiar vital interest)—a ground on which he can talk as a friend and equal—confidentially and sympathetically (another, some work etc.) Says he generally finds some way to approach a boy—but if he doesn't, he feels that his own time and certainly that of the boy is being wasted. Much self abuse among the boys—but he has been astonished at the lack of disease from vice—either inherited or brought on. Says there is very little in case of mountain boys in school. With the boys from the mills it is more prevalent. Many of these go to mills from mountains, find themselves hampered by lack of education and come to school determined to learn. Are then more easy to handle in one sense, but have acquired the vices of civilization. Feels it bad to have so many in one room—especially the little boys with the older—but does not think an industrial school for little boys could be made to pay. Impracticable. Little boys need education but industrial school could not be run with economy. Farm does not pay now, but he thinks it can be worked up to a point where it will pay expenses. Summer work as part of tuition is, of course, expensive.

Has two [?] and is planning a more economical arrangement of crops. Says this land does not make good pasture (have not as high as the Balds.) People would do better to feed stock, save manure, raise more corn and wheat. Oats can be raised if land is manured. Orchards were not placed right here to begin with—but thinks them good and feasible. Has garden and plans to raise enough beans and tomatoes this year—and can them in own cannery, to supply Normal & Collegiate, Home Industrial, etc. Showed me barn, the floor of which he has had cemented to save manure—workshop, boys hauling wood etc. Also told me how he bought spring and with the aid of the boys, piped it away down to the school. (Picked that up himself. Said he often had wondered why he had taken trouble to learn and work at so many things, but thought he knew now.) As a result, when he was away one day, and the steam pipe burst, boys got tools and fixed it themselves.

Has a rule against smoking—a dead letter when he came. He tried penalties and found them ineffective. Decided to expel offenders and after one or two experiences, has had little trouble. Has had to expel one or two for drinking, but does not have much trouble with this now. Wonderful and swift change in boys. Easy to tell 1st from 2nd and 3rd year boy. Says his baseball, football and tennis have been a great help. Boys always try to get him to play with them. Says boys are naturally strong and well can endure any amount of work in what they find interesting. Says mills are bad physically and morally, for boys.

One of the teachers had taught at Concord—a mill town north of Charlotte and said the degeneracy was fearful. No question about the children working under age. Families broken in health, and after a generation or two—quite degenerate. Boys in school corroborate this statement of the youth of workers. Many mountaineers find way to Union and Spartanburg. Said experts who deny this, do not know conditions. Asked me if I did not "find it depressing to study these peculiar peoples"? I replied that I would perhaps, if at the bottom they were not pretty much like the rest of us.

Heard the boys sing and made a call on Mrs. Roger—who is quite young and attractive. Drove back about 3, gathered early sprays of arbutus. Wind had gone down and although air was chill, the ride was delightful. Got in about five.

Saturday morn: John got back having had interesting interviews with Mr. Finley—Miss Phillips—Dr. Boyd—and Mars Hill people.[15] Rainy trip but beautiful.

MARCH 14th, Sunday: Had busy but interesting day. Instead of church meeting in morn, we had a missionary union affair. The service consisting of reports of all the various missionary organizations, interspersed with songs by Farm School boys and the girls of Home Industrial. The Pease Home children came up and recited a set of verses which brought great applause—all amusing and pathetic. The appeal was mostly in the shining scrubbed faces, the neat blue dresses and the knowledge of their history.

I went over to the Pease House to dinner and we sat

round a pretty round table and had a delicious meal carefully served—or rather we were waited on by a fat little girl
whose arms just reached to our plates. Had a pleasant time
with Miss Fuller, Allison, Mrs. Byers, young prof. of Farm
School—Clemens from Maryville—and one or two others—
oh Miss Watson also.

Went over early to Home Industrial, where John was
holding successive audiences with Dr. Roger, Dr. Lawrence,
and Dr. Winston.[16] Dr. and Mrs. Briggs came to tea and John
interviewed the former while I talked to the latter. He is a
brother of Dr. Hensley's wife—and now a famous eye specialist of Asheville. Says tuberculosis is on the increase in mountains. Cannot be otherwise. (Also said a body was shipped
out of Asheville on almost every midnight train). Not the
fault of climate, but living conditions have not kept pace in
improvement—with growth of population. Cases formerly
isolated by nature of things—now in more congested conditions, it spreads rapidly. Moral conditions improving. Says
most people are decidedly not improved by going to mills.
Higher wages but also higher cost of living. People lost everything—and health as well. Could point out in Asheville
20–25 families which had lost property—sold out. Wanted
to go back. Became wanderers and girls became prostitutes.

I had a conversation with two mill girls—one from the
mountains. Had not wished to go to mills—nor mother either—all move of father's part. He a carpenter and got work
and house. The family—all but 3 little ones (oldest six) went
into mill. Father wanted to put in 6 yr old, but mother said
she would go in first. Boy played around in mill and sometimes helped, but got sleepy at nine and one of brothers
had to take him home. One brother did not work much (13
years)—made him sick. Younger sister, (11–12 years) could
only work by two weeks stretches—was a spinner and so low

among machines that she breathed in the lint. Hair white with lint. Was still pale and delicate. Girl herself not well—heavy cold. Said there was a fascination about mill work however. In one mill no running water. Drinking water in pails. Awful little girls with snuff sticks as long as your elbow, would spit right around the drinking water (snuff sticks dipped, wrapped in cotton and dipped again to save trouble of renewal.) Would have to skim lint off top of water before you drank. Little girls brought up in mill, frequently got as much as older people. One girl with aid of little brother under 5 yrs—got $2.50 a night. On Sunday—soft drink places open and great loafing places. Boys hung around and said dreadful things—swearing, etc. Many of girls went wrong. Places in mill where oil dripped so that it could be wrung from girl's skirt which dripped to the knee.

One mill in a hollow with stagnant water about. Many had typhoid. Her mother died and three or four of family—including self—had it. Children working in all the mills. Less in last one (a better mill in conditions—but also after law passed.) Stayed out till inspector had gone through, then were summoned by an older brother or sister. Names did not appear on pay roll. Second girl had lived in mill village always—but had not worked until she was over 12. Appeared pretty well. (Miss Stephenson says as she thinks it over—mill girls do not seem strong—subject to bad colds etc.) She had a bad cold. Liked the mills and enjoyed working. Would go back. Did not know much about children but knew there were some in mills. Did not work in her part. Knew work was bad for little children—but did not think people in general were in specially bad health.

MARCH 15th, Monday: Got off in P.M. to Brevard and went to hotel. Found a prominent citizen girl and Mr. Trowbridge of the Methodist school waiting with him. So we waited gladly until morning, when he came round to see us.[17] School partially inspired by work of Mr. and Mrs. Pease—but Mr. Trowbridge thinks he has an improvement and apparently is catering to old South prejudice of girls working for any one else. Do nothing for teachers or any one else but selves.

We got off at 9.05 and back to Asheville—where we had dinner again at Home Industrial. Got train at 3.35—after affectionate farewell to all household (girls waving to me from window)—and had short conversation with Mr. Smith of the Southern Presbyterian. Then Dr Winston arrived just in time and we pulled out.

Publications by Olive Dame Campbell

Campbell, Olive Arnold (Dame). *Songs and Ballads of the Southern Mountains.* 1915.

———. *Southern Highland Schools Maintained by Denominational and Independent Agencies.* New York: Southern Highland Division, Russell Sage Foundation, 1921.

———. *The Danish Folk School: Its Influence in the Life of Denmark and the North.* New York: Macmillan, 1928.

———. *Southern Mountain Schools Maintained by Denominational and Independent Agencies.* Rev. ed. New York: Southern Highland Division, Russell Sage Foundation, 1929.

———. *I Sing behind the Plough.* New York: American Association for Adult Education, 1930.

———. "The Southern Highlands." *Bulletin of the Russell Sage Foundation Library* 39 (February 1930).

———. *Singing Games Old and New.* Swannanoa, NC: Asheville Farm School, 1933.

———. *The Life and Work of John Charles Campbell, September 15, 1868–May 2, 1919.* Madison, WI: College Printing and Typing, 1968.

Campbell, Olive Dame, Maud Karpeles, and Cecil James Sharp. *English Folk Songs from the Southern Appalachians.* 2nd, enlarged ed. London; Toronto: Oxford University Press, 1932.

APPENDIX

———. *English Folk Songs from the Southern Appalachians.* Reprint. London: Oxford University Press, 1960.

———. *English Folk Songs from the Southern Appalachians.* London: Oxford University Press, 1966.

Campbell, Olive Dame, and Cecil James Sharp. *English Folk Songs from the Southern Appalachians.* New York: Putnam, 1917.

———. *English Folk Songs from the Southern Appalachians: Comprising 122 Songs and Ballads and 323 Tunes.* Whitefish, MT: Kessinger, 2007.

GLOSSARY

Note: Most of these definitions are adapted from the *Oxford English Dictionary* (*OED*), the *Dictionary of Smoky Mountain English* (*DSME*), edited by Michael Montgomery and Joseph S. Hall (Knoxville: Univ. of Tennessee Press, 2004), or the *Dictionary of American Regional English* (*DARE*), edited by Frederick G. Cassidy (Cambridge, MA: Belknap Press, 1985).

Albemarle Pippin. An early-eighteenth-century American dessert apple, said to be prized by Queen Victoria and therefore exported to Britain duty-free. (Vintage Virginia Apples. www.vintagevirginiaapples.com/apples/pippin.htm, accessed November 5, 2010)

Blind tigers. Bars or drinking places, usually illegal during this period. One of them was described as a "tiny log structure, and no one was visible about it. . . . when the requisite sum of money was deposited, a bottle of whiskey was found to be ready for the purchaser." (*Quare Women's Journals,* 76)

Cairngorm. A yellow-brown type of smoky quartz often used in traditional Celtic jewelry, or *cairngorm stone.* (*OED*)

Cinematographs. Series of photographs of moving objects projected on a screen in rapid succession to produce the illusion of a single moving scene. The term is now displaced by its abbreviation, *cinema.* (*OED*)

Clay eating. Clay is also known as "white dirt," "chalk," or kaolin. *Geophagia* (earth eating) has been observed and documented in many areas of the world. People are said to crave clay, especially pregnant women. It is also a key ingredient used in medicines for diarrhea. (*New Georgia Encyclopedia,* www.georgiaencyclopedia.org)

GLOSSARY

Drummers. Traveling salesmen; commercial travelers. (*OED*)

Enceinte. A French word for *pregnant*.

Hackle. A large comb with sharp teeth for processing flax. (*DSME*)

Industrial education. A term used to refer to a practical education, such as agricultural methods, home economics, mechanics, or woodworking.

Kiver. A bedcover. (*DSME*)

Loafers. Persons who loaf around, usually exchanging idle talk. (*DSME*)

Melungeons. A racially mixed group of people centered in eastern Tennessee and Kentucky and southwestern Virginia, sometimes said to be descendants of Portuguese explorers and the native Indians. (*DSME*)

Moonshine still. An apparatus for producing distilled liquor, often illegally. (*DSME*)

Paling. A fence or an enclosed area. (*OED*)

Poke. A bag or sack. (*DSME*)

Poppet. A doll or puppet. (*DSME*)

Postum. A coffee substitute made from grain. Invented by C. W. Post, an American food manufacturer. (*OED*)

Preceptress. A female teacher. (*OED*)

Quoits. A game of throwing rings of flattened iron, rope, or rubber at a peg placed in the ground. (*OED*)

Sentiment, sentimentalism. Personal experience or physical feeling; tendency to be governed by sentiment instead of reason. (Obs. *OED*)

Shagbark. Shagbark hickory, a tree native to the Appalachians with edible nuts and a shaggy bark. (*DARE*)

Sheathed. Covered by siding or a protective layer. (*OED*)

Slays. Wooden pegs used in weaving to separate the threads on a loom. (*OED*)

Sloyd. Training in elementary woodwork, a type of industrial education originally developed and practiced in Sweden. (*OED*)

Spider. A long-handled cast-iron pan with legs to set above a fire. (*DSME*)

Stand. A tavern, inn, or resting place for travelers, for example, Kemmer's Stand, Allen's Stand.

Stereopticon slides. Two images of the same object or scene, projected upon a screen so as to produce the appearance of solidity as in a stereoscope; the procedure is also used to cause the image of one scene to pass into another with the effect of dissolving. (*OED*)

Taximeter. She apparently means "taxi," but a taximeter was a distance recorder fitted on a cab; now the term refers to an automatic device that records the distance traveled and the fare due. (*OED*)

White lightning. Illegally produced or homemade whiskey; moonshine. (*DSME*)

NOTES

Editorial Method

1. The Dame family requested that the literary executors complete the biography and arrange to have it copied. Louise Pitman was a weaver who later became the director of handicrafts at the Campbell Folk School. Olive Dame Campbell (ODC), *The Life and Work of John Charles Campbell, September 15, 1868–May 2, 1919* (Madison, WI: College Printing, 1968), viii. This work is referred to hereafter as *Life and Work*.

2. JCC, *The Southern Highlander and His Homeland* (New York: Russell Sage Foundation, 1921; reprint, Lexington: Univ. Press of Kentucky, 1969, 2003).

Introduction

1. Jane S. Becker, *Selling Tradition: Appalachia and the Construction of an American Folk, 1930–1940* (Chapel Hill: Univ. of North Carolina Press, 1998), 58–60. The quotation is from a letter ODC wrote to Cecil Sharp on December 20, 1916, John Charles and Olive D. Campbell Papers, Southern Historical Collection, University of North Carolina, Correspondence, box 1, folders 56–57, 1916.

2. Louise Pitman, "The Living Word," *Mountain Life and Work* 4, Olive Dame Campbell Memorial Issue (1954): 19.

3. The most definitive account of John C. Campbell's life is his biography *The Life and Work of John Charles Campbell*, written by Olive Campbell herself and distributed posthumously in 1968. A memorial issue of *Mountain Life and Work* published in April 1928

provides details about his work and his contribution to Appalachian social and educational history.

4. Ronald D Eller, *Miners, Millhands, and Mountaineers: Industrialization of the Appalachian South, 1880–1930* (Knoxville: Univ. of Tennessee Press, 1982), xix.

5. Will Wallace Harney, "A Strange Land and a Peculiar People," *Lippincott's Magazine* 12 (1873): 429–38, reprinted in W. K. McNeil, ed. *Appalachian Images in Folk and Popular Culture*, 2nd ed. (Knoxville: Univ. of Tennessee Press, 1995), 45–58. An informative summary of this provocative period appears in *Seekers of Scenery: Travel Writing from Southern Appalachia, 1840–1900*, by Kevin E. O'Donnell and Helen Hollingsworth (Knoxville: Univ. of Tennessee Press, 2004).

6. John Fox, *The Little Shepherd of Kingdom Come* (New York: Scribner's, 1903); Mary Noailles Murfree [Charles Egbert Craddock], *In the Tennessee Mountains* (Boston: Houghton, Mifflin, 1884); Emma Bell Miles, *The Spirit of the Mountains* (New York: J. Pott, 1905); Horace Kephart, *The Southern Highlanders* (New York: Outing, 1913). Still the "image" of Appalachia inspires. The list of books and articles is extensive and still growing. Briefly, they include a Ph.D. dissertation by Cratis D. Williams, "The Southern Mountaineeer in Fact and Fiction" (New York Univ., 1961), published in 2011 in an abridged version in CD-ROM format by the *Appalachian Journal; The Invention of Appalachia* (Tucson: Univ. of Arizona Press, 1990), where Allen W. Batteau avowed that the image of Appalachia as a region apart was invented for political reasons; a collection of essays, *Confronting Appalachian Stereotypes: Back-Talk from an American Region*, ed. Dwight B. Billings, Gurney Norman, and Katherine Ledford (Lexington: Univ. Press of Kentucky, 1997); David C. Hsiung, *Two Worlds in the Tennessee Mountains: Exploring the Origins of Appalachian Stereotypes* (Lexington: Univ. Press of Kentucky, 1997); and in an article by Katie Algeo, where she addressed the reactions of local people to the enduring stereotypes: "Locals on Local Color: Imagining Identity in Appalachia," *Southern Cultures* 9, no. 4 (2003): 27–54.

7. Elizabeth R. Hooker and Fannie Wyche Dunn, *Religion in the Highlands Native Churches and Missionary Enterprises in the Southern Appalachian Area* (New York: Home Missions Council, 1933), 199.

8. John Alexander Williams, *Appalachia: A History* (Chapel Hill: Univ. of North Carolina Press, 2002), 200. See also the monumental *Appalachian Mountain Religion: A History*, by Deborah Vansau McCauley (Chicago: Univ. of Illinois Press, 1995), notably part 4, "The Home Mission to 'Mountain Whites,'" 329–442.

9. John C. Inscoe, "'A Northern Wedge Thrust into the Heart of the Confederacy': Explaining Civil War Loyalties in the Age of Appalachian Discovery, 1900–1921," in *Reconstructing Appalachia: The Civil War's Aftermath*, ed. Andrew L. Slap (Lexington: Univ. Press of Kentucky, 2010), 323–47. Representative selections of writings about the Civil War in Appalachia include Kenneth W. Noe and Shannon H. Wilson, *The Civil War in Appalachia: Collected Essays* (Knoxville: Univ. of Tennessee Press, 1997), which includes Wilson's essay, "Lincoln's Sons and Daughters: Berea College, Lincoln Memorial University, and the Myth of Unionist Appalachia, 1866–1910," 242–69; W. Todd Groce, *Mountain Rebels: East Tennessee Confederates and the Civil War, 1860–1870* (Knoxville: Univ. of Tennessee Press, 1999); and John C. Inscoe and Gordon B. McKinney, *The Heart of Confederate Appalachia: Western North Carolina in the Civil War* (Chapel Hill: Univ. of North Carolina Press, 2000). For a firsthand, intimate family account, see William Albert Wilson, Sandra L. Ballard, and Leila E. Weinstein, *Neighbor to Neighbor: A Memoir of Family, Community, and Civil War in Appalachian North Carolina* (Boone, NC: Center for Appalachian Studies, Appalachian State Univ., 2007).

10. Rebecca S. Montgomery thoroughly discusses the idea that mountaineers were worth saving in *The Politics of Education in the New South: Women and Reform in Georgia, 1890–1930* (Baton Rouge: Louisiana State Univ. Press, 2006), 148–55, as does Andrew Jackson Ritchie in *The Rabun Industrial School and Mountain School Extension Work among the Mountain Whites by One of Them* (Atlanta: Byrd, 1906), 7–10. Other related works include George E. Vincent, "A Retarded Frontier," *American Journal of Sociology* 4, no. 1 (1898): 1–20; C. Willard Hayes, "The Southern Appalachians," in *National Geographic Society Monographs,* vol. 1, no. 10 (New York: American Book Company, 1895), 305–36; Ellen Churchill Semple, "The Anglo-Saxons of the Kentucky Mountains: A Study in Anthropogeography," *Bulletin of the American Geographical Society* 42, no. 8 (1910): 561–89. Mc-

Neil, *Appalachian Images*, includes reprints of Frost's and Semple's articles (91–106 and 145–74, respectively), as well as "The Southern Mountaineer," by John Fox Jr., 1905 (121–44).

11. Williams, *Appalachia*, 207.

12. H. Davis Yeuell, *Moving Mountains: A History of Presbyterian and Reformed Faith at Work in Appalachia* (Amesville, OH: Coalition for Appalachian Ministry, 1985), 6, 10.

13. Quoted ibid., 63–64. Marcia Clark Myers, "Presbyterian Home Missions in Appalachia: A Feminine Enterprise" (master's thesis, Princeton Theological Seminary, 1979).

14. Henry D. Shapiro, *Appalachia on Our Mind: The Southern Mountains and Mountaineers in the American Consciousness, 1870–1920* (Chapel Hill: Univ. of North Carolina Press, 1978), xiv–xxviii.

15. JCC, *Southern Highlander*, 81–82.

16. Samuel H. Thompson, *The Highlanders of the South* (New York: Eaton and Mains, 1910), 58–60.

17. Samuel Tyndale Wilson, *The Southern Mountaineers* (New York: Presbyterian Home Missions, 1906), 66–69.

18. See Ruth Crocker, "From Widow's Mite to Widow's Might: The Philanthropy of Margaret Olivia Sage," *American Presbyterians* 74, no. 4 (1996): 253–64. See also Ruth Crocker, *Mrs. Russell Sage: Women's Activism and Philanthropy in Gilded Age and Progressive Era America* (Bloomington: Indiana Univ. Press, 2006); and her essay "Margaret Olivia Slocum, 'Mrs. Russell Sage': Private Griefs and Public Duties," in *Ordinary Women, Extraordinary Lives: Women in American History*, ed. Kriste Lindenmeyer (Wilmington, DE.: SR Books, 2000), 147–59.

19. ODC, *Life and Work*, 119–20. See John M. Glenn, Lilian Brandt, and F. Emerson Andrews, *Russell Sage Foundation, 1907–1946* (New York: Russell Sage Foundation, 1947), 1:21.

20. Charles Booth is generally considered to be the father of the social survey, as a result of his monumental study of London in 1889. See his *Life and Labour of the People in London* (London: Macmillan, 1902). The *American Journal of Sociology* first appeared in 1895, and Jane Addams established Hull House in Chicago in 1898. See *Jane Addams of Hull House, 1860–1935; A Centenary Study*, by Margaret Tims (New York: Macmillan, 1961).

21. See JCC, *Southern Highlander,* 271, where he lists them as Baptists, Southern Convention; Seventh Day Baptist Brethren; Christians (Christian Connection); Churches of Christ; Disciples of Christ; Congregationalists; Methodist Episcopal; Methodist Episcopal South; Associate Presbyterian; Reformed Presbyterian; United Presbyterian; Presbyterian in the United States; Presbyterian in the United States of America; Protestant Episcopal; Reformed Church in America; and Seventh Day Adventists. Data for these schools was compiled by ODC in *Southern Highland Schools Maintained by Denominational and Independent Agencies* (New York: Russell Sage Foundation, 1921).

22. ODC, *Life and Work,* 171.

23. Becker, *Selling Tradition,* 58–59.

24. For more information about the history of the Conference/ Council, see David Whisnant, first in an article, "Controversy in God's Grand Division: The Council of the Southern Mountains," *Appalachian Journal* 2, no. 1 (1974): 8–10; then as a chapter in his book *Modernizing the Mountaineer: People, Power, and Planning in Appalachia* (1979; reprint, Knoxville: Univ. of Tennessee Press, 1994), 3–39. See also Penny Messinger's in-depth study "Leading the Field of Mountain Work: The Conference of Southern Mountain Workers, 1913–1950" (Ph.D. thesis, Ohio State Univ., 1998).

25. JCC, *The Future of Church and Independent Schools in the Southern Highlands* (New York: Russell Sage Foundation, 1917), 10.

26. For a list of Olive Dame Campbell's publications, see the appendix.

27. JCC, *Southern Highlander,* xiv.

28. Wilson, *Southern Mountaineers,* vii.

29. Shapiro's master's thesis for Rutgers University in 1966 was entitled "A Strange Land and Peculiar People: The Discovery of America." He published *Appalachia on Our Mind* in 1978. Vance's publications include *Human Geography of the South: A Study in Regional Resources and Human Adequacy* (1932; reprint, Chapel Hill: Univ. of North Carolina Press, 1968); and *Regional Reconstruction: A Way Out for the South* (Chapel Hill: Univ. of North Carolina Press, 1935).

30. Claxton was the superintendent of the Tennessee Depart-

ment of Education from 1902 to 1911 and then became the U.S. commissioner of education. His theories were expounded in an article in the *New York Times* in the *Sunday Magazine,* May 10, 1914, "Experts Favor Folk High Schools for United States: Study in Denmark of These Remarkable Rural Schools and the Wonders They Have Wrought Causes National Bureau of Education Officials to Advocate Their Establishment Here." Also see Charles Lee Lewis, *Philander Priestley Claxton, Crusader for Public Education* (Knoxville: Univ. of Tennessee Press, 1948).

31. JCC, *Future,* 19.

32. Philis Alvic, *Weavers of the Southern Highlands* (Lexington: Univ. Press of Kentucky, 2003), 120.

33. The Child ballads are a collection of ballads and songs, mostly dating from the sixteenth and seventeenth centuries in England and Scotland, assembled by James Francis Child and published as *The English and Scottish Popular Ballads,* 5 vols. (Boston: Houghton Mifflin, 1882).

34. ODC and Cecil James Sharp, *English Folk Songs from the Southern Appalachians* (New York: Putnam, 1917). Also see A. H. Fox Strangways and Maud Karpeles, *Cecil Sharp,* 2nd ed. (1933; reprint, London: Oxford Univ. Press, 1955). Cecil Sharp was carrying on the work of James Child in England, but he was adding the music to the lyrics of the English tunes and ballads. Arthur Krim's article "Appalachian Songcatcher: Olive Dame Campbell and the Scotch-Irish Ballad," *Journal of Cultural Geography* 24, no. 1 (Fall–Winter 2006): 91–112, describes her work as "a case study in music geography." To "catch" a song means to write down the music as well as the words of the song or ballad. It is generally thought that the feature film *Songcatcher* (DVD, written and directed by Maggie Greenwald, Lions Gate, 2001) was loosely based on Campbell's ballad collecting. The film credits ODC and Sharp for the ballads used. But it could well have been inspired by the collecting of Dorothy Scarborough, a Columbia University professor who published *A Song Catcher in Southern Mountains; American Folk Songs of British Ancestry* (New York: Columbia Univ. Press, 1937).

35. Allen H. Eaton, *Handicrafts of the Southern Highlands* (New York: Dover, 1973), originally published in 1937 with coauthors

Doris Ulmann and the Russell Sage Foundation. The 1937 edition was subtitled "With an Account of the Rural Handicraft Movement in the United States and Suggestions for the Wider Use of Handicrafts in Adult Education and in Recreation." Alvic, *Weavers of the Southern Highlands,* 19.

36. William Bernard McCarthy, "Olive Dame Campbell and Appalachian Tradition," in *Ballads into Books: The Legacies of F. J. Child,* ed. Tom Cheesman and Sigrid Rieuwerts (Bern, Switzerland: Peter Lang, 1997), 69.

37. Margaret Supplee Smith, "Culture, Altruism, and Exceptionalism," in *North Carolina Women Making History,* by Margaret Supplee Smith and Emily Herring Wilson (Chapel Hill: Univ. of North Carolina Press, 1999), 232–35, biography on 254–57. See also Jess Stoddart, *Challenge and Change in Appalachia: The Story of Hindman Settlement School* (Lexington: Univ. Press of Kentucky, 2002); Frances Louisa Goodrich, *Mountain Homespun: A Facsimile of the Original, Published in 1931* (Knoxville: Univ. of Tennessee Press, 1989); and Lucy Morgan, *Gift from the Hills: Miss Lucy Morgan's Story of Her Unique Penland School* (New York: Bobbs-Merrill, 1958; Chapel Hill: Univ. of North Carolina Press, 1971).

1. October 1908

1. John Glenn was the first director of the Russell Sage Foundation. See Glenn, Brandt, and Andrews, *Russell Sage Foundation,* 1:21.

2. ODC, *Life and Work,* 119–22.

3. "D.U." is unidentified.

4. The Reverend Bruce R. Payne, a professor of secondary education at the University of Virginia, wrote "Waste in Mountain Settlement Work," published in the *Proceedings of the National Conference of Charities and Corrections* in 1908. He advocated the professionalization of social work in Appalachia and urged interagency cooperation in mountain benevolent work. See Shapiro, *Appalachia on Our Mind,* 192.

5. Mayo is as yet unidentified.

6. The Venerable Archdeacon Frederick W. Neve was the rector of St. Paul's Episcopal Church in Ivy, Virginia; he established

the Church of St. John the Baptist and its mission school in the Ragged Mountains. Neve believed that mountain people should stay in the mountains. He suggested alternatives to farming, such as planting orchards or raising stock. See Frederick W. Neve, "The Missions of the Blue Ridge, Diocese of Virginia," in *The Church's Mission to the Mountaineers of the South by Archdeacon Neve, of Virginia, Archdeacon Spurr, of West Virginia, Archdeacon Wentworth, Diocese of Lexington, Reverend S.C. Hughson, O.H.C. of Sewanee Tenn., Reverend E.N. Joyner, Diocese of Asheville, and Reverend W.S. Claiborne*, comp. Walter Hughson (Hartford, CT: Church Missions, 1908).

7. Dr. Claxton was the editor of the *North Carolina Journal of Education*, which became the *Atlantic Educational Journal*. He was instrumental in the establishment of the Southern Education Board and later became the U.S. commissioner of education. See Lewis, *Philander Priestley Claxton*. For more about Dr. Duncan, see note 11.

8. Martin's Academy was established by Samuel Doak in 1784 and was renamed Washington College in 1795. In its convoluted history, it merged with Greeneville and Tusculum College in 1908 to become Washington and Tusculum College, which became Washington College Academy in 1914. See Howard Ernest Carr, *Washington College: A Study of an Attempt to Provide Higher Education in Eastern Tennessee* (Knoxville, TN: S.B. Newman, 1935); and Joseph T. Fuhrmann, *The Life and Times of Tusculum College* (Greeneville, TN: Tusculum College, 1986), xi–xii.

9. Believed to be Mary Clare deGraffenried, 1849–1921, who was trained as a teacher but became a noted women's advocate. Appointed to a position in the U.S. Department of Labor in 1886, she lived in Washington and published innumerable articles on the plight of female labor and working women, the most well-known being "The Georgia Cracker in the Cotton Mills," published in *Century Magazine* in February 1891. See Thomas Pritchett de Graffenried, *History of the De Graffenried Family from 1191 A.D. to 1925* (Binghamton, NY: Vail-Ballou Press, 1925), 10–11. The de Graffenried family was a distinguished one. Originally from Bern, in what is now Switzerland, the first member of the family in this country was Baron Christopher de Graffenried, Landgrave of the Carolinas, who founded New Bern, North Carolina, in 1710. He

was a member of the colonial service and was twice offered the governorship of North Carolina. Many of his descendants in the United States have held important state and national positions. Thomas Pritchett de Graffenried, *The De Graffenried Family Scrap Book, 1191–1956: Seven Hundred and Sixty Five Years* (Charlottesville: Univ. of Virginia Press, 1958).

10. Rabun Gap Industrial School was an independent school in Rabun County, Georgia. See Ritchie, *Rabun Industrial School.* The school is also listed in ODC, *Southern Highland Schools Maintained by Denominational and Independent Agencies* (New York: Russell Sage Foundation, 1921), 6. It still exists as Rabun Gap–Nacoochee School. Rabun Gap–Nacoochee School, www.rabungap.org.

11. The Reverend Calvin A. Duncan is mentioned in Wilson, *Southern Mountaineers,* 160.

12. Opened as Southern and Western Theological Seminary in 1819, Maryville College was chartered in 1842 by the Tennessee State Legislature as a Christian institution and governed by a board appointed by the Presbyterian Synod of Tennessee. Samuel Tyndale Wilson, a prominent minister, citizen, and author, wrote several books about Maryville College as well as *Southern Mountaineers.*

13. Dr. Claxton was interested in the methods used by Nordic schools to educate adults and took several trips to Denmark and Sweden to investigate them. See his biography, Lewis, *Philander Priestley Claxton.*

14. Edwin Alderman was the president of the University of North Carolina and Tulane before he became the president of the University of Virginia (1904–1915). He was one of the most successful of the southern progressives in higher education at making the university an instrument of social reform. He was concerned about the narrow views of religious leaders in charge of church schools. See "Visions of Grandeur: Edwin Alderman and the University of Virginia, 1904–15," in Michael Dennis, *Lessons in Progress: State Universities and Progressivism in the New South, 1880–1920* (Urbana: Univ. of Illinois Press, 2001), 217–45.

15. Young-Harris College, a junior college in Hiawassee, Towns County, Georgia, was then affiliated with the Methodist Episcopal Church, South. See ODC, *Southern Highland Schools,* 9.

16. E. B. Norvell of Murphy, North Carolina, was the superintendent of the schools in Cherokee County, North Carolina. See *The North Carolina Yearbook* (Raleigh, NC: News and Observer, 1908), 76. Nettie Dicky ran a hotel in Murphy. See *North Carolina Year Book and Business Directory* (Raleigh: News and Observer, 1910), 142.

17. Started in 1886 by a Methodist circuit rider, Young Harris Institute was named for one of its benefactors from Athens, Georgia. Its charter was amended in 1891 to make it a college. In 1899, the Reverend Joseph A. Sharp began a twenty-five-year career as president, from 1899 to 1916 and again from 1922 to 1930. After his death, his wife, Ella Standard Sharp, served out his term as president. See Thomas Jackson Lance, *History of Young L. G. Harris College* (n.p., 1935). In 1949 when Sharp Memorial Methodist Church, at the entrance to Young Harris College, was dedicated, Mrs. Sharp and the Sharps' granddaughter were present.

18. Hiawassee High School (also commonly called Hiawassee Academy), Towns County, Georgia, a denominational boarding and day school, was maintained by the Home Mission Board of the Southern Baptist Convention. See ODC, *Southern Highland Schools*, 3. Asbury B. Greene was made principal in 1892. See Southern Historical Association, *Memoirs of Georgia* (Atlanta: Southern Historical Association, 1895), 904. More about the school and A. B. Greene can be found in Walter H. Berg Jr., *A History of McConnell Memorial Baptist Church, Hiawassee, Georgia, 1882–1997* (Franklin, NC: Genealogy, 1997), 33–39.

19. Nacoochee was known for the Nacoochee Mound, a prehistoric mound on the Chattahoochee River in northern Georgia, near Helen. See George Walton Williams, *Relics of a Forgotten Race in Nacoochee, Ga., and Its Surroundings: A Sketch* (Atlanta: Kimsey Bookshop, 1962).

20. The U.S. Geological Survey has produced a map of asbestos production throughout northern Georgia, including Rabun County. See Bradley S. Van Gosen, "Reported Historic Asbestos Mines, Historic Asbestos Prospects, and Natural Asbestos Occurrences in the Eastern United States," 2006, U.S. Department of the Interior, U.S. Geological Survey, http://pubs.usgs.gov/of/2005/1189/pdf/Plate.pdf, accessed March 3, 2010.

21. Demorest, Habersham County, Georgia, was the home of the Campbells and the location of Piedmont College, where John Campbell was president from 1901 to 1907.

22. Because the record of the trip to Atlanta was jumbled in the diary, the typist who first transcribed the diary rearranged it in a clearer sequence. I saw no reason to change the order of events as transcribed.

23. The address to the graduates of the Normal and Collegiate Institute was published in full in the *Asheville Citizen,* June 12, 1907, p. 7, because it included the "very interesting history of Western North Carolina and her early settlers." Jeter Conley Pritchard was a judge on the U.S. Circuit Court of Appeals for the Fourth District. He served in the U.S. Senate from 1895 to 1921, the first Republican to be elected to the Senate from a southern state in twenty years. See *Dictionary of North Carolina Biography* (Chapel Hill: Univ. of North Carolina Press, 1994), 149.

24. Martha Gielow founded the Southern Industrial Education Association in 1905. She was active in the United Daughters of the Confederacy (UDC) organization in Alabama and advocated the promotion of education for mountain white children. See Montgomery, *Politics of Education,* 156.

25. The Berry School was founded by Martha Berry in Mount Berry, Georgia. It was an independent industrial boarding school for boys and girls. See Harnett T. Kane, *Miracle in the Mountains* (Garden City, NY: Doubleday, 1956); and Elisabeth P. Myers, *Angel of Appalachia; Martha Berry* (New York: J. Messner, 1968). In the chapter "Reforming the Mountaineers," Rebecca Montgomery discusses the boarding schools run by female reformers in the mountains. The women felt that having children live at the school and participate in regular school chores was the only way to have any lasting effect on their lives. Montgomery, *Politics of Education,* 165–70.

26. Mission barrels were big round containers used by missionaries to collect donations of used clothing that they distributed to the "needy."

27. Rogers Peet was a British clothing company.

2. November 1908

1. ODC, *Life and Work*, 123.

2. The first settlers in Pleasant Hill, Tennessee, came in 1819, and the Pleasant Hill Academy (1884–1947) educated many of the county youth. The first hospital in the county was established in Pleasant Hill by Dr. May Wharton, wife of Edward Wharton, principal of the academy in 1917. See Kiwanis Club of Crab Orchard, Tennessee, *A Short History of Cumberland County* (Crossville, TN: P.B. Kirkeminde, 1982), 24–25. For additional information, see Iris Webb Glebe, *Thy Loving Children Still: History and Memories of Pleasant Hill Academy* (Allen Park, MI: P.H.A. Book Fund, 1983); and Helen Krechniak [Bullard] and Joseph Marshall, *Cumberland County's First Hundred Years* (Crossville, TN: Centennial Committee, 1956), 151–53.

3. The AMA was the American Missionary Association, a nondenominational group formed to provide opportunities for African Americans and minorities. See *Encyclopaedia Britannica*, www .britannica.com/EBchecked/topic/19996/American-Missionary-Association.

4. Land for the first church in Cumberland County was donated in 1803, and the Grassy Cove Methodist Church still exists. The Grassy Cove Academy (1871–1908) was established in 1871 by the Presbyterian Board of Home Missions. See Kiwanis Club, *Short History*, 30–31; and Krechniak and Marshall, *First Hundred Years*, 128–29.

5. There was a Presbyterian day school and church in Jewett, Cumberland County, Tennessee, which was eventually taken over by the county. See Krechniak and Marshall, *First Hundred Years*, 132. Also mentioned in Wilson, *Southern Mountaineers*, 161.

6. There is a 1906 photograph of a group of county officials, including two Hambys, and a Hamby Hotel in Krechniak and Marshall, *First Hundred Years*, 212. This book is a treasure trove of information about the locations in Cumberland County: Pleasant Hill, Grassy Cove, Jewett, Grandview, Ozone, Pomona, and the infamous "W" Road.

7. "Kimmer" is the old spelling for the name of a prominent

family in Cumberland County, the Kemmers. The Kemmer Stand was a tavern, a stop on the Burke Road. An early post road to Sparta, the Burke Road, like the Walton Road, was in use by 1834. See Krechniak and Marshall, *First Hundred Years*, 26. For a personalized, thorough account of the early history of Grassy Cove, including accounts of John C. Kemmer and his family, see Cora Stratton and Nettie Stratton, *And This Is Grassy Cove* (1938; reprint, Crossville, TN: Chronicle, 1977), 37. A notice in the *Dayton (TN) Herald News Gazette* 19, no. 1,888, July 6, 1893, reads: "J.C. Kimmer has been appointed Postmaster at Grassy Cove, succeeding W.H. Bristow." See TNGenWeb Project, http://tngenweb.org/rheatn/newspaper5. htm, accessed February 12, 2012.

8. The "W," or Walton Road, was a reconstruction of the Anderson Pike, built in 1852 up the eastern bluff of Walden's Ridge in Tennessee. The three switchbacks that formed the shape of a *W* were supposed to make climbing easier. It was completed in 1893 and replaced the old "corduroy road" used by early settlers and by both armies during the Civil War. See James L. Douthat, *Along the Pike: The Story of Walden's Ridge along Anderson Pike* (Signal Mountain, TN: Mountain Press, 1996), 116–24.

9. It is generally agreed that the distance of many mountain homes from schools made it difficult for mountain children to get to school. For a discussion of the difficulties that mountain communities faced due to the lack of good roads, see James Watt Raine, "The Mountains Go to School" in his book *The Land of Saddle-Bags: A Study of the Mountain People of Appalachia* (Lexington: Univ. Press of Kentucky, 1997), 163–88. Dwight Billings, in his introduction to the 1997 edition of Raine's book, comments on the importance of this early firsthand documentary account of mountain people and their mores. This diary's harrowing accounts of the Campbells' travels is a testament to the difficulty of moving around the region in the first decades of the twentieth century.

10. The American Missionary Association first opened the Grandview Academy in 1884; the name was changed to Normal Institute in 1887 to emphasize the school's emphasis on teacher training. A. V. Woodworth was principal of Grandview Normal from 1905 to 1913. See Bettye J. Broyles, comp., *Churches and Schools of*

Rhea County, Tennessee ([Dayton, TN?]: Rhea County Historical and Genealogical Society, 1992), 199–200.

11. Crab Orchard is the oldest established community in Cumberland County, Tennessee. The limestone industry there has been operating since the early twentieth century. See Krechniak and Marshall, *First Hundred Years*, 122–25.

12. Dr. J. S. Kingsley was a professor of natural history at Tufts University in Medford, Massachusetts, from which ODC graduated in 1903.

13. *Child Welfare in Kentucky* (New York: National Child Labor Committee, 1919), a study of conditions in the state by the National Child Labor Board, painted a grim picture of the plight of children in the Kentucky mountains. See the chapter "Rural Life" by Edward N. Clopper, director, on pages 143–67. Shapiro, in *Appalachia on Our Mind*, 172–85, wrote about the ongoing discussion between Alexander J. McKelway, southern secretary of the committee, and August Kohn of the *News and Courier,* a newspaper in Charleston, South Carolina. Kohn was writing a series of articles, quoting Dr. Charles Wardell Stiles, defending the cotton mills against the charges leveled at them about conditions in the mills, especially for children.

14. Lincoln Memorial University was a coeducational independent boarding school for secondary, collegiate, normal, and industrial education. Grace Nettleton Memorial Home and School for Girls provided elementary, secondary, and industrial educational opportunities. They were both in Harrogate, Claiborne County, Tennessee. See ODC, *Southern Highland Schools Maintained by Denominational and Independent Agencies* (New York: Russell Sage Foundation, 1921), 7. On page 130 in *Life and Work,* ODC elaborates: "Where schools lay along the Louisville and Nashville Railroad, as they did to the north of Knoxville, we were able to cover much ground in a few days: Lincoln Memorial Episcopal at Barbourville: Episcopal School at Corbin; Congregational School at Williamsburg; Sue Bennett Memorial (Methodist Episcopal South) at London. We also visited a Swiss Colony near London and found a sturdy people who had succeeded in surviving land exploitation, though not by agriculture alone."

15. Union College, founded in 1879, is a liberal arts college in Barbourville in southeastern Kentucky, affiliated with the United Methodist Church. James Warren Easley was elected president in 1905. See Edwin S. Bradley, *Union College: 1879–1954* (Barbourville, KY: Union College, 1954).

16. The initials stand for Methodist Episcopal South and Methodist Episcopal North. John Campbell discusses this subject at length in his chapter "The Growth of Denominationalism in the Highlands," in *Southern Highlander,* 152–75. Elizabeth R. Hooker also reports on the serious handicap that denominationalism presented. See Elizabeth R. Hooker and Fannie Wyche Dunn, *Religion in the Highlands Native Churches and Missionary Enterprises in the Southern Appalachian Area* (New York: Home Missions Council, 1933), 211–14.

17. Hooker observed that the "mission schools met a real need; although comprehensive public-school systems were adopted during the period of reconstruction, serious obstacles prevented their development[:] . . . the thinly scattered rural population . . . unsound systems of taxation . . . the influence of politics . . . and finally, the fact that public sentiment in favor of the education of all children at public expense, though growing, was still weak." *Religion in the Highlands,* 202.

18. Cumberland College is located in Williamsburg, Kentucky. Originally founded in 1887 as Williamsburg Institute, it was joined with Highland College in 1913 and assumed its present name. Edwin Ellsworth Wood was principal of the institute; he resigned in 1893, returned later as vice-president under John Newton Prestridge, and was elected president in 1898. H. H. Hibbs was the pastor of the First Baptist Church in Williamsburg, also succeeding Prestridge. Hibbs was instrumental in raising money for the institute and in 1906, with the help of Dr. W. C. Buttrick, obtained a matching grant for more than twenty thousand dollars from Rockefeller's Education Society. James Madison Ellison was treasurer for thirty years. See James H. Taylor, *A Bright Shining City Set on a Hill,* ed. Elizabeth Sue Wake (Williamsburg, KY: Cumberland College, 1988), 77–82, 265.

19. Sue Bennett Memorial School in London, Kentucky, was a preparatory high school. It began in 1897 with 75 pupils and in

1917 it had grown to 408. Professor J. C. Lewis was its principal for twenty years. See Mrs. F. H. E. Ross and Mrs. K. J. French, "The Story of the Years in Mountain Work" (Nashville, TN: Women's Missionary Council, M. E. Church, South, 1900), 7. Also see Cloyde C. Jones, "A History of Sue Bennett College" (master's thesis, Univ. of Kentucky, 1940).

20. Will C. Gamble, the first full-time secretary to President Frost, is named in William Goodell Frost's *For the Mountains: An Autobiography* (New York: Revell, 1937), which Frost dedicated to his wife, Eleanor Marsh Frost. William G. Frost became president of Berea College in 1898 and was instrumental in establishing Berea as an educator of white mountaineers as well as Negroes. Established in 1855, Berea was an interracial institution that strived to meet social and individual needs of all races. See Elisabeth Sinclair Peck and Emily Ann Smith, *Berea's First 125 Years, 1855–1980* (Lexington: Univ. Press of Kentucky, 1982). Upon the election of Frost as president, the college changed its primary focus to the redemption of the mountaineer. Williams notes in *Appalachia*, 201: The "religious and educational movement acquired its most influential spokesman" when Frost came to Berea. In his famous essay "Our Contemporary Ancestors in the Southern Mountains," published in the *Atlantic Monthly* in March 1899, Frost preached that Appalachians deserved to be saved because they were the true descendants of the original Anglo-Saxon pioneers.

21. See Hooker's chapter "Environment" in *Religion in the Highlands*, 59, where she discussed the "Inferior Position of Women" in mountain society. Campbell also comments on women and their home life throughout *Southern Highlander.*

22. Isaac Messler, superintendent of Kentucky work for the Women's Board of Domestic Missions of the Reformed Church of America, suggested that the McKee school be turned over to the county high school and that an industrial school be established in Jackson County at Annville; the resulting school became the Annville Institute. See Helen W. Lund, "The Growth of a Mountain School," *Mountain Life and Work* 8, no. 4 (1933): 20. ODC lists the McKee Academy as a boarding and day school for elementary school boys and girls. See her *Southern Highland Schools*, 16.

23. Grayhawk Community School was a coeducational day school for elementary students, also in Jackson County. See ODC, *Southern Highland Schools*, 16.

24. See JCC, *Southern Highlander*, the chapter "Living Conditions and Health," 195–225; table 9 there gives rural death rates in the region. Hooker's chapter "Environment," in *Religion in the Highlands*, also discusses health issues (56–57).

25. John W. Dinsmore was the dean of the Normal Department at Berea. He and Mrs. Dinsmore established a "people's institute" and, with the director of extension work, Professor C. Rexford Raymond, traveled around the state, holding five-day institutes in ten counties. See Peck and Smith, *Berea's First 125 Years*, 169–70.

26. Dr. Robert H. Cowley was made college physician at Berea in 1906. He was "Superintendent of the Gymnasium, Bathrooms, and Hospital" and was charged to "cultivate a variety of athletic interests." Ibid., 104.

27. Winchester, in Clark County, Kentucky, was founded in 1792 with the county itself and named for Winchester, Virginia. See *Kentucky Atlas and Gazetteer*, www.uky.edu/KentuckyAtlas/ky-winchester.html. A note in the margin of the diary says: "Lexington & Eastern R.R. taken over by Louisville & Nashville in 1915."

28. S. P. Lees Collegiate Institute was established in Jackson in 1891 as a preparatory school for Central University, a predecessor to Eastern Kentucky University. See *A History of Eastern Kentucky University: The School of Opportunity*, by William E. Ellis (Lexington: Univ. Press of Kentucky, 2005), 3. Jackson, the seat of Breathitt County, is on the North Fork of the Kentucky River. Founded with the county in 1839 as Breathitt Town, it was renamed Jackson in 1845 to honor Andrew Jackson, who died that year. The Breathitt courthouse post office opened in 1839. Cannel City is a Morgan County community on the Stone Coal Fork of Caney Creek. It grew up around the early-twentieth-century cannel coal mines. The Cannel City post office opened in 1902. See *Kentucky Atlas and Gazetteer*, www.uky.edu/KentuckyAtlas/ky-cannel-city.html.

29. Helechawa, a small Wolfe County town in the Eastern Coal Field region of Kentucky, was established about 1900 as a station on the Ohio and Kentucky Railroad. The name came from Helen Chase

Walbridge, the daughter of the railroad's president. See *Kentucky Atlas and Gazetteer,* www.uky.edu/KentuckyAtlas/ky-helechawa.html.

30. An account of the origin and events of this apparently politically motivated, countywide feud can be found in "Bloody Breathitt," a chapter in *Kentucky's Famous Feuds and Tragedies: Authentic History of the World Renowned Vendettas of the Dark and Bloody Ground,* by Chas. G. Mutzenberg (New York: R. F. Fenno, 1917), 254–324. A more recent rendition names the Hargis-Cockrell-Marcum-Callahan War "The Last and Bloodiest Feud." John Ed Pearce, *Days of Darkness: The Feuds of Eastern Kentucky* (Lexington: Univ. Press of Kentucky, 1994), 31–53. Also see Meriel Daniel Harris's 1940 master's thesis at the University of Kentucky, "Two Famous Kentucky Feuds and Their Causes."

31. The Hazel Green Academy (1880–1983) was the first educational institution in Eastern Kentucky. Hazel Green, a small Wolfe County town, was established in 1849 and named for the locally abundant hazel shrubs. It is located on the Red River about seven miles north of Campton. M. O. Carter was principal of the school, succeeding the Reverend Henry J. Derthick. They were both also ministers of the Hazel Green Christian Church. See Mrs. Roy M. Cecil and compilers, *Early and Modern History of Wolfe County* (Campton, KY: Wolfe County Woman's Club, 1958), 23–25. "Hazel Green, the gem of the mountain towns . . . lies in a great basin on the Upper Red River, with a rim of green mountains around it, like a picture frame," wrote Edward O. Guerrant, *The Galax Gatherers: The Gospel among the Highlanders* (1910; reprint, Knoxville: Univ. of Tennessee Press, 2003), 176.

32. Note 16 in *Life and Work* reads: "Rev. H. J. Derthick, previously Principal of, then a Board Member assigned to speaking and money-raising for, Hazel Green Academy (Disciples of Christ); afterwards Principal of Livingston Academy and later still President of Milligan College, both in Tennessee."

3. December 1908

1. ODC, *Life and Work,* 140–41.
2. Sabbath schools, common all over the country in the latter

part of the nineteenth century, were like the more familiar Sunday schools, held on Sunday to study the Bible and give religious instruction, but many of them were much more than that. Sabbath school missionaries offered training for teachers and complete educational programs, adapting them as much as possible to local conditions. See Fred Eastman, *Unfinished Business of the Presbyterian Church in America* (Philadelphia: Westminster Press, 1921), 165. Edward O. Guerrant mentions a Sabbath school at Middle Fork Church in Kentucky with one hundred pupils. Lewis G. Hensley, "almost unaided," taught "many of them how to read, all of them how to love and serve God." Guerrant, *Galax Gatherers,* 146. Samuel Tyndale Wilson also discussed the Sabbath school missions of the Presbyterian church in *Southern Mountaineers,* 101.

3. Troublesome Creek was well named. It regularly overflowed its banks and separated the Hindman school from the town. A photograph of one innovative way people coped, by walking across chairs, is shown in May Stone, Katherine Pettit, and Jess Stoddart, *The Quare Women's Journals: May Stone and Katherine Pettit's Summers in the Kentucky Mountains and the Founding of the Hindman Settlement School* (Ashland, KY: J. Stuart Foundation, 1997), 299.

4. Hindman Settlement School, founded in 1902, was one of the most important mountain educational institutions of the Progressive Era. Pettit and Stone were icons of the reform movement as they worked to improve the lives of mountain people. See Stoddart, *Challenge and Change.* Richard B. Drake points out that the Settlement School was different from the Mission School, as it was more concerned with community needs than in imposing conventional education and mores on a "needy" people. See "The Mission School Era in Southern Appalachia: 1880–1940," *Appalachian Notes* 6, nos. 1–4 (1978): 1–8.

5. Note 17 on page 139 of *Life and Work* reads: "Miss Katherine Pettit and Miss May Stone were titled the Executive Committee of the Hindman Settlement School, actually its joint Directors."

6. David E. Whisnant discussed ODC's ballad collecting extensively in his book *All That Is Native and Fine: The Politics of Culture in an American Region* (Chapel Hill: Univ. of North Carolina Press, 1983). She was one of three examples he used to analyze

the "cultural drama that was central" to the "multifaceted church and secular missionary enterprise in the mountains" in the early decades of the twentieth century. The others were the Hindman Settlement School and the White Top Folk Festival in Virginia. He wrote: "Mrs. Campbell's cultural work, while more sensitive to political-social-economic context than that of most of her peers and co-workers, nevertheless partook of many of the ironies and confusions that have characterized most organized cultural work in the mountains" (11).

7. On page 142 of *Life and Work,* ODC writes of "the talks, on health conditions, with Harriet Butler, the wise nurse; with Ann Cobb, who wrote poetry and loved carols and folk-songs."

8. The Women's Christian Temperance Union sponsored the school at the Hindman Settlement for the first thirteen years, and it was known as the WCTU School. See Stoddart, *Challenge and Change,* 4.

9. Napier's first name is not given. Both John and M. C. Napier were superintendents of Perry County schools between 1900 and 1910. See Eunice Tolbert Johnson, comp., *History of Perry County, Kentucky* (Hazard, KY: Hazard Chapter of the Daughters of the American Revolution, 1953), 111. The first member of the Napier family in Perry County was Sir William Francis Patrick Napier (1795–1866), who was born in Ireland and moved to America as a young man (227).

10. Note 18 in ODC, *Life and Work:* "Hazard College, Hazard, Perry County, Kentucky, maintained by Home Mission Board and Baptist State Board of Missions, Southern Baptist Convention." The Reverend Asbel S. Petrey came to Hazard in 1898 and by 1902 had organized a movement to establish the Hazard Baptist Institute. His biography was entitled *The Prophet of Little Cane Creek* and written by Harold E. Dye (Atlanta: Home Mission Board, Southern Baptist Convention, 1949). See Johnson, *History of Perry County,* 84.

11. These problems are enumerated at length in the chapter titled "Education" in JCC, *Southern Highlander,* 264–71.

12. According to John Pearce, the French-Eversole War in Perry County began as a business dispute between two lawyer-merchants in 1887 in the hard-living, hard-drinking town of Hazard, Ken-

tucky, and ended in 1913 when Fulton French tried to shake hands with Susan Eversole and was shot by her son Harry. He later died of the wound. See Pearce, *Days of Darkness*, 75. Charles G. Mutzenberg devotes sixty-six pages to the story, noting that more than twenty men were killed, most shot from ambush. See *Kentucky's Famous Feuds and Tragedies*, 231.

13. Hyden, the county seat of Leslie County, was founded in 1878 and named for state senator John Hyden. It is at the mouth of Rockhouse Creek on the Middle Fork of the Kentucky River. The Hyden post office opened in 1879. See *Kentucky Atlas and Gazetteer*, www.uky.edu/KentuckyAtlas/ky.hyden.html. The school at Hyden was supported by the local Presbyterian Church, not the denominational board. See Hooker and Dunn, *Religion in the Highlands*, 300.

14. Lowrie is referring to the Kentucky school law of 1904, the Day Law, which segregated private and public schools. In North Carolina parochial schools worked side by side with public schools in harmony and were considered supplemental. Some of the myriad Presbyterian schools even received state aid. Baptists protested this practice loudly, pointing to the principle of separation of church and state. So in 1896 C. H. Mebane, then superintendent of public instruction, ruled that "the spirit of the law seemed to be against combining Church and State in any way," thereby excluding all church schools from receiving state funds. See Luther L. Gobbel, *Church-State Relationships in Education in North Carolina Since 1776* (Durham, NC: Duke Univ. Press, 1938), 199. Raine observed that there were no organizations in the mountains promoting the value of good schools as there were in the lowlands, such as the PTA and women's and men's clubs. The school terms were so short that pupils forgot what they learned: "The parents become discouraged, the community mildly hopeless." *Land of Saddle-Bags*, 172.

15. London was the county seat of Laurel County, a town of about one thousand in 1890. Judge W. L. Brown, one of its leading citizens, was interested in changing the image of the county as a place full of feudists and vicious revenue officers, which had been perpetuated by news articles in the local paper, the *Mountain Echo*, edited by A. R. Dyche. See Thomas D. Clark, *A History of Laurel*

County: An Account of the Emergence of a Frontier Kentucky Appalachian Community into a Modern Commercial-Industrial Rural-Urban Center (London, KY: Laurel County Historical Society, 1989), 356.

16. Harvey Short Murdoch served as the field secretary of the American Inland Mission, or the Society of Soul Winners, an interdenominational organization formed by Dr. Edward O. Guerrant, a prominent and colorful figure in the Presbyterian Church. Murdoch was a popular and charismatic leader and teacher and was able to raise enough money to establish the Witherspoon Log College in Buckhorn, Kentucky, in 1903, modeled on the log college that Princeton once was. He considered the Log Cathedral on Laurel Point his crowning achievement, and in 1907 it officially became part of the Transylvania Presbytery. See G. Gordon Mahy Jr., *Murdoch of Buckhorn* (Nashville: Parthenon Press, 1946).

17. Mr. M. is not identified in the diary. Probably he is the Mr. Miller in charge of Presbyterian work in Manchester, mentioned in *Life and Work*, 159.

18. See a short history of the Campbell family in Kentucky: Sadie Stidham's *Trails into Cutshin Country: A History of the Pioneers of Leslie County, Kentucky* (Corbin, KY: Sadie W. Stidham, 1978), 35–36. The John Campbells came with the Baker and Couch families to Kentucky from North Carolina in the early 1800s, settling first at Campbell's Bend on the North Fork River. A short time later, they moved on into Cutshin Country, now Leslie County.

19. Mary and Simon Stacy were good friends of May Stone and Katherine Pettit. Mary Stacy is credited with the term "quare women," meaning "strange women," which was used to refer to settlement workers, along with the term "fotched on" women. See Stoddart, *Challenge and Change*, 30, 36–37.

20. The names of Mrs. Cody's girls were Millie and Elsie. Ibid., 41.

4. January 1909

1. ODC, *Life and Work*, 151–52, 155.

2. Jackson, Michigan, was famous for its Jackson wagons, which were made to order. See Charles V. DeLand's *History of Jackson County, Michigan* (Logansport, IN: B. F. Bowen, 1903), 793.

3. In 1897 the Bottle-in-Bond Act was passed by the U.S. Congress, specifying that bonded whiskey had to be aged in government-supervised bonded warehouses, bottled at 100 proof, and the distiller identified. The characteristic flavor is obtained by using charred oak barrels. Bourbon county was named for the French royal family, because France helped the pioneers defeat the Indians. Bourbon whiskey was recognized by the U.S. government in 1904, and it was decreed that the *B* should be capitalized. See John E. Kleber, ed., *The Kentucky Encyclopedia* (Lexington: Univ. Press of Kentucky, 1992), 267, citing William L. Downard, *Dictionary of the History of the American Brewing and Distilling Industries* (Westport, CT.: Greenwood Press, 1980).

4. Frederick Webb was the minister of the Presbyterian churches at Flag Pond and Rocky Fork in Unicoi County, Tennessee.

5. The Beaver Creek area was settled in the nineteenth century and a Mouth of Beaver post office opened in 1854. Further growth occurred with the opening of a Chesapeake and Ohio Railroad station. The Allen post office opened in 1905 and was probably named for a nineteenth-century storekeeper. The town was known as Beaver Creek or Beaver Creek Junction until 1936, when it was named Allen City. See *Kentucky Atlas and Gazetteer,* www.uky.edu/KentuckyAtlas/ky-allen-city.html.

6. The Kentucky General Assembly of 1906 established the Eastern Kentucky State Normal School. The Normal School Commission selected the campus of the old Central University, founded in 1874 in Richmond, as the site of the new school. In 1922 Eastern became a four-year institution known as the Eastern Kentucky State Normal School and Teachers College. In 1930 the General Assembly renamed the school Eastern Kentucky State Teachers College. In 1948 the word *Teachers* was removed from the name, and the college was granted the right to award nonprofessional degrees. On February 26, 1966, Governor Edward T. Breathitt signed into law a bill renaming the institution Eastern Kentucky University and sanctioning the awarding of graduate degrees in academic fields other than education. See "History," Eastern Kentucky University, www.eku.edu/campuses/EKUCampuses/. See also William E. Ellis, *A History of Eastern Kentucky University: The School of Opportunity* (Lexington: Univ. Press of Kentucky, 2005).

7. Dr. James F. Record was president of Pikeville College. Under his leadership (1919–1932), the college "developed a solid reputation for academics in a Christian environment." Ed Maddox and Connie Maddox, *Pike County, Kentucky: A Pictorial History* (Virginia Beach, VA: Donning, 1998), 76.

8. Paintsville is in the coal-field region of Eastern Kentucky. See George D. Torok, *A Guide to Historic Coal Towns of the Big Sandy River Valley* (Knoxville: Univ. of Tennessee Press, 2004).

9. Pikeville College, a Presbyterian school, was in Pikeville, the county seat of Pike County. See Olive Arnold Campbell, comp., *Southern Mountain Schools Maintained by Denominational and Independent Agencies,* rev. ed. (New York: Russell Sage Foundation, 1923), 6. The town was founded in 1823 on the Big Sandy River and was named, like the county, for General Zebulon Pike. The town was always known as Pikeville, although the official name of the town and the post office were Pike and Piketon at various times. See *Kentucky Atlas and Gazetteer,* www.uky.edu/KentuckyAtlas/ky-pikeville.html.

10. The quintessential version of this family/community feud that stretched across the Tug River and two states is told by Altina L. Waller in *Feud: Hatfields, McCoys, and Social Change in Appalachia, 1860–1900* (Chapel Hill: Univ. of North Carolina Press, 1988). She argues that the feud was caused primarily by the changing economic and social conditions in Kentucky and West Virginia at the time. Pearce, in *Days of Darkness,* comments on her "study of the economic transition of the remote valley" and further maintains that the "feud was almost over before the press began its coverage," causing most of the trouble with its "usually erroneous sensationalism" (57). Mutzenberg dates the family enmity back to the bushwhacking that took place during the Civil War, but he proposes the common view that a disagreement over the ownership of a hog was the igniting incident in 1882. It eventually involved the governors of two states, and in *Kentucky's Famous Feuds and Tragedies,* Mutzenberg surmises that, although many feuds had been fought in Logan County, West Virginia, and Pike County, Kentucky, "none equaled in ferocity the bloody Hatfield-McCoy war, during which crimes of the most revolting nature were perpetuated" (29).

11. Frank Phillips, called "Bad Frank Phillips," indeed had an

unsavory reputation to say the least, but he was on the other side. He was raised by an enemy of Anse Hatfield and spent some time trying to kill the old man. For an in-depth version of the story, see Waller's *Feud*. Dr. W. C. Condit was instrumental in the location of schools and churches in the Big Sandy River Valley, including the Pikeville Collegiate Institute. See Maddox and Maddox, *Pike County, Kentucky*, 58–59. Ashland is on the Ohio River in Boyd County in Eastern Kentucky. Beginning in the late eighteenth century, the area was known as Poages Settlement and later Pollards Mill. In 1854 the town of Ashland was laid out by the Kentucky Iron, Coal, and Manufacturing Company and named for the Lexington home of Henry Clay. The Pollards Mill post office opened in 1847 and was renamed Ashland in 1854. See *Kentucky Atlas and Gazetteer*, www. uky.edu/KentuckyAtlas/ky-ashland.html.

12. Morehead Christian School was founded in 1887 by the United Christian Missionary Society of St. Louis, Mrs. Phebe Button, and her son Dr. Frank C. Button, who had been rural school supervisor for the General Education Board. Professor J. M. Robinson was a teacher there in 1909. It became the State Normal School in 1922, changed to Morehead State Teachers College in 1930, and was named Morehead State University in 1966. See Charles O. Peratt, "History of the Morehead State Normal School," in W. R. Thomas, *Life among the Hills and Mountains of Kentucky* (Louisville: Standard, 1926), 202–3. Also see Kentucky Historical Society, Historical Marker Database, www.kentucky.gov/kyhs/hmdb/MarkerSearch.aspx. Morehead, the county seat of Rowan County, is located on Triplett Creek. Settlers were there by the early part of the nineteenth century and a post office opened there as Triplett in 1817. The city of Morehead was founded in 1856 and named for James T. Morehead, a governor of Kentucky. See *Kentucky Atlas and Gazetteer*, www.uky.edu/KentuckyAtlas/ky-morehead.html.

13. This was one of the feuds investigated by Meriel Daniel Harris in his master's thesis, "Two Famous Kentucky Feuds." He cites the sociological customs of mountain life and the lack of exposure to the outside world as roots of the violent tendencies exhibited in mountain feuds (3). Quoting Mutzenberg, who calls it the "Tolliver-Martin-Logan Vendetta," Harris says this Rowan County feud

started in the Civil War and was perpetrated by the kin of the participants (7). Pearce notes that the governor had to send in troops to end the three-year "Rowan County War." He calls it an "unhappy chapter" and a "grisly episode" in the history of Morehead and Rowan counties, which is largely forgotten because no one now keeps personal records such as letters and diaries. *Days of Darkness*, 95.

14. Travelers staying in the inns and taverns along the road often shared a room, and sometimes a bed, with strangers. Meals were served at a common table; a few such establishments offered a bath house. By the 1830s, Kentucky had several inns of note, including the Phoenix Hotel, a Lexington landmark, so named because it was built on the ashes of a predecessor that had burned. From Kleber, *Kentucky Encyclopedia*, 719.

15. Mr. Desha Breckinridge was a member of "Kentucky's premier family of Progressive reformers" and was the "influential editor of the *Lexington Herald* newspaper." His wife Madeline McDowell Breckinridge, a friend of both Katherine Pettit and May Stone, used the *Herald* to publicize the activities of industrial and settlement schools in the region. See Stone, Pettit, and Stoddart, *Quare Women's Journals*, 32, 34.

16. She is referring to Tyndaris in Sicily.

17. She refers to Frances Beauchamp, the "dynamic president" of the WCTU, which sponsored Hindman Settlement School. Stoddart, *Challenge and Change*, 19.

18. The Christian Women's Board of Missions was made up of local church societies to involve women and children in the concerns of missions. See Douglas A. Foster, *The Encyclopedia of the Stone-Campbell Movement: Christian Church (Disciples of Christ), Christian Churches* (Grand Rapids, MI.: Eerdmans, 2004), 201.

19. The governor of Kentucky in 1908 was August E. Wilson, J. G. Crabbe was superintendent of public instruction, and M. E. Rankin was agriculture commissioner. No commissioner of education was listed. See "Kentucky's Governors: 1907–1927" and "Kentucky's Officials: 1901–1925," Kentucky Department for Libraries and Archives, www.kdla.ky.gov/resources/. Note 20 in *Life and Work* reads: "Mr. Crabbe was responsible for the Kentucky School Law referred to previously in this Chapter IV."

20. In 1780 Virginia wanted to expand its educational opportunities to the Kentucky frontier and established Transylvania, a
liberal arts college, the sixteenth college in the United States and
the first college west of the Alleghenies. It opened in Danville but
moved to Lexington in 1789. Due to financial difficulties after the
Civil War, the college merged with Kentucky University, a Christian
Church school in Harrodsburg, in 1858. There was confusion between its name and that of the University of Kentucky, so its original name, Transylvania University, was reinstated in 1908. From
Kleber, *Kentucky Encyclopedia*, 894–96.

21. "Burns of the Mountains" taught at Berea for a short time,
where he met the Reverend H. L. McMurray, a Baptist preacher
from Kansas (the spelling of his name varies from one reference
to another). In 1899 they decided to build a college in the middle
of the mountains. Burns was from Oneida and chose his father's
birthplace as the site of the school. To accomplish their goal, they
had to get the support of feuding families in the area. Burns's own
family had a long-standing feud with the Combs family, and Oneida was the center of the Baker-Howard feud as well. Burns talked
the feudists into meeting in an old mill, where many of the bloody
battles had been fought. Burns reported, "It was a might difficult
meeting. . . . They were the best and bravest men I know. . . . All of
them had bitter memories in their hearts—memories of untimely
graves on the mountain sides." In the famous meeting, Burns con-
vinced the group of fifty enemies to settle their differences for the
sake of their children who would go to school together at Oneida
Institute. Darrell C. Richardson, *Mountain Rising: The Story of James
Anderson Burns and Oneida Institute* (Oneida, KY: Oneida Mountaineer Press, 1986), 136.

22. Josh Carnahan was a merchant. Ibid., 129.

23. Dwight Billings discusses the perpetuation of the upper and
lower classes even after slavery was abolished. He points out that
former planters in the South were still the upper class, economi-
cally and politically, and were bound together by their economic
interests and their social relationships. He goes on to say that prejudice was a "cultural construct of the landed upper class," not a low-
er-class trait, as sociologists suggest. Billings, *Planters and the Making*

of a "New South": Class, Politics, and Development in North Carolina, 1865–1900 (Chapel Hill: Univ. of North Carolina Press, 1979), 91–92. Further, John Inscoe observes that most mountain slave-holders were professionals, either doctors or lawyers, the most influential class in the South before the war. Inscoe, *Mountain Masters, Slavery, and the Sectional Crisis in Western North Carolina* (Knoxville: Univ. of Tennessee Press, 1989), 62. In Madison County, Kentucky, too, the 1900 census showed that "a social caste system very much like slavery flourished." William E. Ellis, H. E. Everman, and Richard D. Sears, *Madison County: 200 Years in Retrospect*, Richmond, KY: Madison County Historical Society, 1985), 248.

24. The oil and gas industry was part of the Kentucky economy as early as the late 1800s. The first year of recorded oil production was 1883. Now more than half of Kentucky's counties produce oil and gas. See Kleber, *Kentucky Encyclopedia*, 692. For a comprehensive review of oil production in Kentucky, county by county, see "Oil and Gas Development of the Mountain Counties, as a Whole," a chapter in Thomas, *Life among the Hills*, 39–77.

25. Note 22 here in the first transcription reads: "Oneida Baptist Institute, Oneida, Clay County, Kentucky."

26. Burns called Professor Louis D. Sandlin "the best worker we ever had." Claude Carson Matlack, Samuel W. Thomas, and W. Robinson Beard, *Dawn Comes to the Mountains* (Louisville: George Rogers Clark Press, 1981), 54. The spelling of Sandlin's name is corrected in pencil in the transcription of the original diary. Sandlin played an important part in the history of Oneida for more than twenty years. McMurray was a partner with Burns in the establishment and construction of the Oneida Institute and was one of the three faculty members when Oneida began operation with classes from the first grade to the eighth. Emerson Hough, *Burns of the Mountains: The Story of a Southern Mountaineer Who Is Remaking His Own People* (Oneida, KY: Oneida Institute, 1927).

27. Burns himself wrote about his family's feud in James Anderson Burns, *The Crucible: A Tale of the Kentucky Feuds by Burns of the Mountains* (Oneida, KY: Oneida Institute, 1928). He tells the story of his family and his upbringing in a log cabin with a dirt floor and little furniture. His father was a Primitive Baptist preach-

er from Kentucky who had moved to West Virginia to avoid the feuds between his family and the Combses. Burns maintained that Kentucky men were "the kindest, gentlest men I ever knew" (45). The feuds were generally started by "reckless boys, or by irresponsible, drunken men, in spite of the combined efforts and energies of the feud leaders and the men of experience" (47). Burns was most proud of the fact that the establishment of Oneida Institute brought the Burns and Combs families together in a combined effort to educate their children: "Let's build a school and teach our children to love each other" (62).

28. The Kentucky River is 259 miles long, formed by the junction of the North and South forks at Beattyville in Lee County in Central Kentucky, and it flows northwest past Irvine, Boonesboro, and Frankfort to the Ohio River at Carrollton. It is partially navigable by means of locks. The upper part of the Kentucky flows through the coal-mining region of the Cumberland Mountains. The lower section flows through the Bluegrass region. The North Fork of the river is 125 miles long, rising in Letcher County in southeastern Kentucky, near the Virginia state line. It flows northwest past Hazard and Jackson and meets the Middle Fork one mile east of the confluence with the South Fork. The South Fork is about 30 miles long, formed by the joining of Red Bird and Goose creeks in Clay County in southeastern Kentucky, and flows north to join the North Fork. The Middle Fork is about 85 miles long and rises in northeastern Harlan County. It flows past Hayden and through Buckhorn Lake reservoir to the North Fork. See two fine books: Thomas D. Clark, *The Kentucky* (Lexington, KY: Henry Clay Press, 1969); and William E. Ellis, *The Kentucky River* (Lexington: Univ. Press of Kentucky, 2000).

29. JCC discusses this "theory of origin" in his chapter "Ancestry" in *Southern Highlander,* 50–71. In Appendix B of his book, "A Misapplied Theory of Mountain Origin," he presents John Fiske's then widely accepted theory that those who could not succeed in Virginia, the poor or the criminal, moved into North Carolina and from there into the Appalachians, where they were known more for their shiftlessness than their criminal nature (349–51). Also see John Fiske, *Old Virginia and Her Neighbors,* vol. 2 (Boston: Houghton Mifflin, 1897).

30. Harold Wilson Coates's little book *The Great Truce of Clay: Stories of Kentucky Feuds* (Cincinnati: Holmes-Darst Coal, 1923) observed that the "deep stain upon Clay County" originated with some of its most prominent citizens. In the early part of the nineteenth century, the Garrards and the Whites were salt barons, and the animosity between them probably originated as industrial competition. But their feud erupted not over economic issues but personal ones. A hound, "yellow and uncertain in breeding," owned by Daniel Bates, had been the object of denigration by a Dr. Baker until "bad blood . . . finally welled to the point" where Baker killed Bates (5). The Howards, relatives of Bates, pushed for Baker's prosecution and were aided and abetted by the Whites. Soon families throughout the county were involved. The Civil War acerbated the antagonism, as politics were then involved. Finally peace was declared in 1901; it lasted until 1904, when old animosities flared during a drinking bout. But by then the "law was beginning to function in Clay County," and the perpetrators were arrested and tried (41).

31. Dr. George A. Buttrick, a prominent New York preacher, was on the Executive Board of the Conference for Education in the South. See Southern Education Board, "Educational Conditions in the Southern Appalachians," *Bulletin of the Southern Education Board* 1, no. 1 (1902): 1.

32. Frank Burns and Levi "Lee" Combs were on the first board. Richardson, *Mountain Rising*, 138.

33. See "Old-Time Baptists of Central Appalachia," a chapter by Howard Dorgan in *Christianity in Appalachia: Profiles in Regional Pluralism* (Knoxville: Univ. of Tennessee Press, 1999), 117–37. In a nutshell, the split derived from the fact that many Appalachian Baptists distanced themselves from the home missionary effort. The Missionary Baptists promoted evangelism and those who opposed it were called "antimissionary" (126).

34. Harlan Presbyterian Academy (1890–1916) played an important role in the educational history of Harlan County. See Torok, *Guide to Historic Coal Towns*, 283–85. Harlan, a record-producing coal town, is located at the forks of the Cumberland River. It was settled about 1796 and was first known as Mount Pleasant, for a local Indian mound. The post office opened in 1828 as

Harlan Court House, was known as Spurlock, for the postmaster, in the early 1860s, and was renamed Harlan in 1865. See *Kentucky Atlas and Gazetteer*, www.uky.edu/KentuckyAtlas/ky-harlan.html.

35. Evarts is about eight miles from Harlan on the Clover Fork of the Cumberland River in southeastern Kentucky and was on the L&N Railroad line. It was incorporated in 1855 and named for a local family. See Torok, *Guide to Historic Coal Towns*, who writes that Evarts is best known for the Battle of Evarts, an extremely violent episode during the struggle to unionize "bloody Harlan county" in 1931 (285).

36. Kentenia Land Corporation from Philadelphia owned eighty-six thousand acres of mineral land in Martin's Fork. See Ronald D Eller, *Miners, Millhands, and Mountaineers: Industrialization of the Appalachian South, 1880–1930* (Knoxville: Univ. of Tennessee Press, 1982), 147.

37. Opened as Southern and Western Theological Seminary in 1819, Maryville College was chartered in 1842 by the Tennessee State Legislature as a Christian institution and governed by a board appointed by the Presbyterian Synod of Tennessee. Samuel Tyndale Wilson, a prominent minister, citizen, and author, wrote several books about Maryville College as well as *Southern Mountaineers*.

5. February 1909

1. ODC, *Life and Work*, 172.

2. Dr. Millard Dudley Jeffries, a Baptist pastor who also had a degree in medicine from the University of Virginia, succeeded Dr. John T. Henderson as president of Carson and Newman College in 1903. Carson and Newman colleges in Tennessee were united in 1889 with Dr. W. A. Montgomery, former president of Carson College, at the head of the resulting college. As a young professor, John T. Henderson was put in charge of a campaign to raise money for new buildings, and in 1893 he became president. With a magnetic personality, he made many improvements in the physical plant and in the academic offerings. See Isaac Newton Carr, *History of Carson-Newman College* (Jefferson City, TN: Carson-Newman College, 1959), 63.

3. Note 26 here in the biography text reads: "Tusculum College." Dr. Charles Oliver Gray served as president of Greeneville-Tusculum College from 1908 to 1931. His term was marked by substantial accomplishments: the budget grew fifteen times over, six major new buildings were built, and the faculty doubled. See Fuhrmann, *Life and Times of Tusculum College,* 167.

4. Frederic Webb was the Presbyterian minister at Flag Pond, the Campbells' destination on this day. In 1901 the Presbyterian Church established a church in Rocky Fork. It added another branch in Flag Pond when the first resident minister, Frederic Lee Webb, arrived in 1905. Miss Jennie started the day school in 1903. She was much beloved by the community, and they renamed the church the Jennie Moore Memorial Presbyterian Church for her in 1942. See the Unicoi County Heritage Committee, *Unicoi County, Tennessee and Its People, 1875–1995* (Erwin, TN: Unicoi County Heritage Book Committee, 1995), 7–8. In William Cooper, *Old Churches of Unicoi County* (N.p., TN: William Cooper, 2003), 49–58, there may be found short histories of the churches in Rocky Fork, Flag Pond, and Devil Fork, with photographs, including ones of Jennie Moore and Frederic Webb. The Sweetwater Church of God in Devil Fork was established in 1903 as the Sweetwater Valley Baptist Church.

5. Suppositions abound about how Flag Pond got its name. The most logical is that it was a swampy area with wild flags (irises) growing around it where three creeks converged. Since creeks were the roads of the early 1800s, it became a gathering place for people living nearby. The name was not official until the Flag Pond Post Office, the first post office in Unicoi County, was established in 1846. See "Flag Pond, Unicoi County, Tennessee," www.flagpond. com, accessed February 26, 2006.

6. The term *digger Indians* generally refers to a low type of humanity. Digger Indians were generally mountain Indians who clashed with those settlers who came to dig gold in the California mountains. See Lisa Emmerich, "California Indians of the Northern Mountains," in *Encyclopedia of Immigration and Migration in the American West* (Thousand Oaks, CA: Sage, 2009), 115–18, also available at *SAGE Reference Online,* accessed February 20, 2012.

7. There are a total of four falls on Spivey Creek and four on

Rock Creek; this is a spectacular part of Unicoi County in south-eastern Tennessee. Spivey Creek Falls, Rock Creek Falls, and Devil's Fork Gap are still popular hiking destinations near the Appalachian Trail.

8. The Sweetwater School was located three miles from Rocky Fork, and the two schools were consolidated in 1957, just before Rocky Fork was consolidated with Flag Pond in 1958. Unicoi County Heritage Committee, *Unicoi County*, 24.

9. Wilson, in *Southern Mountaineers*, provides excellent short paragraphs about the schools in the region. The school in Burnsville was the Stanley McCormick Academy, "ably directed in its formative years by Prof. C. R. Hubbard" (131).

10. The condenser is used to cool the whiskey before it is bottled, just as the Irish and the Scottish used it in the fourteenth century. Copper tubing is shaped like a coil (thus called a worm) and set into a container into which cool water is pumped constantly. Moonshiners guarded their worms closely, since they constituted very incriminating evidence if found by federal agents. To learn how to make a still, see Joseph Earl Dabney, *More Mountain Spirits: The Continuing Chronicle of Moonshine Life and Corn Whiskey, Wines, Ciders, and Beers in America's Appalachians* (Asheville, NC: Bright Mountain Books, 1985), 165.

11. Laurel Country is so named because of the huge stands of rhododendron, called "laurel" by mountain natives, that cover the mountainsides. It blooms in late June or July, spectacularly on the bald of Roan Mountain. Because it is so profuse in this part of North Carolina, it appears in many names of places drained by the tributaries of the Big Laurel Creek: Big Laurel, Upper Laurel, Rich Laurel, Wolf Laurel, Shelton Laurel, etc. Allanstand, or Allenstand, was so named because it was originally Allen's stand, a stand being an overnight or resting place for travelers. See Margaret Warner Morley, *The Carolina Mountains* (Boston: Houghton Mifflin, 1913), who credits Florence Stephenson, principal of the Home Industrial School in Asheville and Frances Goodrich of Allanstand for the prosperity of the Laurel Country (229).

12. The Yale-educated Miss Frances Louisa Goodrich joined the Presbyterian Home Missions Board as a volunteer. In 1895 she be-

gan the first craft shop north of Asheville in Brittain's Cove. Owing to the shift to industrial work, mountain communities were no longer self-sustaining and money was scarce, as were schools, churches, and medical facilities. She came to teach but ended up rediscovering the dying art of weaving, and in 1902 she helped the community revive the craft to sell items in an old log structure once known as "Allen's Old Stand." See Katherine Caldwell and Southern Highland Handicraft Guild, *From Mountain Hands: The Story of Allanstand Craft Shop's First 100 Years* (Asheville, NC: Southern Highland Handicraft Guild, 1995), 2–3.

13. The Farm and Home Industrial School was one of several schools organized in Asheville around 1890. Wilson's *Southern Mountaineers*, 134–46, is a good source of information about all of the Asheville schools.

14. John Sevier was a member of the French Xavier family that fled France during the Huguenot persecution, moved to London, and changed the name to Sevier. In the eighteenth century, his father came to the Shenandoah Valley, where John was born in 1745. A prosperous farmer, John was called to conquer the wilderness of East Tennessee, where he settled his family and became one of the most prominent men in Tennessee history. He was elected six times as governor of the state and four times as a U.S. congressman. See Francis Marion Turner, *Life of General John Sevier* (Johnson City, TN: Overmountain Press, 1997).

15. Penland is in the mountains of Mitchell County, NC, close to Tennessee. The Morgan family lived in North Carolina for several generations before Rufus Morgan founded the Appalachian Industrial School. His younger sister Lucy later began the arts and crafts movement at Penland in the 1920s. The school was under the direction of Bishop Junius M. Horner of the Episcopal Diocese of Western North Carolina, who had approached Morgan when he was still a seminary student, and classes were held in a farmhouse that had been used by a former Baptist school. See Alvic, *Weavers of the Southern Highlands*, 75.

16. Sandra Lee Barney, in her in-depth study of medicine in Appalachia during this period, discusses the role of women's clubs and settlement schools as they tried to coordinate the work of lo-

cal healers and that of the scattered ranks of medical men. There was little difference between the doctors in Appalachia and those in other rural areas at the end of the nineteenth century. Most had little formal education and few relied on their practices for support. Only with the advent of industrial capitalism and new population centers were doctors able to justify acquiring scientific and professional credentials. See Barney's *Authorized to Heal: Gender, Class, and the Transformation of Medicine in Appalachia, 1880–1930* (Chapel Hill: Univ. of North Carolina Press, 2000), 13–15. Earlier, Fred Eastman's *Unfinished Business of the Presbyterian Church in America* (Philadelphia: Westminster Press, 1921) cited the need for hospitals and dispensaries, for community houses with medical care facilities, and for a "religion not of ecstasy, but of brotherhood and service" (36–38).

17. Ledger is a little community near Roan Mountain. About the colorful names of mountain towns, Margaret Morley remarked that "Ledger" does not seem so strange when a place down the road is called "Daybook." *Carolina Mountains,* 332. Towns near Ledger are Cranberry, Minneapolis, Loafer's Glory, and Plumtree.

18. Reformers, often affiliated with women's organizations, were concerned with conditions in jails all over the South during the Progressive Era. See Vivien M. L. Miller, *Crime, Sexual Violence, and Clemency: Florida's Pardon Board and Penal System in the Progressive Era* (Gainesville: Univ. Press of Florida, 2000); and a book published by the Tennessee State Federation of Women's Clubs that featured elegant photographs of socially prominent women and articles they wrote. Among the women included was Mrs. John O. Flautt, who wrote "Prison Reform" and "Juvenile Courts." Tennessee State Federation of Women's Clubs, *Woman's Work in Tennessee* (Memphis, TN: Jones-Briggs, 1916), 151–56.

19. Mrs. Julia Josephine Irving was a professor of the Greek language and literature at Wellesley College and served as president from 1894 to 1899. *New York Times,* June 14, 1894, 5.

6. March 1909

1. ODC, *Life and Work,* 192–93.
2. The Presbyterian School for Boys in Plumtree was estab-

lished by a prominent minister and educator in the region, the Reverend Edgar A. Tufts. The Reverend J. P. Hall, brother-in-law of Mr. Tufts, was made headmaster and later became the first chairman of the Avery County Board of Education. Near the same time, in nearby Banner Elk, a school for girls had been founded, to which the school for boys moved after the fire. Both offered high school courses. They were operated by the Edgar A. Tufts Foundation and eventually became Lees-McRae College and Grandfather Home for Children. See a publication by the Avery County Retired School Personnel, *A History of Avery County Schools* (Newland, NC: Avery County Retired School Personnel, 1989). It also has a chapter on the schools in Montezuma, Cranberry, and Banner Elk.

3. The story of Linville, Grandfather Mountain, and the MacRae families is told in Howard E. Covington, *Linville: A Mountain Home for 100 Years* (Linville, NC: Linville Resorts, 1992). An interest in iron ore and mica mining brought Hugh MacRae as a young man to Mitchell county, where he and his father Donald discovered the Linville River valley. Along with Samuel T. Kelsey, who founded Highlands, they began buying land around Grandfather, Flat Top, and Sugar Mountain (5). In 1888 the name of the post office was changed to Linville from Porcelain (for the deposits of kaolin nearby). William Linville and his son John had been killed by Indians in 1766 when they were camped near the "Great Falls" of the Cherokee (7).

4. Moses Cone was a mill owner who owned thirty-five hundred acres of land north of Blowing Rock, including Flat Top Mountain and Rich Mountain. He donated generously to the public schools, and his contributions to the state teacher's college, which later became Appalachian State University, were instrumental in promoting higher education in the mountains of western North Carolina. He died in 1908 at the age of fifty-one, but his wife lived on the estate for another thirty-nine years. The Moses Cone Memorial Park was donated to the U.S. Government in 1950 and has since become an outstanding feature of the Blue Ridge Parkway. See John Preston Arthur, *Western North Carolina: A History, 1730–1913* (1914; reprint, Spartanburg, SC: Reprint, 1973), 501.

5. Skyland Institute at Blowing Rock was a girls' school with

industrial training, started in 1891 by Emily C. Prudden, who transferred it to the American Missionary Association. In 1912 it was reconveyed to Miss Prudden, then closed. See John Preston Arthur, *A History of Watauga County, North Carolina, with Sketches of Prominent Families* (Richmond, VA: Everett Waddey, 1915), 253.

6. Archdeacon Frederick Neve wrote about Valle Crucis and its Episcopal mission school in "The Missions of the Blue Ridge, Diocese of Virginia," in *The Church's Mission to the Mountaineers of the South,* Walter Houghson, comp. (Hartford, CT: Church Missions, 1908), 80–102. He cited Susan Fenimore Cooper's book *William West Skiles: A Sketch of Missionary Life at Valle Crucis in Western North Carolina, 1842–1862* (1890; reprint, Valle Crucis, NC: Valle Crucis Conference Center, 1992). In 1842 the Right Reverend Levi Ives, Episcopal bishop of North Carolina, gave the remote valley its name, "Vale of the Cross" in Latin. He held the first service in 1842 and established the school in 1844. See also Arthur, *Western North Carolina,* 430–33.

7. Banner Elk was the location of the Lees-McRae Institute, a Presbyterian school established in 1901. The institute became Lees-McRae College. In 1923 the trustees appointed Edgar Hall Tufts, at twenty-three, to organize the school as a junior college. See Margaret Tufts Neal, *And Set Aglow a Sacred Flame: History of the Edgar Tufts Memorial Association, 1895–1942* (Banner Elk, NC: PuddingStone Press, 1983), 108–38. This school is also mentioned in Arthur's *Western North Carolina,* 442.

8. The iron ore deposit at Cranberry, in what was then Watauga County, was discovered by three brothers by the name of Perkins who were looking for ginseng in the woods on Humpback Mountain in North Carolina while hiding out from a Tennessee sheriff. The deposit was owned by the Cranberry Iron and Coal Company, and by 1876 the ore was all shipped by rail to a blast furnace in Johnson City, Tennessee. See C. A. Bowlick, "A Study of the Cranberry Ore Belt: A Thesis" (master's thesis, Appalachian State Teachers College, 1955), 9–10.

9. See Florence Stephenson, *The Home Industrial School, Asheville, North Carolina* (Asheville, NC: The Women's Executive Committee of Home Missions of the Presbyterian Church, 1896).

10. The Reverend and Mrs. L. M. Pease were northerners who were involved in the early work of the Presbyterian Church in western North Carolina. On vacation there, they were struck by the need of mountain children in the Asheville area and organized the Asheville Home Industrial School for Girls in 1887. Shortly thereafter the Normal and Collegiate Institute and the Asheville Farm School for Boys followed. Yeuell claims that there was no overall design by the Presbyterian churches working in the mountains and that the southern and northern churches emphasized different things. The primary goal of northerners was generally "uplift," and education and evangelism were by-products. The southern missionaries began with evangelism to establish churches so that schools would likely follow. Yeuell, *Moving Mountains*, 13–14. See also Arthur, *Western North Carolina*, 439–40.

11. Dr. Chase P. Ambler specialized in diseases of the chest and was an active conservationist. As a result of his efforts to establish the Smoky Mountains National Park, a six-thousand-foot peak was named for him. See Doris Cline Ward, ed., *The Heritage of Old Buncombe County* (Asheville, NC: Old Buncombe County Genealogical Society, 1981), 1:138.

12. The Right Reverend Junius M. Horner was the first Episcopal bishop of western North Carolina. In 1903, when he was bishop of the Missionary District of Asheville, he opened and directed the Valle Crucis School for Girls, where domestic skills were taught as well as academics. Later, he bought a herd of blooded cattle and sent them to Valle Crucis along with a young agriculturist from New York. John Preston Arthur wrote that it was the first practical instruction ever given in any school or college in North Carolina. See Arthur, *History of Watauga County*, 254; Arthur, *Western North Carolina*, 432–33.

13. Dr. Rodney Rush Swope (1897–1916) was the first rector of All Souls Church in Biltmore. George Vanderbilt of Biltmore House himself guaranteed his salary. Dr. Swope led the effort for prison reform when education, medical care, and welfare (benevolence) were more the work of the church than of the government. See Isaac N. Northup and Carole H. Currie, *The Story of a Church: All Souls in Biltmore* (Biltmore, NC: All Souls Church, 1979).

14. This was Dr. J. P. Roger, the head of the Farm School in 1909. He was cited by Arthur in *Western North Carolina* as one of the physicians in the region whose name was known in "many a mountain cabin" (439–40).

15. Mars Hill, founded by pioneers, is the oldest educational institution on its original site in western North Carolina and the first school established by Baptists west of the Blue Ridge Mountains. First named the French Broad Baptist Institute, Mars Hill College was chartered by the state of North Carolina in 1859. John Angus McLeod wrote that the charter had a provision "prohibiting the manufacture and sale of ardent spirits within four miles of the College, so that parents sending their sons to this school will feel assured that they will be secure from influences of this kind." McLeod, *From These Stones: Mars Hill College, 1856–1968* (Mars Hill, NC: Mars Hill College, 1968), 31.

16. Dr. Thomas Lawrence had founded a mission in New York but had moved to Asheville in the 1870s, conducting a school for girls. The Reverend L. M. Pease, encouraged by the success of the Home Industrial School, which he supervised, opened the Normal and Collegiate Institute in 1892 with Dr. Lawrence as president and his wife as principal. Dr. Lawrence retired in 1909 at the age of seventy-five. Arthur, *Western North Carolina*, 439.

17. This Mr. Trowbridge is assumed to be C. H. Trowbridge, who wrote about denominational secondary schools in a master's thesis at the University of North Carolina and also wrote an essay, "Transylvania County as an Educational Center," in *Transylvania County Proposes Railway Connection with Main Line in South Carolina* (Brevard, NC:. n.p., n.d. [19__]). Carl H. Trowbridge was president of the Weaver College School of Opportunity, founded 1872, in Weaverville, North Carolina, from 1922 to 1934. "Heritage," Brevard College, www.brevard.edu/AboutBC/Heritage/tabid/236/Default.aspx, accessed February 20, 2012.

SELECTED BIBLIOGRAPHY

Algeo, Katie. "Locals on Local Color: Imagining Identity in Appalachia." *Southern Cultures* 9, no. 4 (2003): 27–54.

Alvic, Philis. *Weavers of the Southern Highlands.* Lexington: Univ.
Press of Kentucky, 2003.

Arthur, John Preston. *Western North Carolina: A History, 1730–1913.*
Spartanburg, SC: Reprint, 1973. First published 1914 by Ed-
wards and Broughton, Raleigh, NC.

———. *A History of Watauga County, North Carolina, with Sketches of
Prominent Families.* Richmond, VA: Everett Waddey, 1915.

Becker, Jane S. *Selling Tradition: Appalachia and the Construction of an
American Folk, 1930–1940.* Chapel Hill: Univ. of North Carolina
Press, 1998.

Caldwell, Katherine, and Southern Highland Handicraft Guild.
*From Mountain Hands: The Story of Allanstand Craft Shop's First
100 Years.* N.p. [Asheville, NC?]: Southern Highland Handicraft Guild, 1995.

Campbell, John C. *The Future of Church and Independent Schools in the
Southern Highlands.* New York: Russell Sage Foundation, 1917.

———. *The Southern Highlander and His Homeland.* New York: Russell Sage Foundation, 1921. Reprint, with foreword by Rupert
B. Vance and introduction by Henry D. Shapiro, Lexington:
Univ. Press of Kentucky, 1969, 2003. Page references are to the
2003 edition.

Carr, Howard Ernest. *Washington College: A Study of an Attempt to Provide Higher Education in Eastern Tennessee.* Knoxville: S.B. Newman, 1935.

Coates, Harold Wilson. *The Great Truce of Clay: Stories of Kentucky*

Feuds. Cincinnati: Holmes-Darst Coal, 1923.

Crocker, Ruth. "From Widow's Mite to Widow's Might: The Philanthropy of Margaret Olivia Sage." *American Presbyterians* 74, no. 4 (1996): 253–64.

Dennis, Michael. *Lessons in Progress: State Universities and Progressivism in the New South, 1880–1920*. Urbana: Univ. of Illinois Press, 2001.

Douthat, James L. *Along the Pike: The Story of Walden's Ridge along Anderson Pike*. Signal Mountain, TN: Mountain Press, 1996.

Eaton, Allen Hendershott, Doris Ulmann, and Russell Sage Foundation. *Handicrafts of the Southern Highlands: With an Account of the Rural Handicraft Movement in the United States and Suggestions for the Wider Use of Handicrafts in Adult Education and in Recreation*. New York: Russell Sage Foundation, 1937.

Ellis, William E. *A History of Eastern Kentucky University: The School of Opportunity*. Lexington: Univ. Press of Kentucky, 2005.

Frost, William Goodell. *For the Mountains: An Autobiography*. New York: Revell, 1937.

Fuhrmann, Joseph T. *The Life and Times of Tusculum College*. Greeneville, TN: Tusculum College, 1986.

Glenn, John M., Lilian Brandt, and F. Emerson Andrews. *Russell Sage Foundation, 1907–1946*. 2 vols. New York: Russell Sage Foundation, 1947.

Goodrich, Frances Louisa. *Mountain Homespun: A Facsimile of the Original, Published in 1931*. Knoxville: Univ. of Tennessee Press, 1989.

Graffenried, Thomas Pritchett de. *History of the De Graffenried Family from 1191 A.D. to 1925*. Binghamton, NY: Vail-Ballou Press, 1925.

Guerrant, Edward O. *The Galax Gatherers: The Gospel among the Highlanders*. 1910. Reprint, Knoxville: Univ. of Tennessee Press, 2003.

Harris, Meriel Daniel. "Two Famous Kentucky Feuds and Their Causes." Master's thesis, Univ. of Kentucky, 1940.

Hooker, Elizabeth R., and Fannie Wyche Dunn. *Religion in the Highlands Native Churches and Missionary Enterprises in the Southern Appalachian Area*. New York: Home Missions Council, 1933.

Krechniak [Bullard], Helen, and Joseph Marshall. *Cumberland*

County's First Hundred Years. Crossville, TN: Centennial Committee, 1956.

Krim, Arthur. "Appalachian Songcatcher: Olive Dame Campbell and the Scotch-Irish Ballad." *Journal of Cultural Geography* 24, no. 1 (Fall–Winter 2006): 91–112.

Lewis, Charles Lee. *Philander Priestley Claxton, Crusader for Public Education.* Knoxville: Univ. of Tennessee Press, 1948.

Mahy, G. Gordon, Jr. *Murdoch of Buckhorn.* Nashville: Parthenon Press, 1946.

Matlack, Claude Carson, Samuel W. Thomas, and W. Robinson Beard. *Dawn Comes to the Mountains.* Louisville: George Rogers Clark Press, 1981.

McCarthy, William Bernard. "Olive Dame Campbell and Appalachian Tradition." In *Ballads into Books: The Legacies of Francis James Child,* edited by Tom Cheesman and Sigrid Rieuwerts, 283. Bern, Switzerland: Peter Lang, 1997.

McCauley, Deborah Vansau. *Appalachian Mountain Religion: A History.* Chicago: Univ. of Illinois Press, 1995.

McNeil, W. K., ed. *Appalachian Images in Folk and Popular Culture.* 2nd ed. Knoxville: Univ. of Tennessee Press, 1995.

Montgomery, Michael, and Joseph S. Hall. *Dictionary of Smoky Mountain English.* Knoxville: Univ. of Tennessee Press, 2004.

Montgomery, Rebecca S. *The Politics of Education in the New South: Women and Reform in Georgia, 1890–1930.* Baton Rouge: Louisiana State Univ. Press, 2006.

Morgan, Lucy. *Gift from the Hills: Miss Lucy Morgan's Story of Her Unique Penland School.* New York: Bobbs-Merrill, 1958; Chapel Hill: Univ. of North Carolina Press, 1971.

Mutzenberg, Charles Gustavus. *Kentucky's Famous Feuds and Tragedies: Authentic History of the World Renowned Vendettas of the Dark and Bloody Ground.* New York: R.F. Fenno, 1917.

Myers, Elisabeth P. *Angel of Appalachia: Martha Berry.* New York: J. Messner, 1968.

Pearce, John Ed. *Days of Darkness: The Feuds of Eastern Kentucky.* Lexington: Univ. Press of Kentucky, 1994.

Peck, Elisabeth S., and Emily Ann Smith. *Berea's First 125 Years: 1855–1980.* Lexington: Univ. Press of Kentucky, 1982.

Raine, James Watt. *The Land of Saddle-Bags: A Study of the Mountain People of Appalachia*. Lexington: Univ. Press of Kentucky, 1997. First published 1924 by the Council of Women for Home Missions and the Missionary Education Movement of the United States and Canada, New York.

Richardson, Darrell C. *Mountain Rising: The Story of James Anderson Burns and Oneida Institute*. Oneida, KY: Oneida Mountaineer Press, 1986.

Ritchie, Andrew Jackson. *The Rabun Industrial School and Mountain School Extension Work among the Mountain Whites by One of Them*. Atlanta: Byrd, 1906.

Shapiro, Henry D. *Appalachia on Our Mind: The Southern Mountains and Mountaineers in the American Consciousness, 1870–1920*. Chapel Hill: Univ. of North Carolina Press, 1978.

———. Introduction to *The Southern Highlander and His Homeland*, by John C. Campbell, xxii–xxxvi. Lexington: Univ. Press of Kentucky, 1969.

Slap, Andrew L. *Reconstructing Appalachia: The Civil War's Aftermath*. New Directions in Southern History. Lexington: Univ. Press of Kentucky, 2010.

Smith, Margaret Supplee, and Emily Herring Wilson. *North Carolina Women Making History*. Chapel Hill: Univ. of North Carolina Press, 1999.

Southern Historical Association. *Memoirs of Georgia: Containing Historical Accounts of the State's Civil, Military, Industrial, and Professional Interests, and Personal Sketches of Many of Its People*. Signal Mountain, TN: Mountain Press, 1991.

Stephenson, Florence. *The Home Industrial School, Asheville, North Carolina*. Asheville, NC: Woman's Executive Committee of Home Missions of the Presbyterian Church, 1896.

Stoddart, Jess. *Challenge and Change in Appalachia: The Story of Hindman Settlement School*. Lexington: Univ. Press of Kentucky, 2002.

Stone, May, Katherine Pettit, and Jess Stoddart. *The Quare Women's Journals: May Stone and Katherine Pettit's Summers in the Kentucky Mountains and the Founding of the Hindman Settlement School*. Ashland, KY: J. Stuart Foundation, 1997.

Thomas, Samuel W. *Dawn Comes to the Mountains*. Louisville: George Rogers Clark Press, 1981.

Thompson, Samuel H. *The Highlanders of the South*. New York: Eaton and Mains, 1910.

Torok, George D. *A Guide to Historic Coal Towns of the Big Sandy River Valley*. Knoxville: Univ. of Tennessee Press, 2004.

Vance, Rupert B. Foreword to *The Southern Highlander and His Homeland*, by John C. Campbell, vii–ix. Lexington: Univ. Press of Kentucky, 1969.

Waller, Altina L. *Feud: Hatfields, McCoys, and Social Change in Appalachia, 1860–1900*. Chapel Hill: Univ. of North Carolina Press, 1988.

Whisnant, David E. *All That Is Native and Fine: The Politics of Culture in an American Region*. Chapel Hill: Univ. of North Carolina Press, 1983.

Williams, Elizabeth McCutchen. "A Critical Edition of 'Travel in the Mountains—the Survey,' Chapter IV from the *Life and Work of John Charles Campbell* by Olive Dame Campbell: A Thesis." Master's thesis, Appalachian State Univ., 2006.

Williams, John Alexander. *Appalachia: A History*. Chapel Hill: Univ. of North Carolina Press, 2002.

Wilson, Samuel Tyndale. *The Southern Mountaineers*. New York: Presbyterian Home Missions, 1906.

Yeuell, H. Davis. *Moving Mountains: A History of Presbyterian and Reformed Faith at Work in Appalachia*. Amesville, OH: Coalition for Appalachian Ministry, 1985.

INDEX

www.ingramcontent.com/pod-product-compliance
Lightning Source LLC
Chambersburg PA
CBHW031534260326
41914CB00032B/1798/J